THE STATE IN MEDIEVAL KASHMIR

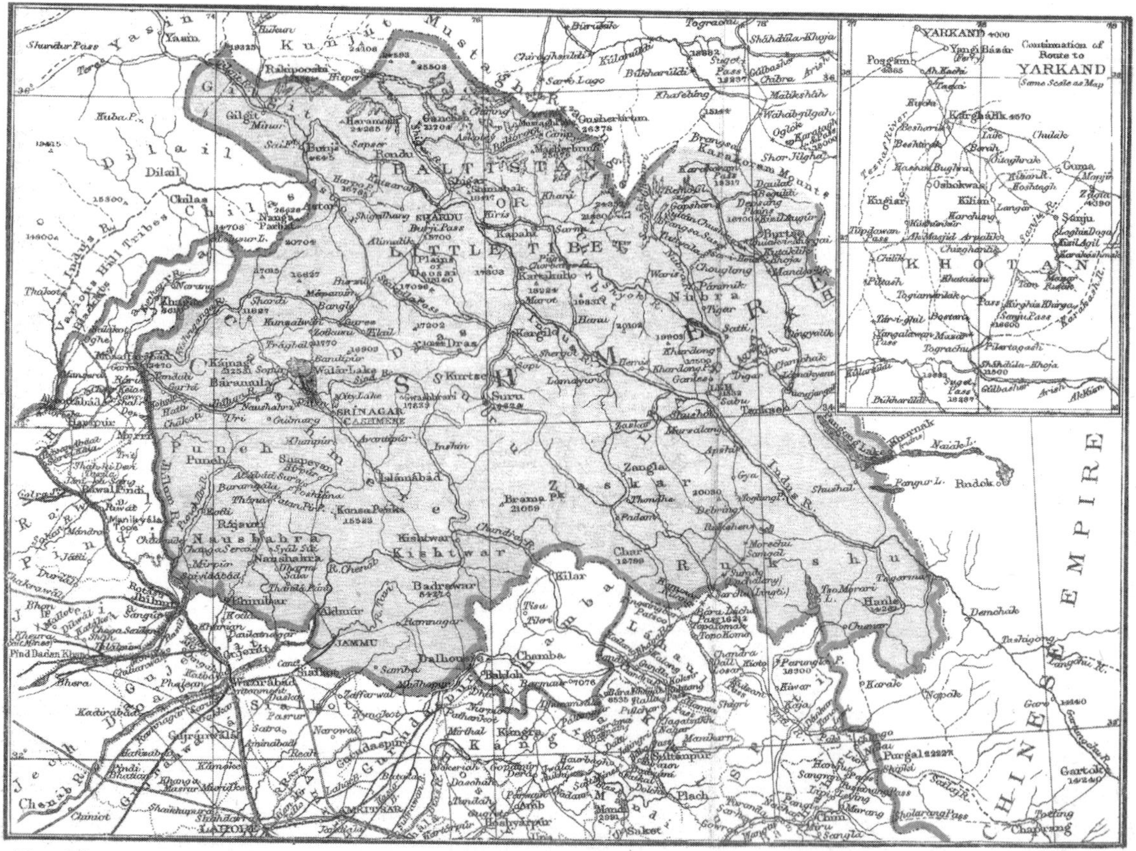

Map: The map shows areas of early Kashmir which were directly and indirectly part of Medieval State in Kashmir [*Source: A Handbook for Travellers in India, Pakistan, Burma and Ceylon*, 8th edn., published by J. Murray, London and Thacker, Spink and Co., Calcutta, 1911]

The State in Medieval Kashmir

(*SECOND EDITION*)

RATTAN LAL HANGLOO

MANOHAR
2023

First published 2000
Second edition 2022, 2023

ISBN 978-81-7304-251-5

Published by
Ajay Kumar Jain *for*
Manohar Publishers & Distributors
4753/23 Ansari Road, Daryaganj
New Delhi 110002

Typeset by
Ravi Shanker
Delhi 110095

Printed at
Replika Press Pvt. Ltd.

To my teacher

PROFESSOR HARBANS MUKHIA

Contents

Map facing p. 3

Preface to the Revised Edition 9

Preface to the First Edition 11

Introduction 13

1. Historical Roots of State Formation in Pre-Sultanate Kashmir 18

2. Conversions to Islam and the Consolidation of a Social Base of Power in the Sultanate 63

3. The Sayyids, Sultans and the State: A Search for Legitimacy, 1339-1470 121

4. The Incorporation of the Sultanate into the Mughal State 154

5. Conclusion 180

Bibliography 185

Index 195

Preface to Revised Edition

The history of medieval Kashmir is considered the most fascinating because this period sketches the evolution of all those complex social and political relationships that gave birth to medieval State in Kashmir. The rise of kings and the priestly class in this tiny valley was always overwhelmed by external forces from trans-Himalayan regions as well as from the rest of India. To characterise the nature of the medieval state in Kashmir I presented in 2000 my understanding of history through this book. I received a lot of appreciation and encouragement from various quarters including students and therefore I am presenting this revised version/edition after carefully elucidating the intricate questions pertaining to medieval state in Kashmir.

It is a pleasure to acknowledge my teacher Prof. Harbans Mukhia for his affection and encouragement. I am deeply obliged to Sri Ramesh Jain and Sri Ajay Jain and their team for bringing out this reprint.

I also owe my gratitude to some of my relations and friends who assisted me in some way or the other in the preparation of this book. These include Sri Sudesh ji Bhat, Sri Ashok ji Bhat, Sri Mohan Lal Wangoo, Prof. R.K. Kaul Bhat, Prof. V. Ramakrishna, Sri P.L. Pandita, Rajesh Raina, Prof. Parvez Ahmad and Dr. Parvez Ahmad.

I thank all my students who always raised very pertinent questions while this book was in progress. These include Prof. Salma Ahmad, Dr G. Nagasridhar, Dr K. Narsaraju,

Dr Mamta Nanda, Dr Fayaz Ahmad, Dr Yasser Arafat, Dr H. Vanlalhruia, Dr K.A. Swamy, Dr C. Swaroopa Rani and others.

My children Akankhsha Bhat Hangloo and Akhil JI Bhat also deserve my thanks.

Finally I owe a debt of gratitude to my wife Sharika Kaul Hangloo, who has always been by my side.

20 October 2021 RATTAN LAL HANGLOO
Hyderabad

Preface to the First Edition

In recent times Medieval Indian historiography has been filled with debates over the effectiveness of concepts characterizing the nature of Medieval Indian State. Viewed from a larger historical perspective, it has been made possible for historians to discern broad trends and identify stages in the evolution and the nature of state formation processes only after exploring the regional patterns. With this perspective in mind this book is devoted to the region of Medieval Kashmir. A book on so limited a scale as this cannot hope to give a full and detailed treatment of all those aspects that need to be covered while exploring the nature of state in Medieval Kashmir. However, this study sets the stage for understanding those broad features which stemmed from the specificities of the region's institutions and facilitated the growth and dynamics of the state formation in Medieval Kashmir.

The preface of this book is a place for me to pay my deep debt of gratitude to my well wishers and my gratitude goes to my parents Sri Radha Krishan Hangloo and Mrs Rupa Hangloo who first encouraged my interest in history and developed in me the ability to recognize that there is an important place in Social Sciences for conscience and humanism. I also owe deep gratitude to my brothers Sri M.L. Hangloo, Sri P.L. Hangloo and Dr Nanajee Hangloo for willingly bearing every burden of the family and in confronting all potential problems effectively. To them I owe more than can be expressed here.

I am most grateful to my teacher Prof. Harbans Mukhia for his insightful comments which helped me to develop the ideas that have eventually found their way into this book. Among others who have placed me in their debt are Prof. M.I. Khan, Prof. B.D. Chattopadhyaya, Prof. Dilbag Singh, Prof. Muzaffar Alam, Prof. Imdad Hussain, Prof. O.N. Koul, Prof. T.N. Madan, Prof. Andre Wink, Prof. G. Haragopal, Dr. G.L. Koul, Dr. Visier Sanyu, Dr. A. Murali, Sri R.K. Koul, Dr. Wolfgang Holtzworth, Mr. Basheer Ahmad Buch, Sri Rajesh Raina and Smt. Sunita Bharti Koul. Their suggestions have been very valuable.

Sri Ramesh Jain and Ajay Jain of Manohar Publishers & Distributors deserve my special thanks for bringing out the book so neatly.

My son Arkaprateem and daughter Arkapravah also deserve thanks for their willingness to bear the burden of arranging and rearranging my source material with minimum chaos while the writing of this book was in progress.

Finally I am pleased to acknowledge the support of my wife Sharika Koul who not only endured the writing of this book with good cheer but also made the hours away from the book more enjoyable than I could have expected. She has always been a great source of inspiration and confidence for me.

RATTAN LAL HANGLOO

Introduction

> Nor can religion be stable without royalty,
> Nor can royalty be permanent without religion,
> They are two foundations interlaced with one another,
> Which intelligence hath combined in one.
>
> Firdousi, *Shahnama*

The strong and positive allegiance that was engendered by popular religious beliefs and practices for a number of ruling dynasties, has rightly come to be seen as one of the basic issues towards understanding the nature of the state in the history of medieval Kashmir. From early times, along with other factors, religion enabled rulers in Kashmir to uphold the view that they were the sovereign rulers of the region. Initially, the social expressions of Brahmanism—the popular belief system and its carefully designed ritual apparatus—were the dynamic, pertinent and creative means in introducing inequalities and in shaping political ideas to maintain and perpetuate the authority of the state. The political inspiration of Brahmanism extended over law, justice, administration, and economic organization. Through these processes it became a privileged instrument and over a period of time increasingly allowed royal intervention. In the process of providing appropriate social conditions for gaining and maintaining the absolute power of Kashmir's kings, the patronization of Brahmanism gradually evolved into a hierarchical landed aristocracy of both religious and secular nature. While elaborating administrative organization and governability, the state's allocation of these religious and secular grants of land and their revenues—a practice which became essential on a wide scale—led to the growth of exploitative structures which used up a large proportion of the state's income. The state's efforts to contain these tendencies led to a perpetual tension between the state and the religious institutions on the one hand, and the state and other dominant social groups (which had grown without the state's support), on the other. In these circumstances it was not the state's authority alone which suffered with the growth of private power, but Brahmanism—the bulwark of social, cultural, economic and political order—also developed cracks and fissures of decay. The process of state formation which had enjoyed a long life by this time, tried to cover all these developments with a veil of apparent unity and political stability in the region. This veil had been in tatters from the ninth century, but the political disorder and social discontent became clearly visible only from the beginning of the eleventh century.

Parallel with this political instability or perhaps as a consequence of it, the impact of Islam from the beginning of fourteenth century strongly affected the region of Kashmir. With this the history of Kashmir entered a new phase. The penetration by Turkish and Central Asian Muslims, which was earlier limited to the occasional visits of merchants, soldiers and craftsmen, now gave way to intrusions by large groups of Turkish, Persian, Central Asian and Arab Muslim migrants with varied professional specializations, who settled in various parts of the valley. These people had not only brought with them an almost fanatic and missionary monotheism, and on the other, they slowly fused ties between themselves and the Kashmiris in the social, religious, economic, technological and cultural sectors. These developments provided a social base for the establishment of the Shahmir Sultanate in the first half of the fourteenth century.

In order to give legitimacy to their dominion and control over the entire stretch of Kashmir, each of the Shahmir Sultans depended not only on the nature of their relations with the local political elites such as the Tantrins, Lavanyas, Magres, Rainas, Dammaras but also on Islam and its preachers. In these circumstances it was natural for these Sultans to patronize and promote the interests of the Sayyids and Sufis who had created the moral universe of Islam in this region. They also established the legitimacy of the Sultan, by prescribing the limits within which the Sultan should be obeyed. The Sultan had to claim popular obedience by right as well as by power, and in this he was successful by offering positions of power and prestige to the local political elites. He had to exercise his authority within the bounds of Shariat and to rule in cooperation with the Sayyids who occupied the positions of *ulama*. Although the Shahmir state was strongly influenced by Islamic practices and traditions, it did not assume a theocratic character because the relationship of the ruler with his religion was primarily linked to the protection of the authority of the Sultan, rather than being the consequence of his religious zeal.

However, the Shahmir state did not succeed in maintaining its power unopposed for very long; the consequence of its management of power relations through steps which did not include the participation of the secular nobility, was acute poverty of the majority, who actually supported the entire structure with their labour and produce. In course of time the Shahmir state became an agency for antagonistic social forces, which tended to uproot the authority of the Sultans one after the other and worsen the social conditions. In these circumstances what seems to have sustained the authority of the Shahmir state at different levels was not the bureaucratically organized, militarily powerful and centralized system, but the religious belief that even if the ruler was impious and unjust, he should still be obeyed, since any kind of order was better than anarchy. The Shahmir state continued to reflect this total disorder, until it was ultimately incorporated into the Mughal state which initiated the control of class relations through patron clientelism—a secular system of exploitation. It is against this background that I undertake to recapture the major trends that have shaped the political trends, patterns of changes in power structure, and the relationship between the religious forces and the political management. This work deals with these specific problems of state in medieval Kashmir and seeks to explore how this problem with all its ramifications would gain from being approached through affiliations to religious institutions, particularly those of Brahmanism and Islam from which it derived their legitimacy. This analysis of the political history of medieval Kashmir confines itself to the study of the region in terms of abstract concepts without establishing any linkages between underlying class forces and their dialectical development over a long period of time. Scholars while dealing with medieval Kashmir's political history have widely neglected the significant role of rituals and belief systems in creating the political ideology of state in medieval Kashmir.

While putting forth my present argument, I am aware of the complex problem created by the lack of conceptual clarity and inconsistency and of certain terminologies of the sources. The central task in this study has been to seek to develop the linkages between the critical areas of polity and religious and secular forces that have a great bearing on the economy and society of the region.

This study essentially focuses on the central function of the state in medieval Kashmir in relation to surplus produce and perpetuation of state dominance through heavy dependence on both Brahmanism and Islam. The state in medieval Kashmir is seen to be firmly situated in the cultural and social traditions of that region.

My views in this book are organized around some main aspects. These are:

1. Historical roots of state formation in pre-Sultanate Kashmir.

2. Conversions to Islam and the consolidation of social base of power in the Sultanate.
3. The Sayyids, Sultans and the state—a search for legitimacy.
4. The incorporation of the Sultanate into the Mughal state.

The degree to which the study of these aspects achieves its purpose may be open to question, but the analysis does provide an introduction to the most important problems which are encountered while reconstructing the nature of the state in medieval Kashmir.

1

Historical Roots of State Formation in Pre-Sultanate Kashmir

Different historical circumstances shaped the process of state formation in medieval Kashmir. During this process various societal institutions facilitated certain class interests and alliances which underpinned and reinforced the patterns of power and domination. The nature of this state formation cannot be understood in isolation from those processes which led to the evolution of complex relationships between the region's economic forces and the role of the political elite in the functioning of the state. Regarding the origins of early state formation, most historians generally believe that there was a transition of human civilization from the hunter-gatherer to the cultivation of land, also referred to as neolithic revolution, which gradually resulted in the growth of complex social relations, sometimes associated with progression in terms of political organization from band level to tribal level formation.[1]

In Kashmir the first complex state formation stemmed from the tribal foundations of Nagas among whom two conflicting and collaborating classes of (a) warrior chiefs and (b) the peasants, pastoralists and craftsmen formed the state structure. The seats of these chiefs became the first centres of political power. These warrior chiefs acquired legitimacy for their authority through kinship lineages and singular ethnicity, to command the resources and loyalty of their subjects.[2] In the case of Kashmir too, the Naga tribal formation appears to have been the earliest political formation from where the early state emerged. The growth of private property and the accumulation of surplus by the Naga tribal chiefs which led to the increasing social differentiation, seems to have brightened the prospects of socio-political dominance of a particular group, which strengthened the power of the Nila Naga over other chiefs in the valley. Much before the Christian era, Kashmir was inhabited by various tribes, among whom the Nagas were the most prominent. *Nilmata Purana* records, 'Thus devoid of grief, thousands and hundred millions of Nagas dwell there without the fear of *Tarkasaya*.'[3]

True, these estimates of *Nilmata Purana* cannot be taken to be as exact because the author is at times prone to such poetic exaggerations. Though plausible at times, yet a critical sensibility of his information does indicate the predominance of Nagas as autochthonous elements in Kashmir from whom evolved the basic preliminaries of socio-political formation. *Nilmata Purana* was written in the seventh century AD. Ved Kumari Gai attributes the authorship of this Purana to Nila Naga, the chief of the Naga tribe in early Kashmir. But a careful study of *Nilmata Purana* reveals that it is a case of pseudo-epigraphy. It is very likely that *Nilmata Purana* was actually written by a Brahmin in order to advance the ritual apparatus among the tribes inhabiting Kashmir as part of the process of Sanskrization, and to popularize it among the tribes, the authorship was attributed to Nila Naga.[4] The bulk of Tantric literature produced during the post-Mauryan period, also indicates the existence of Naga tribal formation which was gradually absorbed and influenced by *Agamas* (Shaivite Tantricism) at the hands of Brahmins and led to a relatively advanced stage of state formation.[5] *Nilmata Purana* states that there were five hundred and ninety-two clan settlements of Nagas sparsely spread across the entire Kashmir valley. The chieftains of these settlements acknowledged the authority of their super-chief

Nila Naga by payment of regular tribute and obedience to him.[6] *Nilmata Purana* refers to Nagas as the progeny of Kashyapa and his wife Kadaru.[7] But scholars have different views regarding their ethnicity and origin. Fergusson takes them as Turanians.[8] Cunningham describes them as Tarkhas who descended from Naga chief Takshaka.[9] Todd mentions them as Toorskas who ruled Arverm in Sakadipa.[10] However, a critical survey of literatures establishes the fact that they were among the indigenous tribes who inhabited various parts of northern India from earliest times.

One of these chiefs, Sadhangula, was even dismissed by Nila for having abducted the wives of other chiefs to satisfy his insatiable lust.[11] Evidence suggests that this vaguely-defined tribal formation was protected from external threat by various chiefs. The Naga chief Bindusara protected the valley from the east, chief Srimadhaka protected it from the south and another chief, Uttaramansa protected it from the north. Nila Naga was thus helped by various subordinate chiefs to hold his co-tribesmen in subjugation and was also assisted in restricting the intrusion of non-Naga tribes into his domain.[12] It is necessary to mention here that the superiority of Nila Naga over others was natural because it was based on lineages and kinship ties, the ideology of power at this stage having no need to look beyond this justification. Such a structure would have based itself on a specific polity but that does not necessarily identify the politically-structured ruling class as such. The protection of the Kashmir valley by various chiefs does not only indicate the nature of their relations with the super-chief Nila but also points to the loosely structured territorial organization which formed an essential element in the process of state formation from early times. This evidence defines the tentative boundaries of Naga kingdom in Kashmir. These territorial limits of the Kashmir valley were never stagnant but kept on shifting, as indicated by literary and numismatic evidence. However, the nucleus was always the main valley, which provided the bulk of its resources and manpower to the state. However, compared with the fully-developed models of early state, this formation does not seem to have grown to that scale in the pre-Mauryan period. The structural model of early state which is derived from a number of empirical case studies, establishes that it was a socio-political organization with definite territorial limits, a centre of governance sustained on agrarian economy, pastoral produce and tributes and taxes derived from trade. It had a two-tier social format comprising: (a) the sovereign and his relations and the aristocracy, (b) the peasants, tenants and craftsmen as their subjects. The position of the ruler in the early state was supported by mythical charters and fake genealogies connecting him to supernatural forces. The administration was carried out by numerous functionaries.[13] But it had certainly attained the features of an organization to enforce its authority. It was from these elements that the structure of the future state was derived.

This tribal level state formation could not possibly remain unaffected by internal and external forces forever. The various forces which helped to break the isolation of Kashmir from the rest of the world included: (a) the penetration of non-Naga tribes of Madras, Tanganas, Darvas, Abhisaras, Gandharas, Juhundaras, Sakas, Khasas, Madaras, Antagiris, Bahiragiris, Kaulindras,Yavanas and Piscas.[14] The cessation of these tribes played a highly significant role in de-tribalizing the Naga tribal formation, (b) the extension of Mauryan rule and spread of Buddhism, and (c) the growth of Agamas at the hands of the Brahmins.

The tribe was only a commonsensical notion, being a political community based on singular ethnicity and kinship ties. With the increasing interaction and intermixing of various other tribes, the existing organization now sought to organize its members (people) by means of concepts which were not familiar from personal experience. It is most likely that the peoples' recourse to demands believed to be super-natural helped the growth of the early state formation process. The Tantric literature that emerged after the dissolution of tribal formation, evolved around the religious institutions and the ritual apparatus at the hands of Brahmins and Buddhist monks, who generated new social and political roles.[15]

All these forces significantlyinfluenced the process of state formation. The intrusion of various non-Naga tribes led to a competition to procure the necessities of life and gradually started reproducing the basic structure. The advent of the Kushanas, Yavanas (Greeks), Pahalvas (Parthians), Tukharas (Tocharians), Hunas and Mauryas between 200 BC and AD 300 integrated tribal formation into a more complicated socio-economic formation of the mainstream type with the partial development of class and *jati* differences and alienation within the community.[16] As a result, the tribal formation witnessed endless disintegration into various settlements growing and spreading over the river valleys and hills in a widely dispersed manner. In their early writings (AD 1846-86), Marx and Engels also noted that only within his own community has each individual the means of cultivating his gifts in all directions; hence personal freedom becomes possible only within the community.

Consequently, the community broke up into various groups based on their social positions. Instead of viewing others as helping co-equals, they viewed them as potential rivals for scarce goods. With the division of the community into exploiting and exploited classes, came the full alienation of its harmony.[17] The old structure began to be expressed in what Laibman calls, 'The gradual dissolution of primitive kinship forms and appearance of rudimentary division of labour accompanied by slow differentiation, the appearance of hereditary priesthoods and invidious ranking of customary status.'[18] On the one hand, these developments destroyed the strength derived until then from the earlier singular ethnicity and kinship lineages, and on the other, posed serious problems to the extending of Mauryan rule in Kashmir. The growth of sparse settlements with varied cults and cultural forms, restricted the physical interaction between the central structure and these areas, particularly when the means of communication (which formed an effective means of keeping the centre's authority intact in these areas) was of a primitive nature. At this stage the Buddhist monks and Brahmins came to the rescue of the regional rulers of the Mauryan state in Kashmir. They provided ideological materials for absorbing these varied cults into a culturally and religiously homogenous populace and rendered acceptance of the new rulership possible. There has always been a close connection between religion and polity because the state was always in need of justifying the inequalities, power differentials, heavy taxations, and tributes. For this purpose invocation of the supernatural or the promise of a better life after death offered powerful legitimation. Herbert Frey rightly observes that the ruling class obtained rents from them and their services by exercising tight control over all the avenues of communication with the so-called extra-human-belief system of their own manufacture. Class division appeared as a differentiation of mental from physical work. While the former by use of religion gave the right to supervising the process of production, the latter enforced the inexhorable routine performance of labouring tasks.[19] The rulers patronized Buddhism and Brahmins for legitimizing their purposes. The foundation of the town of Srinagar in 250 BC and various *stupas* for instance, are attributed to Ashoka.[20]

Regarding Ashoka's measures in Kashmir, considerably details are provided by Hiuen Tsang.[21] The Kushana kings Hushka, Jushka and Kanishka, are also said to have constructed various *viharas, mathas,* and *chaityas* to patronize Buddhism.[22] There are also references to an exchange of ambassadors between Kashmir and China much before the sixth century AD.[23] Even before the sixth century AD there are references to Kashmir in the accounts of Fahien who visited Kashmir and spent more than a year there, while on his way to India. The import of Kashmiri saffron by China dates back to the third century AD.[24] With the growth of Buddhism, majority of Kashmiris also turned towards Buddhism. At this point of time, most of the Kashmiris accepted Buddhism at the popular level and many among the Kashmiri religious elite became Bhikshus (monks) voluntarily and travelled to distant lands including various parts of Central Asia, China and Japan to preach Buddhism. Some of them combined the preaching of Buddhism with their trading activities on the Silk Route. Buddha himself was very impressed by Kashmir's inclination for pursuing spirituality and religion. He says, 'The kingdom of Kashmir is where it will be easiest to lead a religious life. For contemplation and meditation, will that be the best place.'[25]

Although Buddhism overwhelmed religious life of Kashmiris for centuries, unfortunately not much of the literature on early Buddhism in Kashmir has survived; whatever has survived is available in repositories of Tibet which was aggressively taken over by China and one does not know what happened to that vast treasure of information in Tibetan language. There is a lot of untouched literature on early Buddhism in Srilanka but that also remains untranslated and inaccessible to scholars. Therefore our discussion on early Buddhism in Kashmir remains miserably brief. However, that does not belittle the contribution of Kashmiris to Buddhism. The *Great Exegesis* (*Mahavibasha*) which was prepared by various monks under Samghabhadra, a great Kashmiri scholar, mentions 'Having become the holy land of Buddhism, the high Himalayan Valley, in its twin, had to contribute to the "Gift of Law". It did so with honour. Its (Kashmir's) geographical situation, at the boundaries of India, of Persia, and of Central Asia, was destining it to play a great role in the spreading of Buddhism.'[26]

A Kashmiri monk Gunavarman (431-367 BC) was delighted after visiting Java when he received official invitation from the emperor of Song dynasty in China and travelled by ship through the port of Guangzhou and arrived at the Song capital in 431 BC.[27]

Coedes says that the Indianized communities of South East Asia became more Hinduized as well but commerce and Buddhist missionary zeal were the initial impulses driving this expansion of Indic culture.[28]

In AD 458, five Kashmiri Bikshus arrived from Kashmir and introduced Buddhism in China.[29] Interestingly, alongwith Buddhism, the patronization of *Agamas* (Shaivite Tantricism) is also associated with Ashoka's successor Jaluka in Kashmir. He is said to have performed miracles like transforming base metals into gold, arresting the waters of lakes, his queen Isnadevi placing circles sacred to mothers (*matrikas*). These practices can not be dismissed outright. They do contain a grain of truth regarding the synthesis of Tantric Buddhism and Shaivite Tantra. The foundation of the shrine of Jyesthrudra and the agrahara of Varabala (Barawul in Wangath area) is also attributed to him.[30]

All these reveal that there were periods of constant interaction between Kashmir and China, and Kashmir and the Indian mainland from very early times. Before the emergence of the Brahmins as resident nobility, the state was helped in its formative process by Buddhist monks. It would be very interesting to investigate it in as detailed a manner as possible, if and to what extent Buddhism and state formation accompanied and reinforced each other. But the limitations of sources and their chronological unreliability, poses some serious problems. Even if this was counterchecked with whatever evidence has survived, some drawbacks would still remain in the argument. According to D.D. Kosambi:

> The Brahmins were not the only ideological and priestly imports of use to the state. Buddhist monks are supposed to have become powerful from the time of King Jaluka (son of Ashoka) who is further credited with having introduced the four caste class system, legal procedure and central administration headed by eighteen officials which continued as a standard form throughout the Kashmirian history, with later modifications, the monks nearly extinguished the tribal Naga units which would have obstructed any central rule

unless wiped out or assimilitated by state religion. The later step was taken by the Brahmans who had been reduced to helplessness at the time of Bodhisattva Nagarjuna.These priests gained a solid base among the people by writing the (still extant) *Nilmata Purana* which gives official sanction to Naga cult ritual, readjusted comfortably to standard Brahman practice and observances with royal patronage from the time of Gonda III.[31]

The evolution and application of Buddhist and Shaivite Tantricism at the hands of priests made the natural forces appear not only as belonging to extra human sphere, but accessible only through human prayer, sacrifice, rituals and veneration. With developing complexities of social formation, religion became the most important instrument for legitimation. For the subordination of the majority also a religious explanation was sanctified. All these attempts were directed to control the primary producers and ensure their complete subjection to perpetuate the authority of the state.

From literary and archaeological evidences it appears that the worship of Mother Goddess and phallic rituals were the principal forms of devotion among the autochthonous tribal population of Kashmir from very early times. The various art objects obtained from the excavations at Harappa and Mohenjo-daro provide us clear evidence regarding the earliest existence of the Mother Goddess cult. The female figures among these objects are adorned with profuse jewellery and pannier-like management on each side of their heads, pointing to the worship of Mother Goddess even in third millennium BC.[32] Kalhana also refers to worshipping the Mother Goddess in the form of *Matrika* as early as in the Mauryan rule. Under Ashoka they were associated with the queens or the sorceresses.[33] The phallic rituals were supposed to be the means of attaining material objectives. Basically, in the pre-state society of Kashmir, people believed that the collective performance of these rituals would help them overwhelm the forces of nature. But with the commencement of the process of transition to early state formation in Kashmir, these rituals were transformed into the esoteric art of the dominant elements in society. Interestingly, the rituals and symbols of power have never been mere incidental ephemeras but are always central to the structure and working of any society. In fact, various rituals were deployed and transformed by the ruling class as a means of ordering their territorial realms and to sustain their earthly dominance.[34] The varied rituals they performed always played a vital role as they do in every religion even today. Among Kashmiri Pandits, the traditional element in their religion is represented by a host of rituals and that ensures the continuity of its form from generation to generation. Interestingly no single religion is perfect. All religions have their own specificities in terms of rituals, morality, philosophy, ideas of God and priesthood. It is people's needs that gave birth to these different cults, religions, cultures and languages. Like other human societies, religion was needed by Kashmiris too from very early times; even before they evolved as a community of Pandits, they had adopted and accepted Buddhism and Kashmir Shaivism, popularly referred to as *Trika Shaivism* or *Agama*. They required religion for their spiritual satisfaction.[35] The evolution of theistic ideas among Kashmiri Pandits has a long and complex history. Its journey from the very antiquity to the consolidation of Shaivite philosophy, that continues even today as a predominant religious form among them, is not devoid of various stages from the vague divine spirits of primitive times to fetishism, totemism, animism, ancestor and Mother Goddess worship, Tantricism, Shakta, Rishi Pratha (order of saints) and other cult worshipping traditions and myths. In the early stages of societal development, Kashmiris did worship nature and supernatural forces which were not under their control, such as death. It is said that fear of death, above all, was the first mother of gods and it was followed by the fertility goddess cult.[36] Kashmiris indulged in practising such cults at the time of tribal social formation. The primitive Kashmiris regarded the ways of nature as mysterious. In course of time they became increasingly aware of the advantages of procreation. Man and woman thus befriended each other. The woman took the lead and this was not only aimed to satisfy sexual/biological need but more importantly, it was to respond to the everyday challenges posed by material culture in this region and the continuous evolution of life surrounding that, despite several geographical and ecological handicaps. As the women took the lead it led to the development of matriarchy. As a result with women emerging as more powerful and there are reasons for that. Bhattacharya observes,

> The cave man regarded the ways of nature as a mystery. As soon as man had time to notice something beyond the ken of the immediate, he became increasingly aware of the sweetness of beauty, and of a type of rewarding and charming thrill which was not associated just with satisfaction of the demands of the flesh. Eve's demand was impulsive. She just wanted to know more. She refused to be mystified by life.[37]

In its very early stages people viewed and perceived natures' workings as expressions of procreation. In *Rig Veda* there is a beautiful description of this phenomenon when the bridegroom says to his bride, 'I am the sky and you are the earth . . . I shall cast seed unto thee, to mix with your juice and so shall we procreate.'[38]

Phallic worship dates back to the second millennium BC. The earliest evidence of phallic worship in Kashmir is provided by the Neolithic Megalithic culture of Burzoham. It was later incorporated into the Shiva-Shakti cult by Shaivite Acharayas.[39] The phallic emblems were replaced by the symbolic representation of Shiv-Sakti and the installation of *lingam* in a *yoni yantra* indicating continuous growth and regeneration of the universe. . . . The assimilation of various mother goddesses into *Bhairava* and *Bhairavi* was accomplished by means of rituals which while reducing the number of *kuladevis* led to an increase in sacrifice and *chakrapuja*, forcing the clientele to surrender their social surplus to Brahmins, who had acquired a monopoly in performance of highly *tantricised* rituals and the *mantras* associated with them.[40]

Therefore, the evolution of the installation of a stone *lingam* in a *yoni yantram* is not an indication of eroticism in Kashmir but symbolizes a continuous process of regeneration of the universe. It is worshipped in many other ancient societies too. 'The quiescent aspect of Siva is by definition inert. . . . Activity is the nature of Nature (*Prakriti*). For this reason the female form is represented in esoteric sexual union figures as an active partner riding above (*Viparta*) the male, when the Devi is shown as the active power over and above the lying Shiva. It also represents the living aspect of mother. . . . We call ourselves civilized according to a code of behaviour fixed by us. But these people who lived in the past and were mystified by the wonders of sex, stood in an awesome grand regard for its mysteries.'[41]

The Neolithic culture in Kashmir was also dependent on hunting. With the decline of Neolithic culture and transition to food production, women retained their predominant position. This dominant position of women in Kashmir goes back to the Neolithic period third and second millennium BC. The end of Neolithic culture in Kashmir gave birth to the agricultural revolution. In this region because of geographical limitations, agriculture is not possible throughout the year. Therefore there was an increasingly tendency to posses land, plants, trees, sheep, cattle and large pasturage. Development of agriculture and handicrafts had the tendency to split up early Kashmiri tribal society into clans and towards individualism. Domestication of animals was necessitated for sacrifice to deities and spirits. Besides, animals provided protein, clothing and were a source of transportation to Kashmiris in early times.[42] In the absence of agriculture throughout the year, the dependence on cattle wealth required large number of families, women and children to care of the animals and with time even slaves, like in other ancient societies.

Thus Kashmir had a strong matriarchical society and this is not only attested by the fact that Kashmiris are primarily Mother Goddess worshippers even after the growth of

Shaivism. In early tribal societies, while men had to hunt for daily food, women were guardians of the hearth and makers of pottery, apart from producing children. They evolved the knowledge of plants and contributed significantly to agricultural cultivation, caring of flocks, herds and in cattle rearing. Women facilitated the upgradation of men from hunter to a producer of food. Besides, in primitive societies practicing polyandry, women emerged as a predominant force, because they transmitted the life blood of tribes and clans.[43] Will Durant also supports this view when he says that females were more healthy in primitive societies and equal in stature and endurance to men. According to him,

> The difference in strength which now divides sexes, hardly existed in those days, and is now environmental rather than innate in nature. Women, apart from her biological weaknesses was almost equal to men in stature, endurance, resourcefulness and courage; she was robust and capable of performing arduous tasks for long hours, and if necessary to fight to death for her children or her clan. The most economic advantages were made by women rather than men. While for centuries the men clung to the ancient ways of hunting and herding, she cultivated the land adjoining their camps and those busy arts of the home which were to become the most important industries in later days. It was apparently she who developed sewing, weaving, basketry, pottery, woodwork, and building, and in many cases it was she who carried on primitive trade.[44]

In ancient Kashmir, women also directed affairs in society and were thus raised to priesthood and finally became goddesses like in many other early societies. As active participants in agriculture and in course of further evolution, both men and women encountered various challenges like in other societies and began to pay obeisance to the earth, water, fire, the rivers, trees and mountains. As a consequence, stone symbols of gods and goddesses came up as emblems of worship and a medium of expression of reverence to them. *Nilmata Purana*, a seventh century AD text, is full of detail on many of these aspects. The author of this valuable work has assembled and presented interesting information from a wide range of sources. It states, for instance, men possessing horses should worship Revanta, the son of Aditya. 'Persons possessing cows should worship Surabhi and those who have got goats should worship fire. Shepherds should worship the god Varuna, the lord of the waters, and those who own elephants should worship the lord of the Ganas.'[45]

Likewise, each tribe or group or *jatis* had its own set of gods and deities, and some of them continued to be worshipped even in contemporary times after they got assimilated and incorporated into different village settlements, irrespective of varied social and economic changes and growth of knowledge systems. People who had been powerful during their lifetime or belonged to a powerful clan/tribe, family or group or *jati* and therefore were feared or revered, were especially worshipped after their death.[46] This also becomes clear from the megaliths that found in different sizes and shapes on their graves in Kashmir.[47] The worship of sun was also the earliest in Kashmir, which becomes clear from the archaeological evidence from Gufkral and other archaeological sites and Martand Sun Temple in early Kashmir.[48]

In such circumstances, when Kashmiris were in the early stage of tribal social formation, the religious myths were a source to convey a kind of knowledge by explaining natural phenomena that could not be understood by everyone. Obviously, whatever little rational learning the people had at that time, only provided them with distorted information that had plenty of gaps. Such mythification was accompanied by pseudo science, magic and false information. This was the only method to provide answers to questions such as death, excessive rainfall and storms, suffering, and give reasons (false or otherwise) for the natural or manmade calamities, which stuck from time to time. Bhattacharya rightly says, 'Death not in ordinary sense of decay, degeneration and disintegration, but a complete fade out, going out of existence, followed by the decaying life, lingering gradually, but inevitably; the withering flesh, losing its charm of youth, flow of warmth—these as experiences, had long since been accepted. But the other kinds of deaths such as the sudden death of a newborn or youth; through accident, flood, disease and attack. Such deaths created terror in their minds and made man feel helpless. The apparent unreasonableness of such a scheme of things was felt to be out of line, out of joint. Man got suspicious of some lack of order, some miscalculation, some want of arrangement. This aggravated an unacceptable situation and he yearned to know, to master, to control this horrid, unknown power, an entirely uncertain antagonist whose spell was final. These mysterious powers of nature, surely had a source, a central control somewhere. Urge for life's knowledge led to the search for the Divine. Divinity has a rude beginning, in mating, multiplying and separation. Life and the phallus were inseparable and bristled with mystery. Divinity had a phallic source.'[49]

With this kind of framework, the self-styled spiritual elites who emerged in early Kashmiri society, organized the people or groups, monitored their collective thinking, controlled their social relationships, and articulated their dominance the way they wanted.

We must remember that it was out of such an environment that the religious outlook of Kashmiri Pandits evolved for perceiving the world around them, their institutions of worship and their beliefs grew and rituals evolved. Generally speaking, religion was not born in Kashmir out of analytical reasoning. It was only when the people's interaction with various other communities and cultures grew that led to evolution of another religion and began to undermine the previous one. The people began to look for rational grounds. Hence religion was not a set of propositions deriving its sense from criteria of reference or from its verifiability. Whether god exists or not was hardly a religious issue.

At this stage both the Buddhist monks and the Brahmins realized that there were similarities between the tribal Tantric rituals and Buddhist and Shaivite practices. They found them very useful for evolving the Buddhist Tantric rituals. However, in the long run, Buddhism failed to triumph over Shaivism because Buddhism simply turned its back on social Durkheimian aspects of religion. It offered no real guidance. while Shaivism succeeded due to its capacity and with state patronage. The Shaivite Acharayas responded to the challenges of the state and Buddhism by extending and regularizing the services they performed on every occasion in the life-cycle, and their presence became firmly anchored in the locality.[51]

From the Mauryan period onwards, when the interaction of Buddhist monks and Brahmins with the tribal population of Kashmir increased, the Brahmins learned the Tantric lore of Buddhism and Shaivism and absorbed the religious beliefs, deities and cults of tribes in the Shiva-Shakti cult and Buddhism.[52] This superimposition of Buddhist and Shaivite practices over the tribal rituals was encouraged by the ruling elements in order to appropriate to their growing needs, the monopoly of political power, by influencing the religious life of the people.[53] This relationship between the royalty and the priests is very old. Even in *Rig Veda* the nature of the *purohits* duties and functions indicates this indispensability to royalty. He is said to have even accompanied the king and his army to the battlefield and prayed there to ensure the victory of the king.[54] Perhaps they realized that religiosity was an important force which ideologically bind people together in a society. The states hegemonic abilities and capacity to structure its socio-economic and political institutions and behaviour always depended on the type of its legitimacy. Therefore, the state had to base its functioning on a certain degree of acceptance or agreement of its subjects, and to achieve such a situation the royalty had to act more or less in accordance with the existing expectations of the people. At this juncture the state needed an agency to present its functioning and actions as being in agreement with the people's expectations. In medieval societies one finds that it is the priests who generally played a significant role in engineering the consent of the masses, and the state in return, lavishly rewarded the priest. Some times this feature is common to most of the early states.[55] In Medieval Kashmir too the Brahmins began to evolve a bulk of *Agamas* revealing a widespread tendency to extract surplus in the form of gifts from the common people; *dana, dakshina, pratigraha* became ritual practices in which both men and women participated.[56] With this kind of structure the self-styled spiritual elites who emerged in early Kashmiri society, organised people or groups, monitored their collective thinking, controlled their social relationships, and articulated their dominance the way they wanted. On one of the occasions the people were instructed by the priestly thus, 'With their bodies anointed and well adorned, they should worship the Brahmanas and feast themselves in the company of friends, servants, wives and children. Since then the Brahmins should keep the fire kindled in their houses, at night, for a period of six months. . . . On the eleventh night of bright half of the month, the man observing fast should wake up God Hari with songs and dances. . . . On the Pournamasi, nothing should be eaten during the day time. After the rising of moon, Krttikas, Karttikeya, Khadga and Varuna along with Hutasana should be worshipped with garlands, scents, incenses, eatables of various kinds like the rice boiled in milk, vegetables preparations of sugar cane, half ripe barley, cakes of sugar covered with seeds, beautiful trees of lamps and worship of the twice born.'[57]

The dialectic that linked the emergence of various developments in early Kashmiri society to new myths and their diffusion among the general public for stratifying people and then subjecting them by the dominant who ultimately claimed the position of Brahmins, is a very complex relationship. There are many such intervals in history of emergence of religions in Kashmir which involved destruction, innovation, adaptation, distortion patient work and creativity by and the question of dominance and subjection by Kashmiri Pandits within their own community. Nilmata Purana and other Sanskrit texts of Kshemendra Kalhana and others are full of such details on this subject.

Given the nature of Kashmir's geography and the availability of labour, the participation of women was most essential even in a one-crop economy which was supplemented by the pastoral and craft produce. Due to climatic conditions very little time was left for regular agriculture between May to August every year. Every thing had to be carried out during this short period. So the labour of women assumed great significance and was essentially needed to cope with the situation. In early tribal formation the role of women in the raising of crops and in tending cattle was highly significant. The religious texts also emphasized her role of persistence in various social activities.[58] Therefore, the Brahmins continuously exploited all Tantric rites and other rituals to ensure regular labour and the services of men and women for the supply of social surplus.

They knew that women were the most dependable source of labour and were given equal status with men in *Saivagamas* as well. According to *Saivagamas*, the worship of Shakti is the key to all success and a woman occupies equal place with man. She is mentioned as one-half of the man. Like other matriarchal societies, in Kashmir too the general notion about women as coequals of men has in course of time shaped and promoted the organization of social relations between the two sexes.[59]

From Tantric literature and other sources it becomes amply clear that gradually the Shaivites or the Brahmins as *acharyas* came to closely involve themselves in various fields of human activity. Efforts were made to wean the dominant elements among the Nagas from their tribal past so that the superiority of the Brahmanical elements could be asserted. To this effect there are frequent references in *Nilmata Purana:* 'O Nila, the Vedas have sung about you as the eternal one, the essence ofVedas, the object of worship in fire, the fulfiller of desires of those who seek salvation and those who are ambitious of material gain.'[60]

A temple, *matha* or a shrine with the Brahmin *parsada* (corporation) soon became the centre of all religious activities. Apart from conducting all ceremonies from birth to the disposal of the dead, they (Brahmins) consented to conducting marriages, scheduled dates for sowing and harvesting of crops and raising of new structures, dispensed justice and waived laws.[61] Kashmiri kings always acted according to *Smritis* where the Brahmin is always given the key role. Both Kalhana and Khemendra have held Brahmins in high esteem in their works. Kalhana says that even royal fortune could be lost by showing disrespect to Brahmins. He attributes to them a high degree of spirituality, but it was also a manipulating tactic which Brahmins clothed with religion and spirituality.[62] On all such occasions, giving of gifts and sacrificial fee (*dakshina)* was an important aspect of the socio-economic life of the people. Though initially it started with rituals and symbolism, it soon acquired a socio-economic importance. The *dakshina* to the gods and deities may have been symbolic, but to the Brahmins it had to consist of actual objects. On one occasion, it was laid down that 'having made a fish of sand, one should fill it with milk, provide it with jewels and then give it to a brahmana.'[63]

On another occasion, the demand was that 'food preparation of half ripe barley along with purified butter should be given to the Brahmins'.[64] The rituals of *shradha* for the deceased had to be held with offerings of vegetables, meat, and cakes of flour.[65] People were asked to worship Brahmins with varied forms of wealth on all occasions. Thus, through the bulk of *Agamas* the Brahmins laid down a general scheme which would ensure that the ritual and sacrificial observances would result in the well-being and reproduction of social groups, environment and crops. Peasants were asked to commence cultivation only after obtaining prior permission of a Brahmin, for he (the Brahmin) alone practised austerities through which he gained the power to endorse or bestow auspiciousness on time, space and action.[66] The *Malinivijayuttara Tantra* while referring to *vastu-yaga* (household sacrifice and image worship) indirectly indicates the actual motive behind this ritual. It was a perfect way to exploit the resources of household worshippers by a Brahmin guru. This ritual barely left the householder with just enough to survive:

> The *sadhakas* were bound to serve their spiritual teachers, make provision for their food and surrender their right to property dedicated to the deity and the Guru. Household implements like mull, stone, mortar, pestle, etc. used in the worship of gods should never be touched with feet. The feudal obligation of complete loyalty was ensured by rituals designed to maintain the unassailable authority and property rights of the guru. This explains the emphasis laid on the performance of *yagya, homa* and *japas* in one's home to achieve all *siddhis*.[67]

Although the ideology of *Vimarsha* and *Prakasha* was evolved by the Brahmins, yet people were subjected to social inequalities through the ethics of *varna*.

All this evidence lays bare the fact that the application of *agamas* shifted the ground from haphazard and fortuitous conditions of society to a well-organized body knit together by an elaborate ritual apparatus. The social implications of these rituals reveal just how intense were the attempts at shaking the foundations of human existence and conditions which determined the material level of the people. The main aim of these various examples is to illustrate the role played by the *agamas* (rituals) in resting the society on new practices and beliefs produced by the priestly class so that it was to these practices and beliefs that they had recourse to when problems arose.

People were deprived of their basic needs and the ritual apparatus supported only those groups who dominated the forces of production. Among those dominant elements were the *gramadhyakshas* (heads of villages) and *deshadhyakshas* (heads of *deshas)* who looked for patrons and allies to seek protection and to mediate their relations with the peasants,[68] because they occupied important positions in the social and political hierarchy of the early state. The state had direct control over manpower and resources through these agents at different levels of its functioning from pre-Gupta times till the end of the second Lohara dynasty (AD 1101-71). The *agamas* flourished under healthy patrons and helped the Brahmins to play an effective role in supervising the social and political situation with unrestricted objectives. Not only were they effective in facilitating the exercise of paramount influence by kings and other socially dominant elements over the socio-economic and religious life of Kashmir, but they also provided a rudimentary machinery for the perpetuation of state control and authority. It is, therefore, scarcely surprising that the Brahmins were in a position to draw considerable personal and group advantages from the inability of the early state to control the situation without their help. They fulfilled the functions of an ideology for the early state. This is shown even more convincingly by the dictum 'for those who shall act according to the instructions of Nila (King) as far as their means permit there shall be health, long life, much wealth. After death those people shall go to the world of gods and their sons and grandsons shall share the heaven.' This was one of the principal ways through which the ruling elite tried to maintain social order and sustained their own earthly dominance.[69] On the occasion of the coronation of kings, the Brahmins are said to have performed special sacrifices, recited *mantras* for the long life of the king, his fearlessness and prosperity.[70] This was how the Brahmins, after committing themselves to the defence of their roles as rituallegitimizers, helped the state to maintain social order. There is rich evidence to show that the Brahmins supplied the necessary technical materials in the shape of doctrines or religious support by underpinning and propping up the exploitative system. Their role was perhaps the most direct structural link between Kashmir's polity and religion but it was by no means the sole link. The kings and other landed elements representing the state also reciprocated by honouring the community of the Brahmins with large tax exempt *agraharas.*

The earliest *agraharas* granted to them were those of Levera, Kuruhara, Khagi and Khonmusa. The *agrahara* of Levera was granted by King Lava. This is identified with modern Lever village on the right bank of the Lidar river in present Pahalgam tehsil. The *agrahara* of Kuruhara was founded by King Kusa and is the present Kular village in the western part of the Lidar valley. The other two *agraharas* of Khagi and Khonmusa were granted by King Khagendra. Khagi is the present Khag area near Biru and the *agrahara* of Khonmusa is the Khonmoh village a few miles to the north-west of Pampore.[71]

From the Mauryan period up to the end of Harsha's reign (AD 1089-1101) a large amount of land was granted to the Brahmins for the maintenance of *mathas,* shrines, temples and *viharas.* King Godhara granted the *agraharas* of Godhara and Hastisala. These have been identified with the modern villages Gudar an Asthihel in Kulgam[72] King Janaka (who succeeded Suvarna, the tenth king of the Gonda dynasty) gave the *agrahara* of Jalora. The *agrahara* of Jalura is the village Zollur a few miles from Awantipura.[73] The *agrahara* of Samangasa and Sanara are attributed to King Sacinara. Samangasa is the modern Shangas village in Kuthar area in district Anantnag. The *agrahara* of Sanara is the village Kother area near Achabal town. King Sacinara belonged to the Gonda dynasty.[74] Jaluka, the successor of Ashoka, granted the *agrahara* of Varbala and also endowed lands to the shrine of Jyesthrudra for its upkeep.[75] The *agrahara* of Kantkotsa was granted by Abhimanyu I (the last king of the Gonda dynasty).[76]

Mihirakula (AD 515-50), who destroyed the Buddhist *viharas* on a large scale, granted one hundred *agraharas* to Kashmiri Brahmins out of Gandhara land.[77] King Akasa gave the *agraharas* of Aksavala. Aksavala is the modern village of Achabal 5 miles from Anantnag proper, enroute to Breng area;[78] while King Gopaditya endowed the *agraharas* of Khola, Hadigrama, Skandpura and reaffirmed the grant of Khagika and Samangasa. Kalhana attributes five *agraharas* to King Gopaditya but Gopaditya actually gave only three *agraharas* of Khola, the Khull village near Volur area. Hadigrama is the village Aregam near Nagam and Skandpura is identified with Khundur village in Kuthar area. In case of the *agrahara* of Samangasa and Khagika, the grant was only reaffirmed because they were granted by King Khagindra and Sacinara respectively.[79] The Brahmins associated with the shrines of Shiva Buteshvara were granted *agraharas* by King Narendraditya.[80] The *agraharas* of Katimusa and Ramusa were granted by King Tunjana and his queen Vakpushtha. The *agraharas* of Katimusa in modern Kaimuh near Adhvin on the left bank of Vishav river and Ramuh is a place on the high road from Srinagar to Shopian. The lands around Ramuh were till recently the *jagirs* of Dhar family of Srinagar,[81] King Megvahana granted *agraharas* to the Brahmins of Meghamatha.[82]

His queen Amrit Prabha founded the *agraharas* with Amrit Bavana donating large and fertile tracts of land to maintain them. The villages assigned to this shrine were later appropriated by Mamma, the uncle of Cippatayapida, for maintenance of his other temples.[83]

A Brahmin minister of Vikramaditya also founded *mathas* and *viharas* along with the *agraharas* so that the Brahmins could maintain them.[84] The *agrahara* of Bedra was granted by King Baladitya. Bedra is the modern Bidder village in Breng area. The village is presently known for the shrine of ManReshi who is referred as Manshah in the post-conversion period and is revered by both the Muslims and Hindus of Kashmir.[85] Regarding Lalitaditya (AD 725-53) it is said that practically in every town or village he granted *agraharas* to the Brahmins. Prominent among these were Suvarna Parsva, Phelpura and Locantsa.[86] King Avantivarman's (AD 855/6-83) brother and minister Samkarvarman, gave the villages of Suryakunda and Panchata as *agraharas* to the

Brahmins. Panchta is the village Panzath near Devasar area in district Anantnag[87] on the banks of Vitasta (river Jhelum). A number of villages were endowed with as many as 55 *agraharas* by King Yasaskara (AD 939-48). Here it should be noted that the kings in early state had recourse to religious elements to justify royal authority. Therefore, royal power did not appear as an arbitrary imposition on the subjects but the growth of *agraharas* would have certainly appeared as seizure of their territory to the *agraharas*.[88] Queen Suryamati also granted 180 *agraharas* to the Brahmins. Her son Haldra also founded *agraharas* when he became the prime minister.[89] These grants strengthened the financial foundations of the Brahmins apart from providing security to the donors.

Interestingly, the pattern that was set by these *agraharas* in various parts of Kashmir should not be taken as an isolated phenomenon, but as an essential element in the relations and processes of production. The patronage to the priestly sector and the maintenance of the establishments which allowed them material strength should be considered more specifically as the function of a presiding legitimacy in the existing state of affairs of the rule by a given class. The absolute accumulation of the *agrahara* surplus by the priestly sector, beyond certain limits, inevitably resulted in not only social but economic class development. And in course of time, it was this class which emerged as the main link between the state and the subjects, because the state rested on society, which had a fundamental grounding in the religion (Tantricism) preached and practised by the class of Brahmins.[90] Unfortunately, information on the exact amount of land that each of these *agraharas* occupied is not available, but it was indeed from these religious and secular *agraharas* that the first landed aristocracy made its appearance in Kashmir. *Svacchanda Tantra* shows clearly how much interest the gifting of land had acquired in value as compared with other objects of *dana* during the period. The *deshadhyakshas* had to gift away one hundred villages, the *mandalesha* (head of the *mandala*) of hundred villages had to give five, the owner of twenty villages, one, and the owner of one *kshetra* (a single plot of land), had to give away a twentieth part of his land, along with ownership rights as a *dana* or *dakshina.*[91] It will not be out of place to indicate, though firm evidence is still not available, even an approximate casual connection, perhaps establishes that there was a considerable area of commonality of interests between the ritual and economic overloads. Given the primitive levels of development of social formation at that stage, the consolidation of the ritual supremacy does hold a significant key to the understanding of a political formation in general and state formation in particular. However, such a perspective needs to be blended with socio-economic dynamics at work at the same time. For the ruling classes, religion had a useful function, the formation of the priesthood and the maintenance of their establishments contributed to strengthening the beliefs which were unconsciously present in the minds of people. The *agraharas* preserved the people's religious craving for a God and supernatural forces. They emphasized that sacrificial observations were necessary to prevent chaos in society. Life was very hard and constantly menaced by disasters, people only looked for the religion that would give them support in these conditions and compensate for their suffering in the other world after death. As a result, the growth of social awareness among the people was restricted to perpetuating the domination of power.[92] Since the Brahmins had the advantage of having acquired intellectual hegemony, they tried to put forth these beliefs and rituals in such a manner that they had beneficial consequences for the ruling classes. The Brahmins projected their patrons (kings) as people who possessed divine powers and any form of protest against them was considered as sin, since this was an effective mechanism in undermining the magnitude of any social protests. By emphasizing that kings were part of the divinity, the Brahmins ideologically conceived changes conditioning the position of various elements in society, thus necessarily involving a change in the conception structure and purpose of the existing political institutions. Besides, when the structures of a social ensemble are transformed, for any reason whatsoever, the ideology will also be affected. Nevertheless the differential dynamics which rule the structures of social inter-relationships on the one hand and the symbolic systems on the other, will usually result in these changes not occurring simultaneously.[93]

The Brahmins also tended to emphasize the gulf between the producers and non-producers. Since an *agrahara*-based economy was important for their sustenance, the Brahmins perceived land as an essential part of their dignity. Their authority tended to be legitimized by their training in literary and religious texts. This also lent special credence to their roles in states or areas where there was secular functioning. Basically the gradual increase of various grants would have necessitated the need for scribes, record keepers, and other officials connected with the maintenance of records. This provided another opportunity for the Brahmins to occupy secular positions as well. In fact, under King Jaluka, the number of the offices of state rose from seven to eighteen. With this expansion of the state's apparatus, the number of people in the organization of state also increased and led to the furtherance of specialization in societal format.[94] The most striking development came with the state's reliance on these Brahmins as advisors, law givers, ministers and as members of its administrative machinery. With gradual expansion, the number of these people in administration also increased. The Brahmin Mitrasaraman was the *samdivigrahika* (foreign minister) of King Lalitaditya.[95] Devasarman was the minister of King Jayapida.[96]

The Brahmin Bhatphalguna was the courtier of King Semgupta (AD 950-8).[97] Canpaka was the *Dharpati* (Lord of the Gate) of Harsha (AD 1089-1101).[98] Brahmin Ajaka was the minister of King Salhana (AD 1111-12).[99] Manka, the author of *Srikantha Charita* belonged to a family of ministers. His brother Alamkara was *brahadganja* (superintendent of the treasury) and later also held the post of *rajasthania* (chief justice).[100] Judicial positions were mostly the prerogatives of the Brahmins. Sringara was the *brallentrpati* (judge) under King Sussala (AD 1112-20).[101] In King Sangramraja's reign (AD 1003-28), there were a number of Brahmin councillors.[102] King Yasaskara (AD 939-48) was helped by a Brahmin in his political ascendancy.[103] Keshva, a Brahmin from Trigarhata, was King Ananta's (AD 1028-63) minister.[104]

Brahmin Raka rose to the position of the Prime Minister from that of an ordinary soldier.[105] Kalhana mentions that even Brahmins in humbler positions were appointed to very important posts.[106] Khemendra uses the word *Samanta* as a synonym for Brahmins. He has shown how the Brahmins practically monopolized the power of the state.[107] The outcome of this close relationship of state and the Brahmins was the direct exploitation of lands consolidated into compact *agraharas* both religious and secular in nature. By taking charge of the state's administrative machinery, they directly transferred control over the region's economic surplus into their own hands. Particularly at a stage when production relations were based on arbitrary appropriation of the means of production, the kings often submitted themselves to the guidance of the Brahmins and spent their countries' resources on both secular and religious establishments. Some structures and the ruins of others suggest that almost every one in Kashmir must have contributed materials and manpower to these establishments. The structures of Martand, Vijeshvara, Avantipura and others would have been impossible without creating harsh conditions for the peasants and craftsmen who expended the major proportion of their labour on these *agraharas* attached to various temples and *mathas*.

For the rural society, the cultivation of the holdings of Brahmins was an act of reverence towards the deity. Apart from labour services of the peasants and craftsmen, the

Brahmins, as the members of the landed aristocracy, were also entided to receive gifts and customary obligations. In the secular functioning of the world, people would generally believe that their life was in fact protected by divine wisdom. Thus, working on such establishments, had according to them, a hidden meaning which was a bond to be recalled in heaven.[108] Since cultivation of land was possible for only half the year due to geographical and ecological limitations, such labour assumed great economic importance. There must have been periods during which it can easily be said that the demand for labour and other services by religious and secular grantees would have led to a serious labour shortage. This in course of time led to the evolution of forced labour which is revealed in recorded information from King Samkarvarman's time (AD 883-902). Kalhana states that forced labour (*rudhabarudi)* of thirteen categories was in practice. Villagers who abandoned the carrying of loads are said to have been fined the value of the load, calculated according to prices prevailing in that area[109] There is ample evidence to prove that people were reduced to the lowest depths of poverty. On the pretext of offering sacrificial rituals to the images of innumerable deities and Gods for building and rebuilding of various structures of both a secular and religious nature, a large proportion of peasant surplus in the form of labour and produce was extracted on various occasions. *Netra Tantra* gives a detailed description of various items offered to the Saiva Acharyas and other priestly people on different occasions. He says that deities were offered clothes, gold, metals, precious stones, and various kinds of grains on various occasions to avert the effect of evil spirits.[110] This was done largely for reasons. which were not economic. The rights to these *agraharas* came direcdy from the state and this affected the proportions of cultivable waste-from above, setting the degrees of decline in the states' share of revenue and from below, the peasants. Samkarvarman levied special contributions for the pay of village clerks, *gramkayasthas* and *skandkas* as well as other taxes[111] Khemendra is also very critical of the role of *skandkas* in the revenue administration at the village level.[112] Kalhana mentions that at the instigation of the *kayasthas* only breathing was exempt from taxation.[113] King Samgram Raja himself admitted to obtaining such resources by unlawful means. In King Harsha's time (AD 1089-1101) even the Brahmins were made to render *rudabarudi* (forced labour).[114] To maintain the income of the state's treasury, Sussala (AD 1112-20) deprived various officers of the state of their living by dismissing them from the service.[115]

The state needed to derive additional taxes to support its existence; hence, created harsh conditions for those working on these *agraharas*. The Brahmins provided the justification for their dominance by exploiting people who were deeply steeped in superstition, blind belief and fear of the supernatural, in an archaic manner. These Brahmins could effectively put across their indispensability to rulers since they claimed themselves to be the creators of divinity. This is a classic case of the ruling classes selling ruling ideas as the ruling reality. Not surprisingly, therefore, contradictions developed between the non-producer ritual legitimizers (whose claims to social dominance did not last long) on the one hand, and the king, who was burdened with the task of not allowing the centre to fall apart, on the other. While pointing to the situation in medieval Europe, Wallerstein very rightly remarks that the crisis is a situation in which the restitutive mechanisms of systems are no longer functioning well and therefore the system will either be transformed fundamentally or disintegrate.[116] But in the case of Kashmir, except in the case of religious change, there was no thorough transformation in terms of politico-economic structure. Yet the system was in crisis. At times the state did not hesitate in using the crisis for its sustenance

From Samkarvarman's time, one finds a marked decline in the state's grants to these religious establishments. It was now that the state realized how untenable were the claims of the Brahmins to the large wealth locked up in these religious establishments.

However, it was not for long that the alliance of the Brahmins and the state remained intact. The Brahmins acted no more as the ideologues of the state, becoming the prophets of time, trying to cloud the strong consciousness of the masses to legitimize the state's authority. Soon, however, this ritual and economic domination came to be subjected to intra-class contradictions. The phenomenon of this interplay of contradiction, was clearly manifest in its logical consequence of the decline of the Brahmanical monopoly and the subsequent emergence of relatively more secular economic forces in the form of domination by Dammaras and *tantrins*. Apart from Kalhana, the term Dammara has been used by Khemendra to denote the members of landed groups. There would have been some ranking system among Dammaras on the basis of their wealth and power.[117] Khemendra used the terms like *damaravisaya, dammara, dammarapati, dammradhipati* and *tantrapati.*[118] However, it was only during the twelfth century AD that Dammaras came to the forefront as a dominant power. The various areas associated with the Dammaras are Lohara, Selyapura (Modern Silput), Devasara (modern divsar) and Nilasva (Modern Nilav). All these areas are located on the trade routes and also are the fertile zones for the good of agriculture.[119]

The Dammaras were not in receipt of any land grants and, therefore, did not owe their position to the state. The main source of their power was land. Their estates were mostly located in the fertile regions of the valley.[120] Kalhana's description of Jayaka Dammara in the seventh book of *Rajatarangini* throws some light on the material base of Dammaras. Jayaka, a resident of Selyapura, is supposed to have acquired great wealth from the revenue of his land and by the sale of victuals as a trader to distant regions.[121]

King Lalitaditya (AD 725-53) also puts special emphasis on the role of agriculture in augmentation of Dammara power. While addressing his ministers, he says,

> Those who wish to be powerful in this land must guard against internal dissensions. Because of foreign enemies *(parloka)* they are as little in fear of the world beyond *(parloka)* as the *Carvakas*. Those who dwell there in the mountains, and are not easily accessible should be punished even if they commit no offence. Because they are sheltered by their fastness, they are difficult to break up, even if they have accumulated wealth once. Every care should be taken that food for more than one year's consumption should not be left with villagers, because if they should keep more wealth they would become very formidable *Dammaras in* a single year strong enough to neglect the command of the King.[122]

Another factor which facilitated the emergence of the dominance of the *dammaras* was their frequent forays into activities of loot and plunder. They could always replenish their exhausted finances by resorting to robbery on the various trade routes cutting across the main valley. In fact, one of the opinions expressed is that the Dammaras were the descendants of Udambaras who lived on the fertile Karewas *(uddars)* in Kashmir from very early times. They were endowed with such zones on these Karewas which produced commercial crops such as pulses, oilseeds, saffron, etc. Besides most trade routes within the valley and outside Kashmir were cutting across these *uddars* and the Dammaras benefited from trade and also from the commercial crops which helped them to accumulate and multiply their wealth.[123] Kalhana records, 'then the citizens and Dammaras striking at each other with unpraised weapons, plundered the treasures and other valuables of the burning palace'.[124] On another occasion Kalhana refers to the looting of autumn harvest by the Dammaras.[125]

Whatever the nature of their activities, the Dammaras certainly developed as a potential force for the medieval state to contend with. The nature of their response to the state was to create a perpetual tension. They felt that the opportunity for their political ascent had been progressively narrowed down by the Brahmins, who had been running the affairs of the state for a long period. By this time the state had become aware of unholy nature of its alliance with the Brahmins but this did not help resolve the crisis. Drabu feels that the King Jayapida and Samkarvarman adopted various measures to curb the growing power of Dammaras but this was because these two kings extended the apparatus of the state to enforce the collection of revenue which was falling, due to the political turmoil and also to bring the *agrahara* lands under the direct network of taxation.[126] The Dammaras attacked both the secular and religious establishments to undermine the political influence of the Brahmins. Dammara Dhanva is found expropriating the villages endowed to the temples by kings. One of the temple priests on being asked by King Avantivarman to explain the poor state of offerings in the temple, replies, 'In the Lohara district, O King there lives a powerful Dammara, Dhanva by name who is attached to minister Sura and is treated by him like a son. The Dammara, whose power is unrestricted, has taken away the villages (belonging to shrine) and thus we can offer to *buttesha* only the oblation.' This shows that the Dammaras seem to have been confident enough to enter into an open confrontation with the royal power. Kalhana says, 'when that fierce Dammara came out at last before Sura, he made the earth shake with the tramp of his foot soldiers and did not bend his back'.[127] Drabu considers the Dammaras to have been local chiefs who had their own followers and retainers, the 'original appellation of their ancestral homeland'.[128] He also mentions the existence of tradition of *kottarajas* or lords living in fortified castles, the remnents of which are still there. This clearly establishes the fact that Kashmir was at that time divided into small chieftaincies of Dammaravisayas and Damarapatis.[129] There are lots of references to the civil strife which took place among various claimants to the throne, revealing the active intervention of the Dammaras. These interventions in various incidents of turbulent civil strife, offered the Dammaras excellent opportunities to enhance their power by resorting to various manipulative practices. Samgram Dammara while entering into a pact with the king says, 'If you promise to look upon us at all times in kindness I march before you with my troops on the very morrow.'[130] Consequently, the Dammaras came to exercise a decisive influence on the polity of Kashmir.During King Avantivarman's time, a fierce confrontation took place between the Dammaras and the state forces.[131] During tenth century AD the power of Dammaras was so well acknowledged that the deposed King Cakravarman (AD 935-6) entered into an alliance with Samgrama Dammara to seek the help of Dammaras against Tantrins to secure the throne.[132] Queen Dida (AD 980-1003), of the first Lohara dynasty in AD 981 tried to reduce the formidable power of Dammaras in functioning of the state. She had to take varied measures for this. Kalhana writes, 'Hardened by the continuous cruelty, the Queen resolved to kill the sons of Sangrama, who had shown prowess while they were stopping near her.'[133] They fled to Ghasa in Uttara, their own place and killed Kayyaka, the lord of the gate and others who attacked them. Then queen feared a rebellion and began to appease them.[134] These Dammaras frequently aligned themselves with one pretender or the other and had established their complete control over the poliical developments of that period.They made and unmade kings through their manipulative tactics and perpetuated civil strife in Kashmir. Therefore the relations of Dammaras with the state were that of perpetual conflict although some of them were co-opted by the state by giving them powerful administrative positions.[135] Kalhana says that the kind-hearted king Uccala (AD 1101-11) allowed robbers (*dasyus*) Dammaras to rise to high posts in remembrance of their past services just as the sandalwood allows the snakes to climb upon it.[136] Kalhana is very critical of Dammaras. Keeping their character in view he refers to them as *dasyu*, i.e. robbers. Kosambi is very right when he sas that because of weak state the kings were not able to maintain a regularly paid strong army and as a result Dammaras became all powerful by their cooperation and confrontation with the state.[137] While writing about the Dammaras, Kalhana says, 'Trillaka, which was a gathering place for all robbers (*dasyu*), i.e. Dammaras just as the pit is for the owls, consumption of diseases, hell for demons and the ocean for monsters—the great in deceit got the prefect of Devasara area (modern Devsar) over to his side and raised a rebellion.'[138] Dammaras had become too powerful to be ignored by the state. They also entered into matrimonial alliances with the ruling families. A powerful Dammara Gargacandra was offered matrimonial alliance by king Salhana (AD 1111-12) but the Dammaras considered him too weak to be considered for such an alliance.[139] Dammaras became very powerful and were fully participating in power struggles in the state. There was persecution of Dammaras at the hands of some rulers but by and large the kings adopted a policy of conciliation and appeasement towards Dammaras.King Kalasa (AD 1063-89) persecuted some of the Dammaras when he came to power but soon we find that he reversed his policy,when he tried to secure his position by posting Ksirabhupa and many other Dammaras as guards at their respective places Naunahra, etc.[140] During the reign of Ananta (AD 1028-63), Tribhuvana, the powerful commander-in-chief, sought the help of Dammaras to deny the throne to the king.[141] King Harsha (AD 1089-1102) indulged in persecuting some of the Dammaras. From *Rajatarangini* it becomes clear that Harsha excluded Dammaras from benefits of lavish gifts and positions of power. Kalhana writes, 'Then furious like another death, he ordered the governor to slay all Dammaras who had become so powerful.' He first attacked all Dammaras of Holada in

Madavarajya and killed them like birds in their nests. At the gate of the King's palace, there were seen every where rows of triumphal arches with Dammara skulls which appeared like cups. Indeed whoever brought the head of a Dammara received bracelets, dresses and other gifts or rewards which were hanging at the gate at the royal palace. After totally exterminating the Dammaras in Madvarajaya, he hurriedly went to Karamrajya to adopt the same policy.[142] But the Dammaras in Karamrajya rose in rebellion and stopped the governor from taking any action against them. This led to anarchy which was further precipitated by worsening economic conditions in Kashmir. 'Harshas rule though initially witnessing a period of consolidation later due to heavy fiscal exactions necessitated by luxurious curt and cruel persecution of Dammaras saw the rise of grave rebellion under the leadership of Uccala and Sussala, both relations of Harsha from a side branch of Lohara dynasty.'[143]

According to Kalhana, during the tenth century AD the Tantrins, Lavanyas and the Ekangas also came to exercise their influence in the political affairs of medieval state. Hosts of Tantrin foot soldiers formed a confederacy strong enough to punish or favour any ruler of the land.[144] The kings became mere puppets in the hands of the Tantrins and sought each others' favours like village officials, by offering bribes.[145] Kalhana lamented, 'In this land the rulers of which had conquered Kanyakubja and other countries, the kings now maintained themselves by giving bills of exchange (*hundika*) to the Tantrins.'[146] There are plenty of such signs of hostility within the Kashmir nobility at this time. But the obvious division was between the Dammaras and the Tantrins. The former believed that they were the key to the state's prosperity and tried to stress their social pre-eminence while the latter thought that their positions could easily be justified along military lines. But in reality, at the political level, the dominance of both was determined not only by their participation in the active political life of the medieval state but was made more explicit by the official recognition and enlistment of their support by the state for suppressing the other social orders. Since the ideological apparatus of the state had become secure with the decline of the power of the Brahmins, the state continued patronizing the warrior and aristocratic elements in turn in order to safeguard its authority. This is clearly highlighted in *Rajatarangini.* The deposed Chakravarman sought the help of the Dammaras to combat the Tantrin power.[147] Dammara Sangarama while aware of his own powers, discounts the strength of the Tantrins with utter contempt in these words, 'Tantrins are blades of grass, are they counted in battle, which is a last in which I could not help you.'[148] In fact the analysis of the nature of the Dammaras' and the Tantrins' relations with the king and various officers of state that worked in the shadow of that power, and the nature of their attitude towards each other, is a prerequisite for understanding the strong social and political significance of the state in the pre-Sultanate period in Kashmir's history.

One clearly finds that there was a transition from a system produced by singular ethnicity and kinship lineages, to one depending on priestly sanction for legitimization of the political system. The new political system gave autonomy to the priests with regard to productive land and the surpluses produced. In these circumstances, the growth of the state's apparatus and its dependence on the sustenance obtained by appropriation of the produce, which was by right that of the peasants, was but natural. But the increasing need to transfer production to the priestly class and the monopoly of surplus to the state to support its expanding structure, began to affect the positions of the secular economic forces. Consequently, the secular forces tried to assert their positions by forcibly taking over the processes of production. This became necessary as the priests realized that hereditary occupations in the production processes determined the quantum of political power.

Thus, through the evolution of early state formation till the establishment of the Sultanate, a definite pattern of alignments and readjustments is seen among various classes in Kashmir.

Two constants, however, persist through this troubled history. These are the institutions of kingship and the royal domination which persisted *pari passu* due to the blind obedience of the fearful masses. The kings changed but not their hierarchical positions. The masses were taken on a royal ride through this whole process of the legitimization of Shaivite Tantricism without it substantially affecting their socio-economic conditions for a better existence. Classes began to emerge in the process of internal disturbances as well as external intrusions during the resolution of this contradiction. The principal manifestation of such a change lay in the gradual conversion from Shaivism to Islam on a large scale. The game has all along been one not of restructuring power relations, as much as it has been of access to power.

Notes

1. M. Mann, *Sources of Social Power: A History of Power from the Beginning to AD 1760,* 2 vols., Cambridge, 1986, vol. I, Chap. 10.
2. *Nilmata Purana* (Sanskrit), English translation by Ved Kumari Gai, 2 vols., Srinagar, 1973, vv. 986-7, p. 251.
3. *Tārkṣya* is the name of a mythical being in the *Rigveda* described as a horse with the epithet *áriṣṭa-nemi* 'with intact wheel-rims' (*RV* 189.6, *RV* 10.178.1), but alternatively taken to be a bird (RV 5.51) and later identified with Garuda (*Mahabharata, Harivamsha*) or Garuda's father (*Bhagavata Purana* 6.6.2, 21), counted among the offspring of Kashyapa in *Mahabharata* (1.2548, 4830 and 12468). It is also the name of the hymn *RV* 10.178 ascribed to *Tārkṣya Ariṣṭanemi*. I think it refers to Aryans here because they were more powerful and aggressive in the neighbouring regions.
4. D.D. Kosambi, 'Origins of Feudalism in Kashmir', in *Journal of the Bombay Branch of Asiatic Society* (*Fifteenth Anniversary Volume*), Bombay, 1957, pp. 110-11.

5. *Mrgendratantra,* Kashmir Series of Texts and Studies (Sanskrit) (henceforth KSTS), no. I, Bombay, 1930. See also *Gandharva Tantra* (Sanskrit), KSTS, edited by R.C. Kak, Srinagar, 1934.
6. *Nilmata Purana* (henceforth *NP),* vol. II, vv. 915-83, pp. 232-50. Todd mentions them as Toorskas who ruled Arverm in Sakadipa. Alexander Cunningham, *Archaeological Survey Report,* vol. II, 1863-4, p. 10.
7. *NP,* vol. I, p. 49,
8. James Fergusson, *Tree and Serpent Worship,* London, 1873, pp. 60-l.
9. Cunningham, *Archaeological Survey Report,* vol. II, 1863-4, p. 10.
10. James Todd, *Annals and Antiquities of Rajasthan,* London, 1914, p. 45..
11. *NP,* vol. II, vv. 1-92, 1000, pp. 1-27 and 252-5.
12. Ibid.
13. Henri J.M. Classen and Peter Skalnik, *The Early State, Models and Reality,* Hague: Mouton, 1978, pp. 367-650. See also Henri J.M. Classen, 'The Internal Dynamics of Early State', *Current Anthropology,* vol. XXV, no. 4, August-October 1984, pp. 365-76.
14. *NP,* vol. II, pp. 58-76
15. *Svacchanda Tantra* (Sanskrit), KSTS, nos. XXXI, XXXVII, XLIV, XLVIII, LI, LIII, LVI, Bombay, 1921, 1923, 1926, 1927, 1930, 1933, 1935. See also *Netra Tantra* (Sanskrit), KSTS, nos. XLVI, LXI, Bombay, 1926.
16. V.N. Drabu, *Saivagamas: A Study of Socio-Economic Ideas and Institutions,* Delhi, 1990, p. 36; S.C. Ray, *Early History and Culture of Kashmir,* Calcutta, 1957, pp. 1-20.
17. Karl Marx and F. Engels, *Selected Works,* 3 vols., Moscow, 1969, vol. I, pp. 17-24, see also James W. Russel, *Modes of Production in World History,* London, 1988, pp. 44-5.
18. David Laibman, 'Modes of Production and Theories of Transition', in *Science and Society,* vol. XLVIII, no. 3, Fall 1984, p. 268.
19. Herbert Frey, 'Religion as an Ideology of Domination', in *Religion and Revolt,* Manchester, 1984, p. 16.
20. Kalhana, *Rajatarangini* (Sanskrit), English translation with notes by M.A. Stein, 2 vols., Westminster, 1900, vol. I, book I, vv. 101, 107, pp. 19-20; vol. II, pp. 239-41 (henceforth *RT).*
21. Hiuen Tsang; *Si-yu-ki,* English translation by S. Beal, *Buddhist Records of the Western World,* 2 vols., London, 1884, vol. I, pp. 148-

9. See also G.M. Bongard Levin, *Mauryan India,* Delhi, 1985, pp. 21-33.

22. Reinard, *Memoirs Surt>Inde* (French), Paris, 1849, p. 189.
23. Kalhana, *RT,* vol. I, book IV, vv. 102-4, p. 9.
24. P.C. Bagchi, *India and China,* Calcutta, 1944, pp. 72-3; D.D. Kosambi, op. cit., pp. 108-12.
25. Jean Naudou, *Buddhists of Kashmir* (French) Presses Universitaries de France, 1968. English translation by Brereton and Picron. Delhi, 1980, p. 1.
26. Ibid., pp. 2-3.
27. Chu Sanzang Jiji 14; 543. Fozu tong 36.T 49344.
28. G. Coedes, *The Indianised States of South East Asia*, Honolulu, 1968, pp. 19-21, 23, 50, 51, 63-4.
29. Liang Shu, *Dynastic History of Liang* by Yao Silian (557-637) Beijing Zhonghua Shuju 1973.25.256. As a result Shaivism did not receive much patronage and remained in infancy for centuries during the predominance of Buddhism from almost the beginning of seventh century BC to early fourth century AD.
30. Kalhana, *RT,* vol. I, p. 23; vol. II, book I, pp. 110-12, 114, 122, 312, 316; book III, vv 348, 350, 458, pp. 21, 23, 46, 47, 102, 112; M. Marcell, *The Gift,* London, 1954, p. 45.
31. Kosambi, op. cit., pp. 108-20.
32. Sir John Marshall, *Mohanjodaro and the Indus Civilisation,* 3 vols., London, 1931, vol. I, pp. vii, 49-52. See also Plate nos. XII, XCIV-XCV of the same book. Regarding this form of worship in Kashmir also we have a bulk of evidence. The earliest evidence is that of *Sapta Matrika* preserved in Devasar and Pandrenthan (*Purana Adhisthana*) Panels in Sri Pratap Museum in Srinagar. *Nilmata Purana* also mentions various river goddesses. *NP,* vol. II, vv. 82, 145, 159, pp. 22-4.
33. Kalhana, *RT,* vol. I, book I, vv. 122, 123, 333, 335, 348; book III, 99; book V, v. 55. See also T.A.G. Rao, *Elements of Hindu Iconography,* 2 vols., Madras, 1914, pp. 379-85.
34. C. Greertz, 'Centres, Kings, and Charisma, Reflections on the Symbolics of Power', in *Culture and its Creators,* edited by J. Ben David and T.N. Clark (Essays in Honour of E. Shills), Chicago and London, 1977, pp. 34-72.
35. *Nilmata Purana*, vol. II, pp. 22-4.
36. Will Durant, *Story of Civilization, Our Oriental Heritage*. New York, 1963, p. 58.

37. B. Bhattacharya, *Saivism and the Phallic World,* vol. I, Oxford & IBH, New Delhi, 1975, pp. 68-72.
38. Ibid., but see *Rig Veda* also.
39. Drabu, op. cit., pp. 166-70.
40. Ibid., pp. 167-8.
41. Bhattacharya, *Saivism and the Phallic World,* pp. 270-1.
42. Aijaz Ahmad Bandey, *Prehistoric Kashmir: Paleolithic and Neolithic Cultures*, Dilpreet, Delhi, 2008, pp. 34-56.
43. In ancient Iran the matriarchical tradition was very strong and was even passed on to Aryans. R. Ghirshman, *Iran: A volume in the Pelican Archaeological Series,* London, 1954, pp. 27-8.
44. Will Durant, *Story of Civilization. Our Oriental Heritage*, New York, 1963, pp. 33-43.
45. *Nilmata Purana* (Sanskrit), English translation by Ved Kumari Gai, published by Jammu and Kashmir & Academy of Art, Culture and Languages, Srinagar, 2 vols., 1973, vol. I, pp. 102-3.
46. Herbert Spencer, *Sociology*, vol. I, New York, 1910, p. 406.
47. *Indian Archaeology; A Review*, 1962-63, 1966, 1967, 1969 and 1970.
48. B.M. Pande, *Asian Perspective*, vol. 14, University of Hawaii, 1971.
49. B. Bhattacharya, *Shaivism and the Phallic World,* Oxford & IBH, New Delhi, 1975, pp. 69-70.
50. *Nilmata Purana*, pp. 116-17. Having made a fish of sand one should fill it with milk, provide it with eyes of jewels, and then give it to a Brahmana. . . . Then a nice white bull, clothed, endowed with all scents and bearing all sorts of grains should be given to the twice born. Ibid., pp. 116-17.
51. John A. Hall and C. John Ikenbery, *The State*, Open University Press, Milton Keynes, Canada, 1989, pp. 29-30. For dominance of Hindu rituals over the Buddhist ones, which also was a cause for failure of Buddhism to create a stable political process. For details see: David N. Gellner, *Monk, Householder and Tantric Priest,* Cambridge, 1992, 1st Indian edn. 1993, pp. 83-4.
52. *NP,* vol. II, vv. 1175, 1191, 1315, 1316, 1386, 1393, pp. 297-347. See also J.N. Farquhar, *An Outline of Hindu Religious Literature,* London, 1919, pp. 165-7.
53. *Svacchanda Tantra* (Sanskrit), KSTS, vol. II, pp. 326-9, D.D. Kosambi, *Introduction to the Study of Indian History,* Bombay, 1956, p. 275. See also J.P.S. Oberoi, *Politics of Kaula Kings,* Manchester, 1962, pp. 27-33.

54. S.D. Singh, 'The Early Development of Kingship in Pre-Muslim India', in Ian Mabbett, ed., *Pattern of Kingship and Authority in Traditional Asia,* Croom Helm, London and Monash University Press, Melbourne, 1985, p. 88.
55. Jean-Claude Gaily (ed.), *Kingship and the Kings,* London, 1989, pp. 220-49
56. Somananda, *Sivadrsti, Kashmir Sanskrit Granthavali,* edited by Madhusudan Kaul Sastri, KSTS, vol. 54, Srinagar, 1934, VII, vv. 121-5. See also *Svacchanda Tantra,* KSTS, X, pp. 61-6; II, pp. 535-6. Abhinava Gupta, *Tantraloka* (Sanskrit), KSTS, Bombay, 1925, VIII, 155-61 and *Malinivijayottara Tantra,* KSTS, Bombay, 1922, I, p. 697, *NP.,* vol. II, vv. 461, 480, pp. 118-24.
57. *Nilmata Purana,* ibid., pp. 116-17.
58. The study of Kashmir's early geography has rarely been the subject of specialized research. The efforts of M.A. Stein on the subject indicate probable boundaries, seasonal variation and crop patterns. Stein has based his description on Kalhana's *Rajatarangini* and *Nilmata Purana.* M.A. Stein, *Ancient Geography of Kashmir,* Calcutta, 1899. Some useful literature on Kashmir's geography is also provided by Somadeva's *Kathasaritsagara,* English translation under the title *Ocean of Stream of Stories* and notes edited by N.M. Penzer and E.H. Tawney, 10 vols., London, 1924. The literature in the works of F. Drew, *Jammu and Kashmir Territories,* London. 1895; Peer Hassan Shah, *Tarikh-i-Hassan* (Persian), 3 vols., Srinagar, 1885, Research Department Library, is significant in detail and should prove rewarding in scrutinizing some traditional analysis which has been uncritically accepted so far.
59. *Malini Vijaya Uttara Tantra* (Sanskrit), KSTS, no. XVIII, vv. 22, 24, 28.
60. *NP,* vol. II, v. 359, p. 93.
61. There are plentiful references of this nature in early Sanskrit texts on Kashmir. For example, see *Katyayana Smriti,* edited by P.V. Kane, Poona, 1933, pp. 55-6.
62. Kalhana, *RT,* book VII, vv. 12, 13, 15; book VIII, vv. 768-5, 900-94, 2076. Khemendra, *Lokaprakasha* (Sanskrit), edited by Pandit Jagadar Zadoo Shastri, KSTS, Srinagar, 1947, p. 17. See also *NP,* vol. II, pp. 147-212
63. *NP,* vol. II, v. 454, p. 117.

64. Ibid., v. 480, p. 124.
65. Ibid., pp. 189-91.
66. Ibid., vv. 560-3, p. 143
67. Drabu, op. cit., p. 99, for details see also J.N. Banerjee, *Development of Hindu Iconography,* Calcutta, 1956, pp. 220-1.
68. Drabu, ibid., pp. 185-8. For details see Kalhana, *RT,* vol. I, books IV and V, pp. 120-235.
69. *NP,* vol. II, vv. 507, 653, 901, pp. 130-66. The answers to important questions arising out of this type of analysis have been provided by J.R.F. Price, *Rituals and Power: The Roman Imperial Cult in Asia Minor*, Cambridge, 1984.
70. *NP,* vol. II, pp. 13-166
71. Kalhana, *RT,* vol. I, book I, vv. 87-93, pp. 15-17.
72 Ibid., vol. I, book I, v. 96, p. 17. Kalhana does not give the exact period of his rule but places him as the ninth ruler of Gonda dynasty. The date of accession of the first ruler of the Gonda dynasty is assumed to be *Kali Samvat* 653, *Laukika Samvat* 628.
73. Ibid., book I, v. 98, p. 18
74. Ibid.
75. Ibid., pp. 124-6. *Agrahara* of Varabals is the Barawul area near Wangath. Except Kalhana no other sources mention Jaluka as the son of Ashoka. See also Bishop Cowie, *JASB,* 1866, p. 101.
76. Ibid., vol. I, book I, vv. 174-6, pp. 31-3. The *agrahara* of Kantkotsa is modern Kondur village near Biru.
77. Ibid., book I, vv. 307-11, p. 46.
78. Ibid., Aksa ruled for sixty years, the year of his succession according to *Laukika* 2587-6-13.
79. Gopaditya also ruled for sixty years from *Laukika* 2707-6-19. Kalhana, *RT,* vol. I, book I, vv. 89-90, 100, pp. 18, 50-l.
80. Ibid., p. 52.
81. Tunjana ruled for 36 years from *Laukika* 2960, ibid., book II, v. 55, p. 60.
82. Ibid., pp. 72-80.
83. Ibid.
84. Ibid., book III, p. 14. His calculated date of accession is *Laukika* 2599-2-l. He ruled for 35 years.
85. Ibid., vol. I, book I, vv. 480-1, p. 115.
86. He ruled from *Laukika* 3772-6-25 for 36 years, ibid., vol. I, book IV, vv. 126-32, pp. 130-1.

87. Ibid., book V, vv. 23-5, pp. 187-8, Panchta is the village Panzath near Devasar area in the district Anantnag.
88. Ibid., book, VI, vv. 180-207, pp. 282-6.
89. Ibid.
90. *Malinivijayottara Tantra* (Sanskrit), KSTS, no. XXXVII, Bombay, 1922, I, p. 697.
91. *Svacchanda Tantra,* vol. II, pp. 535-6.
92. Abhinava Gupta, *Tantra Sara* (Sanskrit), edited by Pandit Mukundram Shastri, Bombay, 1918, pp. 60-5; for details see also *NP,* vol. II, pp. 117-80.
93. *NP,* vol. II, vv. 507, 653, 655, 900, 903, pp. 113-16, 228.
94. Kalhana, *RT,* vol. I, book I, v. 120, p. 22.
95. Kalhana, *RT,* book IV, vv. 137-8, p. 132. He was the fifth king of Karkota dynasty.
96. Ibid., book IV, vv. 469, 551, 583, pp. 171, 173, 463.
97. Ibid., book VI, vv. 168, 194, 195, pp. 248-52, later he rose to the position of the Prime Minister but was soon ousted by Abhimanyu AD 958-72.
98. Ibid., book VII, vv. 1177-8, pp. 361-90.
99. Ibid., vol. II, book VIII, v. 472, p. 39.
100. Manka, *Srikanthacarita* (Sanskrit) with Jonaraja's commentary, edited by Pandit Durga Prasad and K.P. Parab, *KM* 3, Bombay, 1900, canto XXV, pp. 40-1; Kalhana, *RT,* book VIII, v. 2423.
101. Ibid., book VIII, v. 2422. The *Smritis* also refer to preferential treatment to Brahmins for appointment to judicial and other offices of state, P.V. Kane, *History of Dharmasastra,* 4 vols., Pune, 1960, p. 271.
102. Ibid., book VIII, vv. 576-90, pp. 130-3, see also Krishna Mohan, *Early Medieval History of Kashmir,* AD 1003-1171, Delhi, 1981, pp. 211-25.
103. Kalhana, *RT,* vol. II, book VII, pp. 242-5.
104. Ibid., vol. II, book VII, p. 278.
105. Kosambi, 'Origins of Feudalism in Kashmir', op. cit., p. 111.
106. Ibid.
107. Khemendra, *Lokprakasha,* op. cit., Chapter I, pp. 7-12.
108. David Cannadine and S. Price, *Rituals of Royalty,* Cambridge, 1987, pp. 1-19.
109. Kalhana, *RT,* vol. I, book V, vv. 172-5, pp. 209-10.
110. *Netra Tantra,* KSTS, no. XIX, 53-65, see also *NP,* vol. II, pp. 122-70.

111. Kalhana, *RT,* vol. I, book V, v. 175, p. 210.
112. Khemendra, *Samayamatrika* (Sanskrit), edited by Durga Prasad and K.P. Parab, *KM* 10, Bombay, 1925, canto VI, p. 15.
113. Kalhana, *RT,* vol. I, book V, v. 184, p. 211.
114. Ibid., book VII, vv. 1089-90, p. 352.
115. Ibid., book VIII, vv. 563-7, 1949, 1951, 1961, pp. 151-2.
116. I. Wallerstein, *The Politics of the World Economy, the State, the Movements and the Civilization,* Cambridge, 1984, p. 23.
117. A. Weber, *Loka Prakasha of Ksemendra.* Indische Studien, XVIII, 1898. IVP.60
118. Khemendra, *Lokprakasha,* op. cit., IV, p. 60.
119. Kalhana, *RT,* vol. I, book VII, v. 122; vol. II, book VIII, vv. 15, 17, 424, 591, 733, 1430, 1637, 3115, 2749, 3115, pp. 2, 36, 48, 59, 112, 129, 216, 245.
120. Kalhana, *RT,* vol. I, book VII, v. 494, pp. 307-8.
121. Ibid.
122. Ibid., book IV, vv. 345-8, p. 154.
123. Ibid.
124. Kalhana, *RT,* vol. II, book VII, v. 1572, p. 389
125. Ibid., vol. II, book VIII, v. 795, p. 64
126. V.N. Drabu, *Kashmir Polity,* Delhi, 1986, Appendix I, p. 341. Kalhana, *RT,* vol. I, book IV, v. 628, p. 177.
127. Kalhana, *RT,* vol. I, book V, v. 57, p. 194
128. V.N. Drabu, *Kashmir Polity,* New Delhi, 1986, Appendix I, p. 336.
129. Khemendra, *Lokprakasha,* op. cit., IV, p. 60.
130. Kalhana, *RT,* vol. I, book V, v. 324, p. 225.
131. Ibid., pp. 51-7.
132. Ibid., VI, 280-1, 354.
133. Ibid., 280-2.
134. Ibid.
135. Ibid., vol. II, book VIII, 520, 627, 960, 1640, 1681.
136. Ibid., 2750.
137. Kosambi, op. cit., p. 139.
138. Ibid., book VIII, 2731-2.
139. Ibid., VIII, 441-2.
140. Ibid., book VII, 266.
141. Ibid., book VIII, 154.
142. Ibid., VII, vv. 1228-40.
143. Krishna Mohan, *Early Medieval History of Kashmir,* p. 202.

144. Ibid., vol. II, book V, vv. 304-31, pp. 224-5.
145. Ibid.
146. Ibid., vol. I, book V, v. 266, p. 221.
147. Ibid.
148. Kalhana, *RT,* vol. I, book V, v. 266, p. 21.

2

Conversions to Islam and the Consolidation of a Social Base of Power in the Sultanate

This chapter discusses the problem of mass conversion to Islam in fourteenth and fifteenth-century Kashmir that reshaped the process of constructing and reconstructing identities in the region. This phenomenon also played an important role in the consolidation of the social basis of power in the Shahmir state (AD 1339-1540). The question of conversion to Islam in India is a significant aspect of Indian history which has received very little attention from scholars. Conversion to Islam in medieval India is a crucial historical reality. But until recently research on this topic has been extremely scarce as compared to various other aspects of Indian history.

Conversion to Islam occurred on a mass scale, yet the acceptance of the new religion was seen only in the peripheral regions of pre-partition India: East Bengal, West Punjab, Malabar and Kashmir. In medieval western Punjab, Kashmir, and East Bengal, this phenomenon was very closely related to the social, economic, political, cultural, and even geophysical specificities of these various regions. Thus, for example, the large-scale effort of clearing of forests for extension of agriculture under the leadership of Sufi saints in East Bengal over a period of time led to peasantization and the people taking part in this process acquired not only a new social identity but also religion, i.e. Islam, in association with their masters.[1] According to Ira M. Lapidus, 'In East Bengal, Brahmin and caste influences were weaker, and Buddhism was the dominant religion. Under Muslim rule, East and West Bengal were integrated under a single regime, and the new political environment was permeated by Islamic symbols. Under the leadership of Muslim landlords, warriors and Sufis, the process of agricultural expansion continued into East Bengal making converts out of newly sedentarized peoples.'[2] In western Punjab the numerically dominant caste was that of Jats who acquired economic prosperity based on agriculture but that did not correlate with the social reality within the caste-based Hindu society. To remedy this, *Jats* turned to religion. Many of them accepted Islam, some turned towards Sikhism, and others acquired Hindu identity, like Dhanna the Jat.[3] It has been argued that the hold of the 'Muslim state' over these regions was seldom established for long periods of time, unlike as in the heartland of the 'Muslim state' Delhi, UP and Bihar where the population remained overwhelmingly Hindu. Not more than 20 to 25 per cent turned towards Islam.[4]

It would not be logical to attribute the entire responsibility for these conversions to state' initiatives alone[5] The lack of comprehensive study by social scientists has allowed historical memory to represent the reasons for this conversion differentially from generation to generation. In this process, the earlier versions of historical memory disappeared irremediably and took on new forms that dominated the popular perception. Generally, the memory of events is based not only on the actual event but also on its perception, interpretation, and transmission. While this might suggest a dichotomy between historical reality and memory, which can be problematic, it is important to reiterate here that my interest is also to indicate mediations that oversee the flow of memory into reality. In the process of disappearance of old versions of memory and the rise of new versions there are always remnants that are picked and chosen for various reasons from the oldest strata these take on new meanings in the new context.[6] This is what happened to the phenomenon of religious conversions in Kashmir's history. The historical memory of this phenomenon did not base itself on empirical evidence, but was largely shaped by the popular expectation, the mediator's perception, emotion, and prejudice and always resulted in exaggerating and at times in undermining the actual historical reality.

In Kashmir's context too, when in 1990 the Kashmiri Hindus were forced to migrate to other parts of India because of Pakistan's involvement in cold war politics that impacted South Asia, the medieval phenomenon of conversion to Islam received lot of attention and was interpreted, reinterpreted and misinterpreted by Kashmiri Hindu migrants and Muslims divorcing it from basic historical reality. Whatever of this phenomenon had survived in memory was given new life. Earlier it was this memory also that was given a fixed form in manuscripts by various Sanskrit and Persian chroniclers in Kashmir and outside. Many among the succeeding generation of scholars did not subject the content of these chronicles to scrutiny. As a result, whenever Hindu or Muslim fundamentalists have overexcited people's sensibility to religious identity, interpreted religion for its own ends, divorced faith from its spiritual ethos and created myths and legends without any substance, it has resulted in historical memory gaining legitimacy over the actual historical reality at popular level in society.

Besides, in our age, the manipulation of people's sentiments of deprivation for petty political ends under the guise of religious preaching has become more evident because of the power to propagate fast and over a very wide range of geographical space, especially in South Asia. This is one reason why I shall examine, in this chapter, the phenomenon of the mass conversion to Islam in Kashmir, which took place between the early fourteenth to fifteenth centuries.

Though these conversions from Brahminism to Islam in Kashmir did primarily serve the purpose of the medieval state; it would still be inaccurate to attribute it entirely to the state's initiative alone.[7]

Conversion is a long-drawn, multifaceted process. External and internal stimuli with material bases and socio-cultural dimensions contributed to this process in varying degrees. This took place over a historical period of time. In Kashmir, people are dependent upon different forms of production because their involvement in agriculture offered only a one-crop economy and therefore their dependence on pastoralism, craft production and trade always kept them receptive to external influences and established contacts with various civilizations from very early times. These contacts had been established around 2000 BC. The early metal objects in Kashmir also reflect the Indus Valley/ Harrapan influence.[8] When we look at Indus art forms and hieroglyphics they appear to be intimately connected with tantric motifs. This influence of Indus and give and take between Kashmir and trans-Himalayan regions including Iran, was not limited to material goods alone. The religious practices in Indus valley had also evolved in tribal, pastoral and agricultural practices. One of the earliest evidence is the three-faced prototype of Shiva on an Indus Valley seal wearing buffalo horns as part of his head dress.[9]

Kashmir also had a close relationship with Iran and the region of Indus from prehistoric times. In third millennium BC, it was a well-established practice in Iran to express ones reverence towards various deities and mother Goddesses after victory over their enemies and also after successes were achieved in various other ventures.[10] Invoking of various mother goddesses such as Raegnya, Sharika, Zalla (Jawala), Durga, on several occasions a year has also been an early ancient practice among Kashmiri Pandits. In 2000 BC the inventions of Bronze Age improved the techniques of making metal objects and created increasing demand for raw materials. This source of wealth enabled Iran to enter into trade relations with various regions of India among other countries.[11] Therefore, to assume that Kashmir was not familiar with these developments and remained uninfluenced by them even from prehistoric times, is unacceptable, particularly when many other influences and items from Iran travelled to early ancient Kashmir via Indus Valley too.[12] In 3000 BC trade was in full swing, it is most unlikely that primitive Kashmiris were not part of it. From the beginning Kashmir had strong linkages with Persia, Central Asian regions, China, Egypt and many other civilizations. In strengthening these linkages, Buddhism had also played a strong role.[13] A Kashmiri monk Gunavarman (431-367 BC) was delighted after visiting Java when he received official invitation from the emperor of southern dynasty Song in China and travelled by ship through the port of Guangzhou and arrived at the Song capital at 431 BC.[14] In AD 458 five Kashmiri Bikshus arrived from Kashmir and introduced Buddhism in China.[15]

Therefore the whole process of state formation in Kashmir was not only determined by the local factions, ecological, social, economic conditions but also by external forces and influences from very early times. All these conditions led to the evolution of a polity which had its own strengths and weaknesses, some of which could be generalized in pan-Indian patterns like the large concentration *agraharas* (land grants) of priestly Brahmins for transforming the polity. The varied local factions like Damaras, Ekangas, Tantrins, Rainas, Magres and Lavanyas chose religion as the ideological basis for opposition to the state and the elite. For many of them abandoning their Buddhist and Hindu faiths (along with Tantric, Shakta and other cults) and accepting Islam was a kind of protest against the state of affairs and the state with whose politicians they were in a relationship of perpetual cooperation and confrontation for most of the time. The religious borders were also fluid at that time. On one hand, Buddhists were persecuted by Shaivites on a large scale and on the other hand, Shaivites and Vaishnavites were not ready to see eye to eye with each other. Among the Shaivites, the Kalmukhas, Kapaliks and Tantric cults were also fighting among themselves for religious supremacy.[16] Therefore, the fourteenth century, Kashmir witnessed a religious conversion not only from Brahminism to Islam but also from Buddhism, Tantricism, Shaktaism and other minor cults to Islam.[17] Jean Naudou says,

> It is strange to see our Buddhists participate in that defence of Kashmir, aganist the invader with the 'weapons' of a Buddhist of the 11th century, that is to say with the aid of *mantra*. The Blue Annals tell us in fact that at this epoch, when an army of mlecchas was approaching Kashmir, a Kashmiri master teacher, *Prajnaraksita*, disciple of Naropa, stopped its advance by reciting some mantra. It is quite probable this refers to the campaign of Mamud against Kashmir, which was stopped at Lohara in 1015 to 1021, According to historians. as to the ritual which the Kashmiri monk accomplished, one imagines it quite similar to that of the knife of diamond (*vajrakartari*) described in *Hevajra Tantra* (which we are aware, was at the time, known and studied in Kashmir), and it was not that very simple ritual.[18]

Mohammad Isaq Khan says that Islam in fact became the religion of a great majority of rural Kashmir between fifteenth to eighteenth centuries largely because, through the *rishis,* it allowed the main configuration pre-existing Kashmiri popular religion to adapt itself to the wider Islamic framework.[19] The tradition of *rishis* was introduced in Kashmir by Buddhists. *Rishis* were all Buddhists and Hindus. It was after conversion that they were given Muslim names but after the conversion the *rishis* and their shrines continued to be revered by both the Hindus and Muslims down to present times. The best examples are Manak Rishi of Bedara (the present Bidder village in Anantnag district) referred as Manashah after conversion. Be it Rishi Mol of Anantnag, or *rishi* of Batmaloo (known as Batmaloo Saheb) in Srinagar, or other areas, during the annual Urs (celebration) the people of surrounding villages do not cook or eat non-vegetarian food as a mark of their reverence to the *rishis* which is an ancient practice. As Buddhists these *rishis* never ate non-vegetarian food. These *rishis* were originally Buddhist monks, many of whom were either killed or they turned towards Shaivism and subsequently after conversion the names of their shrines were also changed or modified with Muslim names.

However, we do not deny the role of these *rishis* and Sufis in the spread of spiritual teachings in the valley but it would be wrong to attribute the so-called, 'mass-conversion of Kashmir to their miraculous exploits alone. Of course, certain individual's conversions (who were disciples of some Sufi saints) must have been followed by group conversions. However, such a process of conversion took a long time to progress and mature, extending over centuries, largely owing to the persistence of pre-Islamic customs and beliefs. Islamisation was thus a slow and long process involving initially the converts' passive adherence to Islam but ultimately continuous progress towards bringing one's beliefs, attitudes or modes of conduct into harmony with *Shariat.*[20] This does not necessarily mean that mass conversions did not take place between fourteenth and fifteenth century. What M.I. Khan states is that the process of complete Islamisation took a long period of time, which means that there was a period of transition between accepting the new religion and adopting the principles of *Shariat.* The thesis that most of the people accepted Islam in the eighteenth century is not true because immediately after the Shahmir period we find the names of various local communities like Rainas, Magres, Tantrins, Lavanyas and Damaras, etc., appearing as Muslim names. Besides, the eighteenth-century sources are silent about conversions, except for scattered instances. If the majority of the people had not turned towards Islam why Sultan Zain-ul-Abidin should make an appeal and leave options open for Hindus to return back to their faith and region.[21]

This is an interesting phenomenon which has to be investigated by critically examining the available literature. The efforts of historians like G.M.D. Sufi, R.K. Parmu, Mohibbul Hassan, N.K. Zutshi and S.A.A. Rizvi to reconstruct the history of medieval Kashmir have attributed this mass conversion of non-Muslims to prohibition of *sati* and the application of *gashqa* (*tilak*, a religious mark applied by the Hindus on the forehead)[22]. However, the chief person who prevailed upon Sikandar to adopt an intolerant attitude towards the non-Muslims was Saifuddin, who was in this respect his evil genius. The Sultan at first resisted him, but in the end gave in and allowed himself to be used as an instrument of his minister's religious fanaticism. Saifuddin with the zeal of a new convert called upon not only Brahmins but all Hindus to embrace Islam. As a result, some became Muslims. Those who refused had to pay *jizya*. Others who would not or could not pay, decided to leave Kashmir and take refuge in other parts of India. In their misplaced zeal for their faith, Sikandar and Saifuddin were also responsible for the destruction of images and temples.[23]

Another historian N.K. Zutshi also says, besides the construction of the town of Sikandarpur and the magnificent Jamia Masjid, he (i.e. Sultan Sikandar) studded his kingdom with a number of mosques and hospices. This was the outcome of his devotion to his religion. He was always eager to do what his religion required of him. His encouragement of Muslim learning and to learned men, attracted to his court a large number of missionaries and scholars from Persia and Central Asian countries. They came in groups of which the most important one was of 300 Sayyids and scholars led by Sayyid Muhammad Hamadani, the son of Sayyid Ali Hamadani, who arrived in Kashmir in AD 1393. The Sultan came under the spell of Sayyid Muhammad and became his disciple in 'word and deed'.[24] The Sayyids' resolve to dispel darkness of infidelity from the kingdom formed the basis of the Sultan's subsequent attitude towards non-Muslims. They found in Suhabhatta, renamed Malik Saif-ud-din after converting to Islam, who was the commander-in-chief of the state forces, a spirited instrument with the fiery zeal of a new convert. The outcome was unfortunate for

Hindus—numerous Hindu temples and images were broken. The subjects were forced to abjure idolatry and pay *jizya.* The Hindu usages and customs were debarred from holding high offices.[25]

According to S.A.A. Rizvi, in Kashmir they (Iranian Sufis) seem to have found new avenues for promoting their commercial interests and ransacked Hindu temples in order to enrich themselves and their local followers. The arrival of Sayyid Ali's son, Mir Mohammad, in 1393 reinvigorated the evangelical spirit of the earlier Iranian settlers. Sultan Sikandar (AD 1389-1413) became a disciple of the young migrant and constructed a *khanqah* on the site where his father had first built a prayer platform. One of his powerful and influential Brahmin nobles, Suhabhatta, became Mir Mohammad's disciple, adopted Saif-al-Din as his Muslim name, and married his daughter to his young teacher. Under the influence of Mir Mohammad and Suhabhatta, Sultan Sikandar demolished ancient temples in Pompur, Vijabror, Martand, Anantnag, Sopur and Baramulla. Many puritanical and discriminatory laws were implemented and *jizya* was introduced for the first time in Kashmir. The persecution of Brahmins, their exclusion from the top echelons of government, and their replacement by Iranian migrants, accelerated the process of conversion of the Brahmin elites who were unwilling to abandon the superior position they had held in the administration[26]

These are the only explanations put forward by scholars on this subject. All of these appear to be somewhat simplistic explanations, because they have not taken into consideration the internal problems and the role of external forces which were central to the process of conversion in Kashmir. They rely exclusively on factors unrelated to medieval Kashmiri society which accepted the new religion. These generalizations are based only on Jonaraja's *Zain Rajatarangini* (also referred as the *Jain Rajatarangini*) and Sayyid Ali's *Tarikh-i-Kashmir.*

Jonaraja was a learned Brahmin and judicial advisor

to Sultan Zain-ul-Abidin (AD 1420-70). He wrote in continuation of Kalhana's work and brought his account up to AD 1459. After Jonaraja, his pupil Srivara continued the work from (AD 1459-89). Srivara's account contains the history of only thirty years whereas the work of Jonaraja covers the history of three hundred years. This work was dedicated to Sultan Zain-ul-Abidin and that is why Jonaraja's *Rajatarangini* was named as *Zain Rajatarangini.* His references to Sultan Sikandar and his Prime Minister Suhabhatta spring from his biases. As an orthodox Brahmin, he tended to place great emphasis on the force employed by Suhabhatta to convert people. At one place Jonaraja says, 'Struck by fear, some Brahmins killed themselves by means of poison, some by rope, others by drowning themselves in water and others again by falling from a precipice and others burnt themselves. . . . The country was contaminated by hatred and the king's (favourite) Suha could not prevent one man in thousand from committing suicide'[27] The Brahmins by their corrupt and immoral practices had reduced Kashmir to the lowest depths of poverty and immorality. I am not denying the fact that coercion was not exercised by Sultan Sikandar or his Prime Minister Suhabhatta to force some people to accept Islam. But force alone does not provide a satisfactory explanation because when non-Muslims were in majority why they did not protest? Even Laleshwari who was a contemporary of this period does not express this cruelty, instead criticises the nature and role of the priestly Brahmins and the overall system prevailing at that time. Besides, if this was the situation then how did Brahmins survive and wander and visit holy places during the period of turmoil, as stated by Jonaraja himself in the same text[28] From his account it becomes amply clear that he was not ready to visualize the concrete situation in Kashmir that had brought about this shift from one religion to another at the popular level. Jonaraja was among the *agrahara* (land grant) beneficiaries because he held a position at the court of Sultan Zain-ul-Abidin (AD 1420-70) and Sultan

Sikandar's fiscal policies aiming at obtaining wealth from the temple establishments and the confiscations of *agraharas* ánd destruction of temples such as Martanda, Vishaya, Ishana, Chakrabhrit, and Tripureshvara affected his position and that of his community.[29] Perhaps this was why Jonaraja accused Sultan Sikandar, and more so Suhabhatta, of having adopted an anti-Hindu policy. Basically there are various factors that converged.

Sayyid Ali was related to the Shahmir dynasty from his mother's side. He completed the *Tarikh-i-Kashmir* during the period of Yusuf Shah Chak (AD 1580-6). Sayyid Ali's account has legendary overtones and not all inferences in the *Tarikh* are convincing. It is generally these opinions that have been accepted by other scholars without any critical examination. Sayyid Ali, who was in the service Mirza Haider Dughlat (AD 1530-7), begins his work with the arrival of Sayyid Taj-ud-din who came to Kashmir during the reign of Sultan Shihab-ud-din (AD 1354-74). The work gives an account of the role of the Sayyids who came to Kashmir during the Shahmir period. It also throws light on the nature of Sultan Sikandar's attitude towards non-Muslims and provides the biographical sketches of various *sufis* and *rishis* in Kashmir. Sayyid Ali seems inclined to see the appearance of Islam and its spread in Kashmir in the light of miracles and attributes the overwhelming success of Islam to the preaching of the Sayyids and the force used by Sultan Sikandar, portrayed to the common man as *butshikan* (idol breaker).[30]

Such interpretations have primarily served to legitimize stereotypes in Kashmir's historiography; as a result no alternative explanation of this phenomenon of conversion has developed so far, despite attempts by various scholars to explore the medieval history of Kashmir. Although this problem has been elucidated in terms of the explanation given by the sources, but the sources were never subjected to new sets of questions; for example, when we study Jonaraja's account, it clearly reveals that Suhabhatta, a Hindu, was more enthusiastic in destroying temples and oppressing the Brahmins than Sultan Sikandar. He also tries to establish that the oppression was directed only against the priestly Brahmins, who, in fact, alone did not constitute the entire societal format of Kashmir and a majority of converts were from non-Brahmin hindu and Buddhist stock. Jonaraja calls Suhabhatta a low born.[31] To quote Jonaraja: 'Suhabhatta disregarded the acts enjoined by the Vedas and was instructed by *mlecchas,* who instigated the king to bring down the images of gods.'[32] At another place, Jonaraja says, 'There was no city, no town, no village, no wood, where Suha, the *turushka* left the temple of Gods unbroken' [33]But Mirza Haider Dughlat who ruled over Kashmir from AD 1540-50 and visited many parts of the valley, says that in and around Kashmir there are more than one hundred and fifty temples.[34] However, temple destruction alone does not necessarily account for conversions in Kashmir because even prior to the arrival of Islam, temple and Buddhist Vihara destructions took place in Kashmir at the hands of Hindu rulers of the valley, among whom King Harsha was very notorious on this activity[35]

The religious life of Kashmir, which at present is dominated by Islam, underwent major changes from early times down to the fifteenth century AD. From the third century BC, the faith of the majority of the population in Kashmir was Buddhism and it continued to be so for the next millennium or so. From antiquity, Kashmir was subjected to diverse influences, contacts with neighbouring regions, conquests, migrations, etc. With the new order, i.e. (Buddhism) had come new theistic ideas, institutions and culture, as a result of which whatever nature and form of *Agamic* tradition (Shaivism) was there in early Kashmir, taking that to further levels of higher spiritual plane, was not possible.

The mythic-religious concepts of the Vedic Aryans covered cosmic worship and fire worship, which were shared by them in common with Indo-Iranians, as also hero worship, which they evolved in course of their victorious advance.

The *mantras* of these Vedic people revolved round these three aspects of their religion.[36] The emergence of Krishna cult in Punjab and also the *ahimsa* sects like Buddhism, Jainism and Ajivikas also inhibited the expansion of Vedic rituals. When a declining Buddhism coincided with the invasion of Alexander, it devastated things on the periphery of Kashmir, if not in the valley, and these problems did not go without impacting Kashmir's religious, social and cultural life. According to Hiuen Tsang, 'Mihirakula, having lost all, was welcomed by the king of Kashmir, but the cruel Hephtalite assassinated his host and then attacked Gandhara, where he destroyed all the convents'. Kalhana does not mention the persecutions of Mihirakula against the Buddhists; with equal cruelty he used to pursue everybody. Moreover, it is certain that he more willingly attacked the shaven heads.[37] Kalhana describes Mihirakula as 'a man of violent acts', 'a scourge of God on earth, who killed people without compassion or discrimination'.[38] He even broke the begging bowl of Buddha which was being preserved piously in a *vihara* in Srinagar.[39] Despite all these actions, the Brahmins of Kashmir were quite disposed to pardon the evil he had done to Buddhists because they were given land grants by him to have them by his side.[40] As per Hiuen Tsang's record, at the time of Mihirakulas persecutions of Buddhists there were a hundred monasteries in entire Kashmir sheltering nearly a thousand monks. Hiuen Tsang stayed at the *vihara* of Che-ye in-to-lo (Jayendra) (what is referred to now as *zeether* temple, establishment now on the banks of Dal Lake near the hill in Srinagar.[41] With this persecution of Buddhists by Mihirakula in sixth century AD, Shaivism got a new lease of life and began to consolidate itself in the entire Kashmir valley. This decline of Buddhism also opened up alternate space for Shaivites to operate. A careful study makes it clear that Mihirakula's violence was deliberately diverted against the Buddhists because he was an outsider and with the help of Shaivite Brahmins he got legitimacy to perpetuate his rule. His land grants to Brahmins helped them to revive the custom and traditions of Brahminism, which revolved around only obtaining of material favours from state.[42] By fifth century AD, Brahminism started reasserting itself in various forms like Shaivism, Vaishnavism, Tantra and Shaktaism.[43]

Conversions to Islam were an important element in the social history of medieval Kashmir and must be studied in terms of the changes taking place in the social structure as well as in the realm of ideology and socio-political consciousness. Interestingly, the majority of the people who converted to Islam in medieval Kashmir, were non-Brahmins, Buddhists and Kayasthas, comprising peasants, share croppers, craftsmen, pastoralists, village menials and people of other professions such as weavers, blacksmiths, washermen, barbers, woodcutters, saw holders, carpenters, tribal's, etc., and belonging to various religious denominations like Buddhism, Shaivism, into what is today perceived as the monolithic structure of Hinduism. The divergent strands like Shaivism, Vaishnavism, etc., are all accepted as Hinduism and in popular understanding many people do not have knowledge of the total pantheon or practices. The practices of Hindus are contextual and region-specific and not Shastric or textual; therefore, the monolithic character of Hinduism is a recent phenomenon, which is confined to the urban classes. Because urban societies do not have long standing tradition they therefore popularize this because they shun their other regional and religious identities and want a national religious identity which also mirrors the national political identity of Hindutva today.

Without careful or incisive and contextual reading of the *Rajatarangini* of Kalhana, we may be drawn towards the bipolar opposites of specificities versus monotheism. Kalhaṇa's *Rajatarangini* clearly establishes that the Kashmiri society during the period was no less stratified and caste-based than the Indian mainland.[44] In the Islamist discourse, the millenarian and emancipatory factors were the message that struck a responsive chord rather than theological Islam.

If conversion from one religion to another could be viewed in terms of each individual's search for spiritual salvation according to his own understanding, this indeed might be so wherever the changes of religion were confined to a few individuals and where non-religious elements could be shown to be equal; but in the context of vast masses deserting the religion into which they were born and opting for another, the phenomenon surely assumes social dimensions of great significance. In such a context, the social, political and ideological, all interact with one another to make one religion more attractive than the other. Conversion in Kashmir also symbolized a protest by extending the dream of a new order where there would be stability and equality as opposed to hierarchy and warfare. Conversion is easy to define in the Semitic religions of Judaism, Christianity, and Islam because they have a clear notion of who is a believer and who is a non-believer. Conversions are also a long-drawn process rather than a single episode as K.Z. Ashrafyan has very rightly remarked, in the context of spread of Islam, 'Conversion to Islam has passed through an important process of evolution.'[45]

Therefore, in order to understand the question of conversion to Islam in Kashmir, it would also be fair to examine the nature of state and societal relations in this region before the fourteenth century. I have used the term State instead of Hindu rulers, since it is historically unintelligible or incorrect to call the pre-fourteenth-century rulers of Kashmir 'Hindu rulers', as has been wrongly interpreted by historians like H.H. Wilson and Krishna Mohan[46] The rulers of Kashmir and those who represented the state, like Brahmins, Damaras, Lavanyas, Magres, Rainas, Tantrins, Khasas Khokhars and Ekangas and many tribes were not all Hindus by faith because among them there were Buddhists and varied tribal cults also. For centuries Buddhism remained a dominant religion in Kashmir and despite Mihirakula's atrocities, it was most unlikely that Buddhism was destroyed in Kashmir completely. Besides, in the absence of any statistical information in such a fluid situation, it is very difficult to say what faith the majority of the rulers and representatives of the state professed because the nature of the state cannot be characterized in terms of religion but by examining for whom (which class of people benefited most from the state) the state existed. The understanding of these problems is invaluable because it also enables us to recognize the subtle dangers and disguised communal influences that have crept into the writing of Indian history.[47] These were the main narratives in popular historical memory. The Sayyids used these as reference points in their discourse with larger audiences at the popular level in different areas of the valley.[48]

In pre-fourteenth century, Kashmir's poverty among the lower sections of the society was doubly embedded in the ecology and in the politico-social organization. For an economy dependent on agriculture, craft making and pastoral production, the amount of arable land in the valley was rather meagre, and much of this land was given in lavish religious grants to priestly Brahmins and secular *agraharas* and other officials of the state respectively.[49] *Agrahara* was an area of cultivable land, the ownership of which rested with the temple deity, but it was cultivated by the peasants and a major portion of the resources of that land was used by the priestly Brahmins for their own purpose under the pretext of the maintenance of temples and *mathas*. These were termed as religious *agraharas*. The various *agraharas* granted by Kashmiri rulers in the pre-Sultanate period were those of Levera, Kuruhara, Khagi, Khonmusa, Godhara, Jalora, Hastisala, Samangsa, Sanara, Varabala, Kantkotsa, Aksavala, Bedara, Khola, Hadigrama, Skandpura, Katimusa, Nadavana, Khadua, Samma, Galuna, Kamalahatta, Kamla keshava, Parihaskeshava, Phalapura, Locantsa, Suvarnaparasva, Adisthana, Vijeshvara, Khaduya, Hastikarna, Panchatta, Sureshverikshetra, Avantivara, Suryakunda, Nandikshetra, Vitasta, Trigami.[50]

The secular *agraharas* were the ones where the land was

owned by the peasants but the major portion of the revenues was given in salaries to officials of the state.[51] The non-*agrahara* holdings were very small holdings of peasants. The pasture lands were commonly used by pastoralists for cattle rearing. The amount of land under the peasants' plough was perhaps not very large. Since the *agrahara*-based economy was important for their sustenance, the priestly Brahmins perceived agrarian surplus as an essential part of their status and dignity; their authority tended to be legitimized by their training in literary and religious texts. This also lent special credence to their roles in larger society and the state's administrative functioning. The most striking development came with the state's reliance on these priestly Brahmins as advisors, law givers, ministers, members of the administrative machinery and priests. Kalhana mentions that even Brahmins in humbler positions (poor) were appointed to very important posts.[52] The outcome of this close relationship between the state represented by the king and the Brahmins was the direct exploitation of the lands consolidated into *agraharas* of both a religious and secular nature. By taking charge of the state's administrative machinery, the Brahmins transferred the control of the region's economic surplus into their own hands, particularly at a stage when production relations were based on the arbitrary appropriation of the means of production.[53] The kings often submitted to the guidance of priestly Brahmins in spending the country's resources on secular establishments like the state's administrative machinery and religious establishments such as temples, *mathas,* shrines, *viharas,* etc. Kalhana says, 'in the king's palace, councillors, chamberlains and other attendants, moved about adorned with gold chains and bracelets'.[54] For the rural society, the cultivation of holdings of the priestly Brahmins was an act of reverence towards the deity. Apart from labour services of peasants and craftsmen, the priestly Brahmins in these *agraharas,* as members of region's landed aristocracy, were also entitled to receive gifts and customary obligations in the form of labour and products from various sections of the society on festivals and ceremonies from birth to death.[55] *Nilmata Purana* is full of details on such aspects. Contributions through *dana* and *dakshina* on birth, marriage, and other ceremonies till death and after, continues till now but is fast disappearing because of decline of population among Kashmiri Hindus after their forced migration from their homes in Kashmir because of terrorism in 1990s.

The burden of taxation levied on the peasant proprietors in kind could hardly be described by any other term than oppressive. Jayapida (AD 753-82), for example, brought his subjects all conceivable misfortunes by exacting every penny from them, though his officers delivered only a small portion of it to the state.[56] Since the cultivation of land was not possible for the entire year due to geographical and ecological limitations, human labour assumed great economic importance and this, in course of time, led to the evolution of forced labour which is recorded by Kalhana from King Samkaravarman's time (AD 883-902) and more wealth by oppressing the peasants'[57] King Samkaravarman reduced people to the lowest depths of poverty. He did not hesitate to raise revenues from the incense and sandalwood of the temples. He introduced the forced carrying of loads (*rudabarudi*). Those who refused to render this forced labour were subjected to economic extortions.[58] During the famine of AD 917-18, 'Thousands died for want of food and prices rose sky high, one *khari* (equal to 80 kg.) of rice selling for a thousand *dinars,* corpses were thrown into the Jhelum, the entire land laid waste and parched. Bones covered the open spaces making the country look like a huge burial ground. Meanwhile the officials aided and abetted by Tantrins acquired and sold grains (rice) from the royal stores at phenomenal prices and amassed wealth at the cost of the people.'[59] Samkaravarman established two new offices of revenue called *atta patibhaga* (Department of the Lord of the Market) and *grhakrtya* (domestic affairs). He also received special contribution for pay of the village clerks (*grama kayasthas*) and *skandkas* as well on other land taxes.[60] In addition to the usual land taxes he introduced new cesses for *gramakayasthas* (village clerks) and *skandkas* (*lambardars*)'.[61] Likewise, Partha (AD 906-21), Cakravarman (AD 923-33) and Unmattavant (AD 937-9) cast all moral obligations to the winds and oppressed the masses through tyrannical extortion.[62] Kalhana mentions that at the instigation of the *kayasthas* (state officials) only breathing was exempted from taxation. About the nature of eleventh century Jean Naudou says, 'The Kashmiri people had only to suffer from rigorous economic conditions,which Kalhana attributes to bad management and the rapacity of functionaries.'[63]

Kalhana's and Khemendra's account is full of accounts of malpractices by *kayasthas* in Kashmir. King Samgram Raja (AD 1003-28) himself admitted to obtaining such agricultural resources by unlawful means[64] 'Oh shame', writes Kalhana in indignation, 'that he possessed his grandfather's treasures and those which Utkarsha at the commencement had brought from Lohara and those he had confiscated from the temples, the riches bestowed by former kings. Yet he endeavoured to secure more and more wealth by oppressing the peasants. The reference is obviously to King Harsha (AD 1089-1101) who under the pretext of protecting his subjects, plundered the country for years together.[65] Harsha levied new imposts through several prefects of property *nayaka* who seized property of all sorts so much so that he 'appointed a prefect on night soil'.[66] When Ananta abdicated the throne in favour of his son Kalasa, it turned out be disastrous for Kashmir. The reign of Kalasa (that of Utkarsha lasted only 22 days) was darkened by the struggle he carried on aganist his father and the latter's lamentable end.[67] To maintain the income of the state's treasury, Sussala (AD 1121-8) deprived various officers, belonging to various caste groups, of their living by dismissing them from service[68] King Suhadeva (AD 1301 20) is referred to by Jonaraja as a *rakshasa* for his cruel and avaricious nature.[69]

The priestly Brahmins in particular and the other landed groups in general continued, however, to be honoured and privileged in the social hierarchy. They worked out everything to their advantage since they were free from punishments, forced labour and taxation.[70] 'Brahmin offenders were treated with leniency while offenders against them were treated with ten-fold severity.[71] The *agraharas* had given them a considerable measure of strength and stability. Even after the death of a Brahmin his property was not escheated by the state if he died heirless, while this was not so in the case of people belonging to the lower castes.[72]

The landed property that came to the priestly Brahmins as free gifts provided material comforts and pleasures to them and a sense of security to the donors. The *deshadhyakshas* (heads of areas), *gramadhyakshas* (heads of villages), etc., looked for a patron, an ally powerful enough to offer them protection and act as a mediator in disputes with their peasants.[73] This accounts for a gift of a village or so in favour of their patrons. This was clearly indicated by frequent troubles and uprisings of Damaras and other powerful landed groups from the Karkota period onwards. Interestingly, the heads of *deshas* and villages placed themselves under the protection and care of Brahmins and agreed to surrender a part of their wealth in lieu of such protection. The Brahmins acted as the 'strategic ally' of the rulers, kept their economy afloat and provided an ideological base for inducing the peasants to pay the social surplus to their lords (*deshadhyakshas*)[74] This surely was not the way to inculcate a religious outlook!

The Brahmins thus seem to have never hidden their willingness to assist their feudal lords-turned-vassal disciples in acquiring this surplus, a part of which, in the form of *dakshina* of a village or so, was sufficient to maintain them and their alliance with the *rajputras*.[75] The Brahmins exercised moral and ideological pressure on the peasants in all parts of the valley to part with their surplus and render allegiance to their lords. The heads of villages or districts seem to have reached an understanding with their protectors, but on their own terms, to get their authority recognized in those belts where the peasants were difficult to control. This also helped them obtain tacit recognition from their peasants, which normally they would have failed to get with force in such inhospitable areas where tribal loyalties among Dammaras, Lavanyas, Ekangas, Khasas, Khokhars and Tantrins were still strong.[76]

Whatever the amount of land or number of villages donated or gifted to the priestly Brahmins, it appears that the peasants posed a serious threat to the authority of *deshadhyakshas*, where lack of military credibility led them to willingly surrender a major part of their social surplus in favour of the priestly Brahmins to deal with their peasants. The *deshadhyakshas* who were much revered lords and who had learnt the art of survival realized how unwise it would be to deal with their peasants. They seem to have found from experience and the recurrence of frequent Damara revolts, that no agreement with their peasants in the sharing of social surplus would stick unless the priestly Brahmins and peasants combined and were committed wholly to it. An agreement with the Brahmins was a necessity for them to safeguard their feudal militia against attacks by Damara peasant alliances and other radical elements.

The political history of the post-Karkota period reveals how, compelled by circumstances, the landed elements transferred their allegiance from kings to Brahmins and made all possible concessions to maintain their precarious hold over the refractory popular base of peasants and others. Even though the lay *sadhakas* (disciples) engaged priestly Brahmins as tools to contain the simmering discontent of the people, as time progressed the Shaivite Acharayas, priestly Brahmins and their *sadhakas*, despite the efficient articulation of their Shaivite religious preaching and teaching, failed to dispel the darkness and could no longer exploit primary producers.[77]

In such circumstances the Brahmins provided the justification for their dominance by exploiting people who were deeply steeped in superstition, blind belief, and fear of the supernatural, in an archaic manner. These Brahmins could effectively put across their indispensability to rulers since they claimed themselves to be the creators of divinity. This is a classic case of ruling classes selling ruling ideas as the ruling reality. Not surprisingly, therefore, contradictions developed between the non-producer ritual legitimizer whose claims to social dominance did not last long because of the penetration of Islam in the valley on the one hand, and the king, who was burdened with the task of not allowing the centre to fall apart, on the other.

However, from the beginning of the ninth century onwards, the alliance of the Brahmins and the state began to show cracks. The Brahmins no longer remained as the ideologues of the state, becoming the prophets of time, trying to cloud the strong consciousness of the masses to legitimize the state's authority. Soon, however, their ritual, economic, and political domination came to be subjected to intra-class contradictions and their alliance with state was viewed as unholy. Thus the economy of pre-fourteenth century Kashmir was so organized as to transfer resources upwards into the hands of the rulers, and their highly bureaucratized machinery, the landed aristocracy, Shaivite *mathas* and the priestly Brahmins. Such a state of affairs could hardly have promoted rapport among the different groups in society. And since the Brahmins were among the beneficiaries of this economic organization, their preaching's, based on so much of exploitation, were unlikely to promote their religious cause for a long time.

The other landed groups in the valley were those of Damaras, Lavanyas and Tantrins. Being materially very rich, they felt that their political ascent was being undermined by the Brahmins who were collaborators of the state, therefore, they intrigued to bring about the collapse of the state. The Damaras indulged in looting of temple establishments much before the commencement of the Shahmir Sultanate.[78] This contradiction was clearly manifest in the decline of Brahmin monopoly and the subsequent emergence of relatively more secular economic forces in the form of domination by Dammaras, Tantrins, and other groups.[79] These groups were the virtual kingmakers in Kashmir down to the end of the thirteenth century. The rebellions of the Damaras led to serious civil wars under Sussala (AD 1112-20) and Jaisimha (AD 1128-49) when the Damaras took away the whole harvest, the people fled in various directions abandoning their possessions and households.[80] In Ucchala's time (AD 1101-11), *kayasthas* set the town of Buteswara on fire five times, which resulted in terrible discontent in the kingdom.[81] 'In Kashmir, the palace intrigues recommenced. Excessive opulence and misery rubbed shoulders more than ever. Capital and countryside fell prey to scourges denounced by Kalhana: the great military corps, Ekangas and Tantrins, the Kayasthas, the Damaras.'[82]

Affairs took a turn for the worse when unity among the dominant groups was completely shattered after the death of Avantivarman (AD 855-83), and there was a serious loss of control of the central government.[83] Once the alliance of Brahmins and the kings was destroyed, the secular landed groups could not make headway because the state started using one group against the other. The revolts of the Damaras, the uprising of Tantrins, Ekangas, Lavanyas, and the *prayopavesa* (hunger strikes) of the Brahmins became frequent. The solemn *prayopavesa* was the chief instrument of the Brahmins for pressing their demands and politicizing simple things which in the long run damaged their reputation and ruined the state [84] The *Rajatarangini* is full of such court intrigues and Brahminical hypocrisy. Here it should be understood that these constant conflicts must have created a lot of insecurity for the common man.

This internal strife and the open enmity of these groups to the kings led to the appearances of large claims to the royal authority resulting in them waging war against each other. With the weakening of the system and their power, the kings resisted the domination of the Brahmins and their religious claims to the huge wealth of temple endowments, and this led to the plundering of temple property at the hands of Samkarvarman (AD 883-902),[85] Ksemgupta (AD 950-1109), Vigaraja (uncle of King Ananta), Kalasa (AD 1063-89), his son Harsha (AD 1089-1101) and Dammara Janakaraja.[86] The destruction of all these temples, *mathas* or *viharas* was not concerned with the theological question, with the exception of King Nara, who ruled Kashmir before King Mihirakulla.[87] Samkarvarman plundered sixty-four temples under the pretext of supervision and even robbed the temples of the revenues of sandalwood. He resumed the villages of these temples and is said to have cultivated them for himself against the *pratikara*, i.e. compensatory assignment. The king demanded a fixed amount as compensation from the revenues of these *agraharas* and thereafter brought these lands under direct fiscal management[88] Ksemgupta (AD 950-8) burnt the *vihara* of Jayendra and snatched the money and the copper of Sugata Buddha. He also took away thirty-six villages granted to this *vihara*, one of the reasons given for this being that this *vihara* had provided refuge to rebellious Damaras like Samgram Dammara[89] (Even Vigharaja, the maternal uncle of King Ananta (AD 1028-41), burnt the Lothika *matha* because of political differences with his mother, Queen Srilekha[90]

This certainly tended to devalue the position of the Brahmins as priests in religious matters. It is from then onwards that priestly Brahmins in Kashmir began to be looked down upon by the rest of the Hindus who survived conversion and claimed the identity of Kashmiri pandit. It is these priestly Brahmins who were intimidated and oppressed by Suhabhatta and his colleagues and some of the sultans of Shahmir dynasty. Jonaraja says, 'The kingdom of Kashmira was polluted by the evil practices of the mlechchhas, the Brahmins, the *mantras*, and the gods relinquished their power. The gods who used to make the glory of their prowess manifest, even as fireflies manifest their light, now hid their glory on account of the country's sin. When the gods withdrew their glory, their images became mere stones, and the *mantras* mere letters. Owing to the sin of Kali Yuga, the merits of those who did virtuous acts were lost, and the gods deserted the images, even as serpents cast off their skins.[91] 'While as in caste based society in the mainland they continued to be upper strata. It was during the second Lohara dynasty that the Damaras who had made several attempts to come to power really came to the forefront as a formidable power. Kalhana narrates in detail, the turmoil of the wars of succession of this period, in which the various factions of Damaras played a leading role. He gives us a vivid description of how these kingmakers (Damaras) of medieval Kashmir operated by resorting to clever, manipulative tactics and by perpetuating the civil strife in Kashmir. The *Rajatarangini* relates an incident where the powerful Damara, Dhanava, is found expropriating villages belonging to the temples. The temple priest, on being asked by King Avantivarman to explain the poor state of offerings in the temple gave the following reply. 'In the Lohara district O King, there lives a powerful Damara, Dhanava by name, who is attached to the minister Sura and treated by him like a son. This Damara, whose power is unstrained, has taken away the villages (belonging to the shrine) and thus we can offer to Bhutesa only this oblation'.[92] That the Ḍamaras were already well entrenched in the valley and were ready for any kind of confrontation with the state is evident from Kalhana's narration. He further writes, 'when the fierce Damara came at last before Sura, he made the earth shake with the trample of his foot soldiers and did not bend his back'.[93] The references to the private armies maintained by the Damaras reveal another aspect of their power.

An important factor which helped the Damaras to augment their riches was their frequent raids to loot and plunder. They could always replenish their exhausted finances by resorting to such wild activities. The *Rajatarangini* documents innumerable such instances. Kalhana writes, 'Then the citizens and Damaras striking at each other with upraised weapons plundered the treasures and other valuables of the burning palace'.[94] Referring to the time of Bhiksacara's encroachment on the kingdom, Kalhana writes, 'When the autumn harvest had been carried away by the Damaras, the people fled in every direction abandoning all their possessions and households.'[95] Describing the siege of Srinagar, Kalhana writes, 'They invested the city, and shouting day and night set fire to some places, and in others plundered the inhabitants.'[96] In the course of describing a famine, the *Rajatarangini* tells us that 'the people's savings were exhausted by their long troubles; their houses were burnt and outside the city the Damaras seized their produce and blocked the roads.'[97]

By dint of such circumstances, the general population of Kashmir quite naturally was kept in a state of fear and apprehension by the Damaras and other dominant groups. Since the people were often the victims of Damara aggressions, they professed great hostility towards them. The following passage in the *Rajatarangini* renders an eloquent description of the people's reaction to the arrival of Gargacandra, a Damara leader. 'Once when Garga had come from Lohara into the king's presence, all the people in the city were agitated and distressed by fear because at that time, the message was spread that Garga had arrived in anger to kill all in the king's employment, by impaling them on boats. For two or three days all the people appeared as if shaken by fever, in consequence of such a terrifying rumour which made pregnant women miscarry.'[98] It is clear that the general public felt threatened by the Damaras whose activities heaped misfortunes on them. Thus when the royal forces led the attack against Gargacandra, they were greatly helped by the general population. Kalhana describes the scene thus, 'The whole people in great excitement rushed on with raised weapons, but Damara Gargacandra received them all with dismay. Following a defeat of the royal troops, however, the town folk everywhere in the land were again and again dreading the return of Garga and barricading their houses'.[99]

During the tenth century, the Tantrins and Ekangas became all powerful in politics. Kalhana relates how during that period, hordes of Tantrin foot soldiers had formed a confederacy and was strong enough to punish or favour rulers of the land. The kings who were mere puppets in their hands ousted with each other like village officials by offering greater and greater bribes.[100] He goes on to lament, 'In this land, the rulers of which had conquered Kanyakubja and other countries, the kings (now) maintained themselves by giving bills of exchange (*hundika*) to the Tantrins.'[101] These incessant conflicts among the dominant groups, plundering of temples and undermining of the priestly Brahmins' religious authority could perhaps have lingered on without much popular reaction if only an alternative had not presented itself to Kashmir's society. The alternative came in the form of Islam, which presented only a hope of political stability and a new world-view comprehending social, political, ideological, and cultural aspects. Popular reaction, indeed popular protests against the goings on at the higher ends of the social ladder took the non-violent form of mass conversion to this new world-view, i.e. Islam.

In these conditions, Kashmir was clearly a fertile ground for the growth of Islam among the people, who had become familiar with the new religion which was being brought to Kashmir from ninth century AD onwards by traders, soldiers and craftsmen from various parts of Central Asia. Similar effects seem to have followed from the conflicts of the Damaras, Tantrins, Lavanyas and Ekangas as well.

The other factor that also facilitated people's receptiveness towards Islam was the increasing presence and role of Turks in Kashmir. The Turks and other Muslims who came from trans-Himalayan regions accompanying Muslim armies that invaded India and Kashmir from early tenth century onwards, also terrified the ordinary people in Kashmir.

From the eighth century onwards we get consistent

information about the presence of Turushkas, 'Turks', in Kashmir. Kalhana says, 'by his (King Lalitaditya, i.e. AD 725-53) command to display the mark of their bandage that the Turushkas carry their arms at their back and shave half their heads'.[102] Between AD 883 and 903, King Lalliya Sahi in the Sahi kingdom in the neighbourhood of Kashmir (in present Afghanistan) perceived the Turushka leader as the greatest threat to his authority.[103] At another place Kalhana refers to Turushka girls being brought to the seraglio of King Kalasa (AD 1063-89).[104] In early eleventh century AD, Trilochanpala, the ruler of the Sahi dynasty, sought military help from Kashmir's King Sangram Raja (AD 1003-28) against the Turushkas.[105] By this time Turks had established their reputation as great soldiers not at the courts of Kashmiri kings but as far as Bengal, Deccan and rest of south of India. After the expedition of Mahmud of Gazni, the Islamized Turks remained implemented in the Punjab, henceforth the vicissitudes of internal history of the Musalman dynasties must have had very serious repercussions on India. The Turkish horsemen unleashed their destructive fury and chased out monks from both Central Asian and Indian monasteries.[106] In AD 1186, after the decline of Mahmud of Ghazni, when Lahore fell to Muizz-ud-din of Gori dynasty and Rajputs continued to fight among themselves rather than putting a united resistance, many Kashmiris who were away in various parts of India noticed the tragic events that took place in various regions of India under Turkish oppression. Tarnatha says,

> At Odantapuri and Vikramasila, at certain moment the king installed a kind of fortress and therein placed men of war in order to ensure protection. A school of the Greater Vehicle was founded at *Vajrasana* and during the summer retreat, nearly 10,000, *saindhava-sravaka*, were assembled there. As to the other universities, for the most part they were nearing their decline. At Vikramasila and Odantapuri, one could count on affluence equal to that of the time of Abhayakara. After the death of King Rathika, when Lovasena excercised royal power, some years of peace followed, but soon appeared in the

Antervedi, between the Ganga and Yamuna, the Turkish King Moon (zla-ba) and through the medium of various *bhikshus* [*sic* Schiefner] who were envoys of the king, he joined some other little Turkish kings living in Bengal and other regions. He conquered the Magadha entirely, massacred at Odantapuri numerous religious people and destroyed that university as well as that of Vikramasila. On the site of the Odantavihara was erected a citadel of Tajikas.[107]

It was most likely that the Turks had also established their settlements in many areas in India and Kashmir. Though tension existed at the level of the rulers, apparently no such relations existed at the more popular level, for when some years later Harsha (AD 1089-1101) tried to establish peace and order by suppressing the Damaras and Lavanyas, Kalhana says that the people fled to the lands of the *mlecchas* where they ate beef and worked on hand-mills and water wheels.[108] The terms *mleccha* and *turushka* denoted Muslims, the latter having established themselves in the lower hill regions neighbouring Kashmir, probably Rajouri and Poonch.[109] In King Sussala's reign (AD 1111-21) foreign horse dealers and artisans (most of them were Turks) are said to have become rich because the king was fond of horses and new construction works. King Bhiksacara, a grandson of Harsha who occupied Sussala's throne for some months, did not hesitate in appealing to a contingent of Turks.[110] He depended on Turushkas during his expedition to Lohara also. When King Kalasa of Kashmir wanted to put a gilded parasol over the temple of Shiva, he sought the help of Turushka craftsmen from Turushka country.[111] King Harsha of Kashmir employed hundreds of Turushka captains in his army for their military skill and strength[112] 'The people suffered there, and it is beyond doubt that the conditions created by the political anarchy hardly lent themselves to an intense cultural life. On the other hand, the political feebleness of the Kashmiri state offered very many dangers, at a time when Islam was encircling Kashmir from nearly all sides, although the poverty which was the consequence of it preserved it from dangerous concupiscence's. . . . In 1128, on Sussala's death, Kashmir which had until then been spared invasions by Mohammedans, was not less torn exhausted, and miserable.'[113]

Even though the contacts between Kashmir and Central Asia were on a collision path due to some invasions, including that by Dulucha in AD 1320, also referred to by some of the Kashmiri and Persian chroniclers as Zulachu or Zulqadr Khana, the Mongol invader who entered Kashmir during King Suhadeva's reign from the Baramulla side with 17,000 horsemen and also some foot-soldiers, referred as mlechchha, Turk and Tajika with total 60,000 forces caused widespread disturbances in Kashmir, plundering all and forcibly took away all the women judged worthy of their harems and the men whose resistance led to conjecture that they would be appreciated in the slave market.[114] Kalhana says that Kashmir became almost chaotic, a vast territory with few men, little food and lots of grass.[115] Abul Fazal says Dulcha was the general of the king of Qandahar. But according to Marcopolo, he was most likely the general of Negudar, the grandson of Chengis Khan who deputed him to Kashmir when he himself proceeded to India.[116]The Mongol invasion fully exposed the then rulers when they could not protect their subjects from its onslaught. It was during this period that Rinchana and Shahmir came to prominence because they played a significant role in preserving at least a semblance of authority of the state to avert the future consequences of Mongol disaster. But this collision never meant the end of the contact between Kashmir and Central Asia. Instead, it resulted in enlarging the range of Kashmiri contacts with Central Asia and also in expanding the volume of Kashmir's response to Central Asian culture in general and Persian culture in particular.[117] Since a variety of contacts had existed for a long period of time, the Turkish arrival with the Muslim religion this time, did not appear as a cultural shock to Kashmiris, the only thing that was new this time was that the Turks from Persia and Central Asia had associated themselves with Islam as an important historical experience and the Kashmiris who interacted with them in various capacities also did not represent a monolithic Hindu identity as is perceived today.

All these pieces of evidence suggest that there was a constant cultural exchange, a commercial relationship and mutual dependence in artisanal skills and military techniques, from the middle of the eighth century. It also suggests that from an early period, the preaching of Islam also ran parallel to the traditions of Buddhism, Brahminism and other cults. By the thirteenth century, Kashmir appears to have come to possess permanent Muslim settlements of both migrants and converts, otherwise Shahmir (AD 1339-42), who was from Iran (Qutb-ud-din Shirazi refers to him as *Muffakhari Iran,* Grandeur of Iran), was unlikely to have thought of becoming king of Kashmir without a little support base within the valley.[118] Srikanth Koul also appears to have made a fair statement that there was a colony of Muslims when Shahmir became the king of Kashmir. This is further attested by the presence of Bulbul Shah's mosque and the free communal kitchen (*langar khanah*) in Bul Bul Lanker near the Alikadal part of the old city in Srinagar at the time of King Rinchana (AD 1320-3), who converted from Buddhism to Islam. The basic fact is that when Rinchana entered Kashmir, the entire Kashmir Valley was totally devastated because of Mongol invasions, as stated earlier, and Rinchana found it an opportune time to kill Ramachandran and proclaim himself king because Ramachandran appeared to him a weak ruler as he had proved incapable of protecting his subjects and therefore lost his legitimacy. Some scholars say that he expressed the desire to accept Hinduism. Some scholars say that Rinchana was not accepted by the Hindu priest, Brahmin Devaswamin, in the Hindu fold so he turned to Islam and sought the help of Bulbul Shah for his legitimacy.[119] Some scholars say he had accepted shaivism in Tibet already. The fact remains that Rinchana was basically motivated by his political ambition since he remained in the close company of Shahmir, and was watching that a gradual shift was taking place at the societal level in Kashmir with the Damaras having burnt down the *mathas* and temples and the Turks the monasteries. This indifferent attitude of non-Muslims and Muslims in Kashmir was sufficient hint to Rinchana to accept Islam because when social basis of power was increasingly shifting from Hindus to Muslim Turks, he felt it reasonable to accept Islam to seek legitimacy for his authority.[120] Rinchana was hoping to found a new dynasty. For this he relied on Shahmir, a Turk who was the premier servant of the then Kashmiri king but Shahmir did not support his (Rinchana) son born from Kotarani, instead he facilitated the descendant of Kashmiri dynasty Udayanadeva.[121] Shortly after the death of Udayanadeva, things further worsened and Shahmir who had already spread his tentacles exploited the situation and founded the first Muslim sultanate in Kashmir.

Before proceeding further to examine those aspects of Islam that appealed to the population and the contribution of the Sayyids to the conversion of people, the question arises as to why the people did not turn towards Buddhism. To answer this question it becomes necessary to look into the daily religious life at the popular level in Kashmir during this period, which was dominated by conflict and confusion. For example, by the twelfth century, Buddhism had lost its organizational structure in India. The Turkish troops had chased away Buddhists from their monasteries, and in such circumstances the state also did not extend its patronage to Buddhists. When the Maha Pandita Saskya Panchen (AD 1182-1251) went on a pilgrimage to holy places he found Vajrasna had deserted all having fled before the *Karluks*, i.e. Turks at the end of his life when he came back to Kashmir along with his master Rahul Sribhadra, aged 89, he found that Buddhism in Kashmir had fully declined.[122]

The study of early Sanskrit chronicles and the *mahatmyas* suggests that in the early period of idolatry, rituals and reverence to Nagas and deities formed the main theme of religion. It had lost its former subtlety and vitality and with the change of time, had split into a number of different religious sects such as Shaivism, Vaishnavism, Shaktaism, and Tantrism. All these embodied a number of principles none of which had undisputed supremacy. Thus religion in Kashmir also lacked the dynamism of a universal religion that Islam was exhibiting at that time and therefore could hardly claim society's allegiance. Besides, the Shavite *acharyas* kept themselves busy in evolving and interpreting Shaivism and its metaphysics and kept it only confined to literary elites known as pandits.

So far as Buddhism is concerned, the Sarvastivada School of Buddhism was prevalent in Kashmir. Besides, its nature had become overladen with the indigenous superstitions of the people who professed it. Earlier too, Ashokan patronage of Buddhism in Kashmir had brought it into open conflict with Brahminism which hostility between the two continued for centuries. King Nara burnt thousands of *vihāras*, and Mihirakula too hated Buddhism wholeheartedly.[123] With the growth and spread of Shaivism, which was accompanied by a variety of rituals, the state extended patronage to Shaivism because in the initial stages it helped in incorporating various tribal cults into its fold and facilitated their subjection to the state. Besides, Muslims were not persecuted; rather they persecuted the Buddhists, which is why the common people did not turn towards Buddhism[124]

Besides this, the conditions created by the politico-economic anarchy could hardly have fostered an intense cultural life. On the other hand, the political feebleness of the Kashmiri state offered many dangers at a time when Islam was entering Kashmir. A grandson of Harsha, Bhiksacara, who succeeded in occupying King Sussala's throne for some months, did not hesitate to appeal to the contingent of Turushkas for help. The two years that followed the Damaras burning of the temple of Chakradhara, close to which had worked so many Kashmiri and Tibetan monks, and the monasteries that also became easy targets.[125] On the eve of these events Kashmiri Buddhism was far from having the same lustre as at the commencement of the century. We must not forget that Kashmiri Buddhism was of the Mahayana type in which various cults dominated and the local variations that crept into it made it more diffused.

Keeping in view the developments in Tibet and Central Asia, where Islam had made great strides after destroying other religious establishments, in Kashmir none of the new political groups like the Damaras, Lavanyas, Ekangas, and Tantrins felt it appropriate to patronize Buddhism; they all facilitated the spread of Islam. There was a kind of universal decline of Buddhism; to confront the Turks the Indian garrisons were kept in the monasteries, and this time it was out of fear that many Buddhists migrated to various places for safety and the preservation of their religion [126] It was partly because of this insecurity that even the preachers of Buddhism in Kashmir, like Kunkavarman, Tilakakalasa and Jayananda, undertook far-off journeys to draw closer to the centres of Buddhism rather than stay in Kashmir.[127] Learned Brahmin preachers like Kumarila Bhatt, Shankaracharya and Abhinava Gupta showed great disrespect to Buddhism in Kashmir.[128] Buddhist monks instead of reviving their faith made it corrupt. The degeneration of Buddhism in Kashmir can well be imagined from the fact that each Dhyani Bodhisattva began to have a consort.[129] The great patrons of Buddhism in Kashmir, such as Emperor Ashoka, King Matragupta, and King Meghavana wanted their subjects to sacrifice, but also stressed that instead of bloody sacrifices a 'meal of pulverized gold should be offered to Gods'.[130] King Avantivarman (AD 855-83) prohibited the hunting of birds and fish.[131] These edicts were unlikely to promote the cause of Buddhism in a society which was seriously being influenced by new ideas under Muslim Sufis and Sayyids. Besides, the wrath of anti-Buddhism displayed earlier by Shaivites, was deeply enshrined in the public mind—therefore turning towards Buddhism was unthinkable for the larger public.

Shaivism and Vaishnavism were also increasingly catering to the elite culture by turning to the acquisition of knowledge at the elite level, and at the popular level, nothing was done to relieve people from the age-old burden of rituals. Creative intellectual attention was lacking and it became ossified as the path to true liberation. Swami Tejomayananda, while referring to the means of attaining liberation through Shaivism, says that it is intellectual knowledge which can be obtained from scriptural study for avoiding ignorance and thereby beginning a process of liberation.[132] This pursuit of liberation through the acquisition of scriptural knowledge inevitably put it beyond the reach of the masses and limited its appeal to the select few who had the leisure for intellectual pursuits. Besides, the Shaiva philosophers concentrated on the study of various philosophical and intellectual aspects of Shaivism; indeed, the masses were increasingly burdened with cumbersome rituals and ceremonies.[133] Many villages were surrendered to *tantric* gurus who as a class of new beneficiaries came to have direct control over the means of production in the course of time. Those beneficiaries soon converted their titles into possession and treated the donated villages as their estates.[134]

The *tantric* gurus played a crucial ideological role in reconciling the masses to the surrender of their surplus. The landed property that came to the Shaiva Acharyas as free gifts, provided material comforts and pleasures to them, because gift giving was an important aspect of the social and economic life of the age of *Agamas*. The word *agama* means coming near or approaching (*agam*), and would literally imply a sense of achievement or accomplishment. By Manu's time this word seems to have acquired a definite meaning: specific traditional doctrine or a collection of such doctrines, sacred works like the *Brahmana,* used in wider sense. Subsequently, the word *agama* came to mean anything handed down or fixed by tradition, on the reading of a text or record and specifically a Tantra or work inculcating the mystical worship of Shiva Shakti class of works teaching the highest *yoga* and mystical formularies, mostly in the form of dialogues between Bhairava and Bhairavi, are said to have treated five subjects in its generalized framework: (1) the creation; (2) destruction of the world; (3) worship of Gods; (4) attainment of all subjects, especially of six superhuman faculties; and (5) the four modes of union with the supreme spirit by meditation. These doctrines were ascribed to Shiva, who in the course of time of his dialogues, is said to have revealed them to Devi and this entire discourse came to be regarded as divine and was known as *Agama*. The *Agamas* claimed primacy over the Vedas both in point of time and in performance of ritual. But it appears that *Agamas* were posterior to the Vedas. The practice of the *Agamas* gradually led to the decline of Shaivism and acquired socio-economic importance. The behaviour pattern of Shaivite gurus shows that they had no social pretensions. The old tradition of life-long celibacy maintained by the fourteen saints of the monistic school of Shaiva philosophy in Kashmir was broken by the fifteenth saint, i.e. Tryambakaditya, aged seventy, who married a very young Brahmin girl of fifteen years, according to Brahminical rites, rituals, and traditions.[135]

Added to all this were the animistic principles of Buddhism, Shaivism, Tantra, and Shakta, which had only inculcated the spirit of superstition among the people at the popular level. They believed in a host of spirits and stood in awe of the spirits of their ancestors. They paid a portion of their produce to Brahmins for remission of sins, for the peace of the ancestral souls, as well as for a ceremonial and sacrificial fee.[136] Among the Kashmiri Brahmin families most of these beliefs still continue. Not only on the twelfth day after one's relative's death, but for generations afterwards, offerings in little cash as *dana/dakshina* and kind continue to be given to *purohitas*. Some Hindus in villages used to offer milk cows to *purohitas* on the first *shradha* to buy peace for the departed souls. But after the mass migration of Kashmiri Hindus to various parts of the world as a result of the crisis in which Kashmir has been since 1986, these practices are not only getting diluted but also disappearing fast. In the post-mass conversion period, the profession of *purohitas* (gor) was also not treated with dignity among Kashmiri pandits while as in Indian mainland they are considered Brahmins of high order in the caste hierarchy. The other reason for their disappearance is the erosion of the institution of priesthood among Kashmiri Hindus as a result of modernization and urbanization, which made alternate avenues of employment available to them. Besides the spirits of human beings and animals, there were countless others. The mountains, the rivers, the crops, all had their animate spirits. It was believed that the neglect of some tradition or ceremony would annoy the spirits. To the peasants the harvest was of supreme importance but the crops were supposed to possess spiritual essence which was to be propitiated by offerings.[137] Likewise in the early ancient period it was firmly believed that even routine matters were under the control of the gods. Seed time (*gongul*) and harvest (*helcrav*) were linked with ritual acts and special days were chosen by priests for commencing these activities. Similarly, the practice of medicine and the beginning and completion of buildings, were associated with auspicious date, time, prayers, offerings and people were charged for these. The priestly class alone had the authority and the vision to bestow auspiciousness on time, space and action and control human society.

In such circumstances, the new preliminaries of Islam at that time appeared to the Kashmiris as nobler knowledge and a better ordering of life than they had known.[138] It created a psychological climate for political stability which made it comparatively easy for people to abandon Brahminism.

Every monotheistic religion implicitly lays stress on social equality and consecutively its ideological appeal is the greatest among the lower sections of society, which is the victim of social inequalities. Islam initially revolutionized ideology and contemporary society by its championship of social equality and concept of brotherhood, the *millat.*[139] While in the Hindu religion *karma, dharma* and the observance of rituals were the main principles known to some people at popular level, in Islam the common prayer was formalized as one of the five principles of Islam, which was not the case with Hinduism.

It is generally recognized by historians that as Islam spread to distant lands and adjusted itself to the customs and practices of the political, social, and economic life of different regions, it began to lose much of its content of the concept of brotherhood, though it remained a part of its dogma.[140] However, one section among the Muslims still strove to revive and reinforce the pristine purity of Islam represented by the Koran, especially its egalitarian traditions which looked upon all human beings as the sacred creation of God. This tradition survived in the hands of Sufi saints who sought to personify in their everyday life all that was noble in their religion.[141] It was through their stimulating personalities, living among the poorest of the poor, learning their language, being sensitive to their smallest woes, avoiding putting any pressure on them to change their religion 'except by setting examples, that the spread of Islam was facilitated as a social and religious force in Kashmir long before it acquired political power.

Among the earliest who brought the message of Islam to Kashmir was Bulbul Shah, who first attracted the attention of the harassed masses.[142] After him a Turk named Shahmir laid the foundation of Muslim rule in Kashmir for which he was even able to obtain the support of Hindu chiefs such as Kottarajas, and the chiefs of *dvara* (gate) and Bangila. He is said to have entered into matrimonial alliances with Hindu chiefs. He married his granddaughter (daughter of his son Ali Sher) to Lusta, chief of *dvara,* and another son's (Jamsheed) daughter to the chief of Bangila. Some of the daughters of his family were married to Lavanyas. From then onwards the Lavanyas assumed Muslim names which clearly establishes the fact that they had entered into the fold of Islam.[143] These matrimonial alliances not only accelerated the process of conversion but also helped Shahmir in establishing his power.[144] Sayyids from Isfahan, Hamadan, Bokhara, and Balkh appeared on the scene during the reign of Qutb-ud-Din (AD 1374-89), and further facilitated the spread of Islam. Sultan Shihab-ud-Din set up the first *Madrasat ul-Quran* (a school for study of the Koran) and *madrasas* in many other places of Kashmir for teaching the basic tenets of Islam. Sultan Qutb-ud-Din (AD 1370-89) founded a college at Qutb-ud-Dinpora along with a free boarding house for the teachers and the taught. Sayyid Jamal-ud-Din Muhi-al-Din opened an institution, *Urwat-al-Waga* in Fateh Kadal, Srinagar, for Islamic teaching.[145]

The other Shahmir sultans also established *khanqas* and *madrasas* with *langar-khanah* and patronized the Sayyids who taught the rudiments of Islam to the people.[146] It was Sultan Sikandar (AD 1389-1413) of the Shahmir dynasty and his Prime Minister Suhabhatta, a converted Brahmin, who took much firmer steps to consolidate Muslim rule. Generally, it is believed that Suhabhatta accepted Islam because he was impressed by the simple religion of the Sayyids. But the more convincing reason for his conversion to Islam was that the Sayyid domination was increasing at the court of Sultan Sikandar (AD 1389-1413). They exercised considerable influence in state policies. In such circumstances, Suhabhatta who had no ideological relationship with the Sayyids must have felt that his alienation from the prime ministership was inevitable. So in order to preserve his official position he thought it better to accept Islam and was re-named Malik-Saif-ud-din. To please the Sayyids he had no other alternative but to execute the wishes of Sayyids more strictly, like the imposition of *jizya,* which has been termed by Jonaraja as the employment of force.[147] For this he along with them and Sultan Sikandar challenged the basis of the authority of the Brahmins by demolishing their temples and confiscating the *agraharas* and temple wealth, a practice introduced by King Harsha earlier. This they proceeded to do rather systematically. It is significant that there is no evidence of popular indignation at these steps of the sultan and his prime minister. Islam clearly flourished in the fourteenth century and later. In fact, there is evidence of Hindus, including Brahmins, converting to Islam and the transformation of their temples into mosques with a slight architectural modification.[148] Sultan Sikandar, in taking these coercive measures against Brahmins and their temples, was of course only continuing a century-old tradition in Kashmir begun by Hindu rulers, as stated earlier in this chapter. It is therefore hardly surprising that in pursuit of these goals he was ably aided by his Hindu prime minister, Suha Bhatta, who was later to become a Muslim himself.[149] The Sultan extended patronage to the Sayyids from Persia, Turkistan, Kashgar, and many other parts of Central Asia, who entered Kashmir in large numbers along with their disciples and dependants.[150] Some of the prominent Sayyids among them were Sayyid Hassan Shirazi, Qazi of Shiraz (Iran), Sayyid Ahmed from Isfahan, Sayyid Mohammad from Khwarizm, Sayyid Jalaluddin from Bokhara, Baba Haji Adham and Baba Hassan from Balkh, and Sayyid Mohammad Hamadani from Khatlan. He was accompanied by three hundred people.[151] Sayyid Ali has listed various anecdotes in his work *Tarik-i-Kashmir*. He says that after his arrival, when Sayyid Ali Hamadani visited Alauddinpora, he found that there was a large temple establishment attached to an inn which was controlled by a Hindu saint and his large group of disciples. The saint and his establishment were routinely fed by the residents of the locality among whom were both Hindus and Muslims. Sayyid Ali involved the saint in religious discussions and after defeating the saint, he asked his disciples to break the idols. They destroyed 120 idols. While breaking the biggest, the saint dubiously or cunningly took out a paper from his pocket on site on which he had written the *Kalima* and he gave an impression as if this paper had come out from the large idol that they broke, to convince the public of his self-claimed miracles. On seeing this, the Hindu saint is said to have cut his sacred thread and accepted Islam along with all his disciples.[152] The community of the Sayyids had a far-reaching influence in Kashmir many of whom were also joined by local Brahmin converts.[153] The people who migrated from Persia and Central Asia brought with them new technology and skill and provided work to large numbers of the lower echelons of society. They brought with them new designs of wooden architecture, one of the famous architects who introduced these new designs in the construction of mosques, *khanqahs*, and other buildings was Sadr-ud-din Khurasani from Khorasan.[154] The proof of wooden architecture of Sultan Sikandar's time is Jamia Masjid in Srinagar, which was founded by Sultan Sikandar as early as AD 1400 and completed by Sultan Zain-ul-Abidin (AD 1420-70). The chief architect of Jamia Masjid was Khwaja Sadur-ud-Din from Khurasan.[155] They also introduced new fashions in stone-cutting, stone polishing, instruments of ginning, and cleaning cotton.[156] Sultan Zain-ul-Abidin (AD 1420-70) organized Kashmiris socially to undertake the systematic manufacturing of various arts and crafts, such as bottle making, window cutting, gold beating, manufacture of fireworks, new designs in shawl making, carpet weaving, etc. In order to promote calligraphy in Kashmir, Sultan Zain-ulAbidin brought calligraphists from Samarkand and Balkh and gave them lands in pargana Phag for their maintenance. [157]

There is also evidence to show it was only in the thirteenth and fourteenth centuries when wooden worm-worked rollers were introduced by Turks in Pakhli in the neighbourhood of Kashmir. The Silk Route also encouraged trade between Kashmir and Central Asia, and Muslim traders subsequently came to Kashmir in increasing numbers with the establishment of the Shahmir Sultanate. These developments broke the extreme social and economic immobility of the peasants and the artisan class. This was a new experience for them; they learnt new crafts for which there was adequate demand hence they were able to move up economically. Hence it was under Sultan Sikandar and Sultan Zain-ul-Abidin that the growth of small industries took place[158] A new town life emerged with new social classes. All these measures also weakened the traditional bonds of the peasants with the Damaras and Brahmins as they floated towards new towns where they found employment. For the craftsmen, increased economic security and a plentiful supply of food was incentive enough to devote their time and skill to new techniques. All these techniques had a great effect on their lives and also on the new literature that began to be produced.

Equally important was the experience and feeling of community life like eating together and going to the mosque, a great delight to people coming from the lower rungs of society. The common prayer, especially on Fridays, encouraged craftsmen who exchanged their goods and organized trade on new lines.[159] This tradition has survived down to the present. In every town and village, on Fridays, people come from various areas and exchange their goods. The rural artisans and craftsmen come to sell their small articles like knives, sickles, butter, pulses and other articles of domestic use. On Fridays there are a lot of rural craftsmen and even peasants around the Jamia Masjid and Dargah Hazratbal in Srinagar as well.

The other aspect that proved of major inspiration to people of all castes was the role of the local ascetics. Among them the major contribution was of Lalleshwari (Lalded) and Sheikh Nuruddin (Nund Rishi)[160] Lalleshwari, when she realized that Brahminism was incapable of reforming, thought it better to welcome religious innovations rather than to try to redress the deep-seated abuses in the existing religion. She had no intellectual background but her ideology was conditioned by the crises amidst which she lived.

The exact date of birth of Lalleshwari cannot be established, but it is generally believed that she was born in AD 1335. She suffered due to the abuses in the then prevailing social order, which is clear from her poetry. She says, 'Let them abuse me or call me names/Let them say whatever suits them/They may even worship me with thousand flowers/ what do they gain thereby spotless that I am.'

The original text in Kashmiri reads:

Gal gadienam bole padinam
dopnam yas yoth rochai
sahaz kosmow puze karinam
bo amlani kas kya muchai[161]

As a result, she chose the path of a wandering ascetic.[162] Her poetry explains her readiness to break with tradition and to defy socio-ecclesiastical authority and put forward what she saw as a new and better way of life. She says, 'The soul is ever new, the man is ever new, so do I see the world ever new and new since I (Lalla) scoured my body and mind (all yesterdays and tomorrows faded away). I live in ever present new, forever new and new'[163] She attacked idol worship, the condition of priesthood, the claim of high birth, and the viciousness of aristocratic life. All these aspects had significantly dented Kashmiri society and culture. She says, 'Oh fool! Right action does not lie in fasting and ceremonial rights. The idol is but a stone, the temple is but a stone, from top to bottom is all but stone.[164] Her poetry also prepared the mood of the masses to abandon the age-old exploitative rituals and look for monotheism as the guiding principal in pursuing spirituality.

In the Foreword of this book, T.N. Dhar Kundan rightly says,

> Her writings are relevant on mundane platform as also in the realm of spirituality. These contain lessons of tolerance, message of love and harmony, revolt against falsehood and a strong case for pursuing the truth. She has also underscored the importance of the preceptor and expounded the tenets of Kashmir Trika philosophy in

> simple diction so that it is intelligible to even a common man. Her poetry is so comprehensive, so deep, and meaningful, so enchanting and melodious, so varied and so rich that one can write volumes explaining and analyzing the hidden meaning and purport of each verse.[165]

Thus a culture, technically competent, modified the religious understanding of the common man.[166] The most striking ideas of Lalleshwari and Sheikh Nuruddin penetrated Kashmir, radicalizing the process of reformation at the popular level.

Sheikh Nuruddin was equally concerned about establishing a community where equality, though not recognized in principle, was realized in real life.[167] Sheikh Nuruddin is much respected among the Sufi saints of Kashmir and is considered to be the founder of the Rishi Order in Kashmir. He was born in AD 1377.[168] His preaching seems to have stirred the populace unconsciously or consciously and helped to ready the people for the reception of a new faith. In view of these circumstances, people increasingly felt that deserting their religions, i.e. Buddhism, Shaivism, Tantra, Shakta would solve their problems because under the Agrahara, priestly Brahmins and Shaivite *acharyas* were justifying the ongoing exploitation of the people and also legitimising the then existing political order by their complete silence about larger society from beginning. Jayratha in his *viveka* of *Tantraloka* clearly states, 'the theory and practice of 'Saivagamas' becomes intelligible only through constant exertion and practice under a *guru,* as the very nature of *agamas* suggests that these are not theoretical manuals to be committed to memory but are basically action-oriented, the *Siddhatantra* being principally *Kriya Pradhan* (a spiritual practice-oriented), *Namaka Jnana*-oriented (*Jnana Pradhana*) and the *malini*—the essence of the two. It is the command of the *gurunatha* alone that can initiate a *sadhaka* into the secrets of *agamas* and not otherwise.'[169] These priestly Brahmins and Acharyas were evolving, interpreting reinterpreting and debating philosophical aspects of

Shaivism, and to the ordinary people these philosophical aspects and tantric ritualism and yoga remained vague mysteries. Therefore, accepting Islam meant establishing a new identity and legitimizing one's position in the new social order, facilitated by the processes of vertical and horizontal mobility ensured by the penetration of Central Asian elements who had accepted Islam much before the Kashmiris.

The foreign missionaries who entered Kashmir from time to time, did not perhaps need to make much effort. The majority of the population was ready to rally for the cause of Islam with enthusiasm. The task of the missionary Sayyids was to teach the rudiments of religion and establish *khanqahs* to carry out their activities. Among all the foreign Sayyids after Bulbul Shah, Sayyid Ali Hamadani's visit marked an unparalleled growth and development in missionary ventures in Kashmir. Sayyid Ali Hamadani was accompanied by seven hundred of his followers. It is generally believed by historians that the Sayyids came to Kashmir along with their leader Sayyid Ali not just to propagate Islam because they were imbued with religious zeal, but the fact that Sayyid Ali Hamadani was a refugee from Hamadan, Persia. He and his order were expelled by Timur in AD 1380, because they could not prove their spiritual worth as Timur expected them to and it was in Kashmir that they found avenues for promoting their interests.[170] Apart from this, the thirteenth century is considered to be one of the most critical periods in the annals of Islam. No doubt during this period Islam was fast growing on Indian soil but in Central Asia, it faced decay due to various factors such as intra-tribal warfare.[171] Thus, in these strifes and conflicts Kashmir also served as an asylum for the persecuted, restless but technically advanced Turks, Persians and Central Asians. In this pre-Sultanate period also, when successors of King Samkarvarman (AD 883-902) led a campaign against the Shahi power at Udabhanda, the princes of the Shahi dynasty found refuge at the Court of Kashmir.[172] According to Sadat, Sayyid Ali and his followers converted 37,000

Hindus to Islam.[173] Many learned Sayyids, such as Sayyid Jamal-ud-Din Atrani, Sayyid Kamal, Sayyid Nuraldin, Sayyid Muhammad Qureshi, Sayyid Abad-Allah, Sayyid Muhammad, and Sayyid Muhammad Shirazi, who accompanied Mir Sayyid Ali Hamadani to Kashmir, now resided in almost every part of the valley.[174] These various Sayyids established *khanqahs* and taught people the basic tenets of Islam and gave them all possible help.[175] Hazrat Baba Zain ud-Din openly appealed to the masses that whoever rejected idolatry and accepted Islam would be given the status of the *khalifah* of the wise and would be highly respected.

The original text of the appeal reads:

Har An Kase Taft O Az Kufur Dina,
Khalifa be Shak Ast An Pesh Dana,
Chun Kase Ayad ba Islam
Sharf payad Ziman name Maula.[176]

The Sayyids also indulged in destruction of temples. There are instances of Sayyids publicly smashing idols in some of the temples. In the vicinity of Alauddinpora in the city of Srinagar, during the reign of Sultan Qutb-ud-din, a group of Sayyids destroyed idols in temples. Similarly, Mir Sayyid Qazim destroyed the temple in village Letapora near Awantipora town. The temple in Bijbehara faced the same fate. In this temple some of the idols that were made partly of silver and other precious metals were sold off. Sayyid Ali says that a large temple at Sikandarpora in Srinagar was destroyed on the instructions of Sayyid Muhammad Hamadani.[177] But from an examination of the sources it becomes clear that behind these activities there was no other reason except the fact that the Sayyids wanted to convince the common people that these idols did not possess any spiritual power but on that pretext huge wealth was being accumulated by the custodians of Brahminism by demanding free labour, offerings, and grants.[178] Unfortunately in the post conversion period they indulged in much worse exploitation of the peasantry and other artisans in the valley till most recent times. The Sayyids did transform and modify many temples and shrines by removing the statues and converting them into *khanqahs* and mosques.[179]

The painting shows *Mahakali* temple on which the *khanqah*/mosque was superimposed after destroying and modifying the temple structure. The temple structure and it exists in same building in present day Khanakah Mohalla, near Nauhatta in Srinagar.[180]

There appears to have been no opposition or protest from local people to these attrocities of the Sayyids and the sultans. Besides, in pursuance of their objectives, the Sayyids passed on many advanced skills and knowledge of various things to the local people. Sayyid Ali Hamadani wrote a treatise, *Zakhirat-ul-Mulk* on the political ethics and the state system which must have helped the Sultans to work out various activities for consolidating their power. He also wrote *Gayat-ul-Makan and* a book *Fika-i-Ahvat* on medicine.[181] They also spoke in a cultured language which drew on imageries of the Kashmiri mysticism preached by Lalleshwari and Sheikh Nuruddin.

The converts mostly came from the various artisan classes—craftsmen, peasants, pastoralists and village menials spread over the entire valley. This is further attested by the complete absence of local Hindu butchers, barbers, cobblers, blacksmiths, weavers, etc. Now local Hindu carpenters and tailors are very rare. These professions have also disappeared among the local Hindus. Beside the above-mentioned people, the Kayasthas also seem to have totally embraced Islam because after the conversions we do not come across any references to Kayasthas in Kashmir's history.

It would thus seem that the reasons for turning away from ones faith were diverse. They were certainly not confined only to external elements like the use of force or persuasion; indeed, these had their effect only because the Kashmiri priestly Brahmins and Hindu political elements such as Dammaras, Lavanyas, Tantrins Ekangas, Magres, and Rainas had created favorable conditions for them. The fundamental change brought about by Islam was that it replaced a religion which had been reduced to a highly hypocritical set of liturgy with a community of common worship. Islam gave a new sense of direction. Since there were not many cults in Islam, turning to it meant turning to a new social morality without any grave tensions at the popular level. The existing system had become rotten, with internal contradictions in society, especially for those who suffered from social and economic deprivation. The only alternative seemed for to them to shift to a new order.

Thus, Islam at the hands of Turks from various parts of Central Asia, was a process which extended from the middle of the eighth century to the first half of the fifteenth century and temporarily it was found to be an answer and a solution to the problems of injustice, disharmony, misery, and instability of the people facilitated by the local political factions and their conflicts with the state and among themselves. But in the long-term perspective, for village menials such as Dombs and Chamars (*vetalas*), it merely provided what P. Masterson calls, 'a deceptive justification and illusory consolation for an unhappy state of human society'.[182] Because Kashmiri Muslims continue to carry the cultural baggage of the pre-Islamic period in terms of social differentiation, the only difference was that in theory, *jati* and *varna* were replaced by *taifa* (a term used locally) for discriminating and distinguishing, in real life, one social category down to the present day. The Dombs and Chamars (locally referred to as *vatals/vetalas* in *Rajtarangini.*) in Kashmir still suffer from the hierarchical order of the Muslim social organization and serious discrimination at the hands of the dominant groups within the Muslim community. The caste and professional differences have been retained by Kashmiri Muslims in the valley down to our own times.

In the political sphere, the emergence of new groups like the Damaras, Lavanyas, Tantrins, etc., brought about more contestation for power and therefore conflict in society. There was an urgent need for order in the political sphere and the Islamic religion with its stress on monotheism was understood, by extension, as a monolithic order transcending local and petty loyalties and thus was well received as it gave the vision and direction for an alternate polity in which the priestly Brahmin had no role to play. The austerity and puritanical lifestyle of the Sayyids set an example and prepared the ground for the new discourse, and the Sayyids were in turn patronized by Muslim rulers and thereby indirectly legitimized their patrons. Thus we may say that the people of Kashmir had been open to diverse cultural influences for a long time, and by virtue of these influences, Kashmir was the ground where Buddhism, Shaivism, Shakta, Tantra and a varied mother goddess cults were practised and the introduction of Islam was also initially adopted by Kashmiris as the adoption of a new culture.

Notes

1. Richard Eaton, *Essays on Islam and Indian History*, New Delhi, 2000. Introduction, pp. 1-5 also pp. 249-75. For details see by the same author *India Rise of Islam and the Bengal Frontier (1204-1760)*, Berkeley, 1993.
2. Ira M. Lapidus, *A History of Islamic Societies,* Cambridge, 2002, 2nd edn., pp. 362-4.
3. Irfan Habib, 'The Technology and Economy of Mughal India' Delhi, 1969 (Dev Raj Channa Lectures), *Indian Economic and Social History Review,* January-March 1980, 17(1): 6-7.
4. Lapidus, A *History of Islamic Societies,* p. 361.
5. Harbans Mukhia, 'Communalism: A Study in Its Socio-Historical Perspective', *Social Scientist,* no. 1, August 1972, pp. 45-57.
6. Pandit Jonaraja, *Rajatarangini* (Sanskrit), English translation by J.C. Dutt as *Kings of Kashmir,* 3 vols., Calcutta, 1879-1898, (rpt. Delhi, 1990), vol. III, pp. 60, 99, 165, 206.
7. Mukhia, 'Communalism: A Study in Its Socio-Historical Perspective', op. cit., pp. 45-57.
8. H.D. Sankaliya, *Pre- and Proto-History of India and Pakistan,* Poona, 2nd edn. 1974, p. 303. See also H.D. Sankaliya, 'New Evidence on Early Man in Kashmir', *Current Anthropology,* vol. 12, nos. 4 and 5, 1971.
9. D.D. Kosambi, *The Culture and Civilization of Ancient Indian Historical Outline,* Delhi, 1970, p. 40.
10. R. Ghirshman, *Iran: From Earliest Times to the Islamic Conquest. A Volume in the Pelican Archaeological Series,* London, 1954, p. 55.
11. Ibid., p. 72.
12. Ibid., p. 292.

13. Jean Naudou, *Buddhists of Kashmir* (French), Presses Universitaries de France, 1968, tr. J.P. Brereton and Claudine Picron, Delhi, 1980, p. 1.
14. Chu Sanzang Jiji 14; 543. Fozu tong 36.T 49344. Quoted in Naudou, *Buddhists of Kashmir,* op. cit.
15. Liang Shu. *Dynastic History of Liang* by Yao Silian (557-637) Beijing Zhonghua Shuju 1973.25.256.
16. Kapalikas worshipped the Hindu deity Bhairava-Siva and his consort. They also worshipped bones, blood, flesh and skulls while as Kalmukhas ate from a skull bowl, be smeared their body with the ashes of corpse and kept a part for traditional wine (sura) and ate from same. David N. Lorenzen, *The Kapalikas and Kalmukhas,* Berkeley and Los Angles, 1972, pp. 2-5, 31-39 and 97-130.
17. D.L. Snellgrove, *Hevajra Tantra: A Critical Study,* London, Oriental Studies VI, Part I, Introduction and translation XV, p. 149 also Part I Oxford I XI, 1959, p. 188.
18. Naudou, *Buddhists of Kashmir,* op. cit., p. 157.
19. Mohammad Ishaq Khan, *Kashmir's Transition to Islam: The Role of Muslim Rishis,* Delhi, 1997, pp. 177-8.
20. Ibid.
21. N.K. Zutshi, *Sultan Zain-ul-Abidin,* Lucknow, 1976, pp. 15-51.
22. G.M.D. Sufi, *Kashir,* 2 vols., Lahore, 1949, vol. 1, pp. 75-116. Sufi has traced these references from early Persian sources of Baba Daud Mishakti, *Asrar-ul-Abrar,* Khawaja Muin-ud-din Naqushbandi, *Maqamt-i Mahamadiya;* Muhammad Ali Khan Marin, *Tazkirat-ul-ulma,* and other reliable sources. S.A.A. Rizvi, 'Islamic Proselytization', in G.A. Oddie, ed., *Religion in South Asia,* Delhi, 1977, p. 28; R.K. Parmu, *A History of Muslim Rule in Kashmir (1320-1819),* Delhi, 1969, pp. 119-26. The other works which have attributed conversion to force or the efforts of Sayyids are T.W. Arnold, *Preaching of Islam,* London, 1912, pp. 291-2. P.N.K. Bamzai, *A History of Kashmir,* Delhi, 1962, pp. 320-1. Even earlier works such as *Tarikh-i-Rashidi; Baharistan-i-Shahi* and *Ain-i-Akbari* are of the same opinion. See Mirza Muhammad Haidar Dughlat, *Tarikh-i-Rashidi* (Persian). English translation by Sir E. Denison Ross with an Introduction by N. Elias, London, 1895, p. 433. *Baharistan-i-Shahi* (anonymous) Persian Ms., Research Department Library, Kashmir University,

Srinagar, p. 24; Abul Fazl; *Ain-i-Akbari* (Persian), 3 vols., English translation by Blochmann and H.S. Jarrett, Calcutta, 1894, vol. II, p. 387.

23. Mohibbul Hassan, *Kashmir under the Sultans,* Srinagar, 1967, (2nd edn. 1974), pp. 64-6, 218-19.
24. N.K. Zutshi, *Sultan Zain-ul-Abidin,* pp. 14-15
25. Ibid.
26 S.A.A. Rizvi, 'Islamic Proselytization', in G.A. Oddie, ed., *Religion in South Asia,* Delhi, 1977, pp. 28-33.
27. Jonaraja, *Rajatarangini* (Sanskrit), English translation by J.C. Dutt as *Kings of Kashmir,* 3 vols., Calcutta, 1879-98, vol. III, p. 66.
28. Ibid., p. 67.
29. Ibid., pp. 60-1.
30. Sayyid Ali, *Tarikh-i-Kashmir,* pp. 2-23.
31. Jonaraja, *Rajatarangini,* pp. 66-7.
32. Ibid., p. 59.
33. Ibid., p. 60.
34. Mirza Muhammad Haidar Dughlat, *Tarikh-i-Rashidi* (Persian), English translation by Sir E. Denison Ross with an Introduction by N. Elias, London, 1895, p. 426.
35. Kalhana, *Rajatarangini,* English translation by M.A. Stein, 2 vols., London, 1900, rpt. Delhi, 1961 and 1979, vol. I, pp. 220-6, 234, 238, 264, 358, 392, 364-5. vol. II, pp. 5, 10, 53, 56, 62, 65, 74, 172, 215.
36. *The Cultural Heritage of India,* vol. I: Introduction by Sarvepalli Radhakrishnan, Calcutta, 1937, p. XIVIII.
37 Naudou, *Buddhists of Kashmir,* op. cit., pp. 4-5.
38. Kalhana, *RT,* vol. I, p. 34.
39. Naudou, *Buddhists of Kashmir,* pp. 4-5.
40. Ibid.
41. Ibid., pp. 39-40
42. Kalhana, *Rajatarangini,* vol. I, book I, vv. 290-3. See also Hiuen Tsang, *si-yu-ki,* English translation by Samuel Beal, 2 vols., *Buddhist Records of the Western World,* vol. I, London, 1884, p. 171.
43. V.N Drabu, *Saivagamas: A Study in Socio-Economic Ideas and Institutions in Kashmir (200 BC to 700 AD),* New Delhi, 1990, pp. 31-54.
44. Kalhana, *Rajatarangini,* vol. I, pp. 1-2.
45. K.Z. Ashrafyan, 'Historical Significance of Turkish Conquest', in

Kunwar Mohammed Ashraf: An Indian Scholar and Revolutionary, edited by H. Kruger, Delhi, 1969, p. 77.

46. H.H. Wilson, *Hindu History of Kashmir,* Calcutta, 1960 p. 145. and Krishna Mohan, *Early Medieval History of Kashmir,* AD *1003-1171,* Delhi, 1981, p. 305.
47. Harbans Mukhia, *Perspectives on Medieval History,* Delhi, 1993, pp. 33-44.
48. Sayyid Ali, *Tarikh-i-Kashmir,* pp. 2-16.
49. *Rajatarangini,* vol. 1, book I, pp. 15, 18, 23, 26, 31, 34, 46, 49-51, 60, 68, 72-4, 80, 110, 113, 115, 120, 123, 125, 139, 141, 148, 164, 167, 181, 184, 187, 189, 190, 192, 202, 207, 219, 224, 231, 242, 246, 256, 260, 261, 275, 277, 279, 282, 311, 313, 323, 342; vol. 2, pp. 7, 21, 47, 83, 133, 262, 263.
50. For the *agrahara grants* to the priestly Brahmins and the temple priests see Kalhana, *Rajatarangini,* vol. 1, book I, pp. 15, 18, 23, 26, 31, 34, 46, 49-51, 60, 68, 72-4, 80, 110, 113, 115, 120, 123, 125, 139, 141, 148, 164, 167, 181, 184, 187, 189, 190, 192, 202, 207, 219, 224, 231, 242, 246, 256, 260, 261, 275, 277, 279, 282, 311, 313, 323, 342; vol. 2, pp. 7, 21, 47, 83, 133, 262, 263; vol. 1, book I, p. 50, v. 340, p. 52, vv. 347, 348; book II, p. 60, v. 55, p. 67, v. 132; book III, p. 72, v. 8, p. 105, v. 376, pp. 115, vv. 480, 481; book IV, p. 123, v. 38, p. 181, v. 673, p. 183, vv. 696-9; book V, p. 187, v. 16, p. 188, vv. 23-4, p. 229, v. 4004, p. 230, v. 426; book VI, p. 242, v. 87-9; book VII, p. 282, vv. 180-1, p. 285, v. 207, p. 317, v. 608, p. 342, vv. 955-6; book VIII, p. 21, vv. 243-4. The alphabet v. refers to verses and not to the Tarang of *Rajatarangini.*
51. Ibid., vol. I, book V, vv. 165-83, pp. 208-10.
52. Kalhana, *Rajatarangini,* vol. I.VII, vv. 881-3.
53. Ibid.
54. Ibid.
55. *Nilmata Purana* (Sanskrit), English translation by Ved Kumari Gai.Published by Jammu and Kashmir and Academy of Art, Culture and Languages, Srinagar, 2 vols., 1973, vol. I, pp. 102-3.
56. Kalhana, *Rajatarangini,* vol. I, book IV, v. 29, p. 177.
57. Kalhana, op. cit., vol. I, book V, vv. 165-83, pp. 208-10; Kalhana, op. cit., vol. I, book, vv. 175, 271-4, p. 221. See also Kosambi, 'Origins of Feudalism in Kashmir', op. cit., pp. 109-20.
58. Kalhana, op. cit., vol. I, book V, vv. 165-83, pp. 208-10
59. Saxena, op. cit., p. 126.

60. Kalhana, op. cit., vol. I, book V, vv. 175, 271-4, p. 221. See also Kosambi, 'Origins of Feudalism in Kashmir', op. cit., pp. 109-20.
61. Kalhana, op. cit., vol. I, book V, vv. 165-83, pp. 208-10
62. Ibid., vv. 245-448, pp. 219-31.
63. Naudou. *Buddhists of Kashmir,* p. 156.
64. Kalhana, op. cit., vol. I, book V, pp. 268-79.
65. Ibid., vol. II, book VIII, pp. 353-4.
66. Ibid., vv. 245-448, pp. 219-31.
67. Naudou, *Buddhists of Kashmir,* p. 159.
68 Kalhana, op. cit., vol. 1, 75-106.
69. Jonaraja *Rajatarangini,* edited by Srikanth Koul; Hindi translation by Raghunath Singh, Varanasi, 1972, stanza no. 173.
70. Krishna Mohan, op. cit., p. 221
71. Wilson, op. cit., p. 145.
72. Brij Narayan, *Social Life of North India,* Delhi, 1966, p. 35.
73. Kalhana, 1900: Books IV-XII, pp. 61-2.
74. *Svacchanda Tantra* 1921, pp. 61-2.
75. Ibid.
76. Drabu, *Shaivagmas,* pp. 185-200.
77. Ibid.
78. Kalhana, op. cit., vol. 2, v. 795, p. 64.
79. Ibid., vol. 2, p. 64, v. 795.
80. Ibid.
81. Ibid.
82. Naudou. *Buddhists of Kashmir,* p. 158.
83. Ibid., v. 10, p. 110
84. Ibid., vol. 1, pp. 127, 234, 238, 264, 268, 352, 358, 392; vol. 2, pp. 5, 10, 53, 56, 62, 65, 74, 172, 215.
85. Ibid., 10, v. 110.
86. Ibid., vol. 1, pp. 207-8, vv. 165-70.
87. Kalhana, op. cit., vol. 1, p. 34, v. 200.
88. Ibid., vol. 1, pp. 207-8, vv. 165-70.
89. Ibid., vol. 1, 248, v. 171-3.
90. Ibid., vol. 1, 323, v. 696-7.
91. Jonaraja, *Rajatarangini,* vol. II, p. 59.
92. Ibid., vol. I, 193.
93. Ibid.
94. Kalhana, op. cit., 389.
95. Ibid., vol. II, 59.
96. Ibid.

97. Ibid., p. 96.
98. Kalhana, op. cit., p. 36.
99. Ibid., 37.
100. Ibid., 224.
101. Ibid., 221.
102. Kalhana, op. cit., 138.
103. Ibid., 206.
104. Ibid., 310.
105. Kalhana, op. cit., 272.
106. Naudou, *Buddhists of Kashmir*, pp. 243-4.
107. Tarnatha, pp. 254-5.
108. Ibid., vol. 1, 364.
109. Ibid.
110. Naudou, *Buddhists of Kashmir*, p. 238.
111. Kalhana, vol. 1, p. 311.
112. Ibid., vol. 1, p. 357.
113. Naudou, *Buddhists of Kashmir*, p. 238.
114. Ibid., pp. 253-4.
115. Kalhana, *Rajatarangini*, vol. II, pp. 152-5.
116. Naudo, pp. 253-4
117. R.L. Hangloo, 'Indo-Central Asian Relations', *Journal of Central Asian Studies,* vol. IV, no. 1, Fall/Winter 1999, Okalhoma University, Still Water, Okalhoma, pp. 14-29.
118. Kalhana, vol. II, v. 87, p. 59.
119. *Baharistan-i-Shahi:* folio 14b Bulbul shah is said have been a disciple of Nimatullah Farsi of the *Suhrawarddiya* order.
120. Naudou, pp. 238, 240.
121. Ibid., p. 254.
122. Ibid., pp. 245-6.
123. Kalhana, *Rajatarangini*, vol. 1, p. 34, v. 200.
124. Naudou, pp. 240-2.
125. Ibid., p. 238.
126. Ibid., pp. 240-4.
127. Ibid., p. 240; P.V. Bapat, *Twenty-five Hundred Years of Buddhism,* 1956, p. 63. From the frequent grants of *agraharas* to temples and the massive construction of Shavite temples it becomes clear that even though Buddhism, Vaishnavism and Shakta were among the prevalent religious forms, the Tantra Shaivism was the relatively dominant religion from fourth to the fourteenth centuries is Kashmir, if one were to go by

the numerous references scattered in the *Rajatarangini* to the construction of Shaivite temples.

128. Pandy, 1951, pp. 151-3.
129. R.C. Temple, 1924: 88. See also Sarla Khosla (1974: 53). For a detailed study of the Decline of Buddhism in Kashmir, see Jean Naudou (1980).
130. Kalhana, op. cit., vol. 1, 92.
131. Ibid., 195-201.
132. Tejomayananda, see also V.N. Drabu, op. cit. N.J. Demerath and Philip H. Hemmond, *Religions in Social Context,* New York. V.N. Drabu, *Kashmir Polity,* Delhi, 1986, p. 26.
133. S.K. Dass, *Shakti or Divine Power,* Calcutta, 1934. R.G. Bhandarkar, *Vaishnavism, Shaivism and Other Minor Religious Systems,* Strassburg, 1913.
134. Drabu, 1990, pp. 164-200.
135. Ibid.
136. Kosambi, p. 112.
137. *Nilamata Purana,* op. cit.
138. Sayyid Ali, 5-20, 29.
139. Ahmad Hassan, *The Doctrine of Ijma in Islam,* Lahore, 1976, pp. 11-18.
140. G.E.V. Grunebaum, *Classical Islam (600-1258),* tr. K. Watson, London, 1970, pp. 177-9.
141. For details see S.A.A. Rizvi, *A History of Sufism in India,* 2 vols., Delhi, 1978.
142. *Baharistan-i-Shahi,* f. 14b; see also *Majmua dar Ansb Mashaikh-i-Kashmir,* Anonymous, f. 106; see also *Tarikh-i-Hassan,* vol. 1, f. 136b and vol. 2, f. 84b.
143. Jonaraja, 1898, 25-7.
144. S.A.A. Rizvi, 'Islamic Proselytization', in G.A. Oddie, ed., *Religion in South Asia,* Delhi, 1977, rpt. 1992, p. 28.
145. Sufi, 1949: op. cit., vol. 2, 345, G.M.D. Sufi has traced this evidence from the early Persian sources of Baba Dawud Mishkati Kh. Muin al-Din Naqshbandi *Mahamidiyyah*; Mohd. Ali Khan Matin and some other reliable sources. All these are available at the Research Department Library at Kashmir University, Srinagar and many of them also with the author.
146. Ibid.
147. Jonaraja, *Kings of Kashmir,* p. 60. See also stanzas 606, 607, 673.

148. Sayyid Ali, *Tarikh-i-Kashmir*, pp. 3-4.
149. Jonaraja, op. cit., p. 60. See also stanzas 606, 607, 673.
150. *Baharistan-i-Shahi*, f. 34.
151. Ibid.
152. Sayyid Ali: 45.
153. *Baharistan-Shahi*, 29-30; Sayyid Ali: 10; Jonaraja 1898: 370).
154. Sayyid Ali, op. cit., p. 11. See also Percy Brown, *Indian Architecture*, Calcutta, 1942, p. 81.
155. *Baharistan-i-Shahi:* 32-5.
156. Irfan Habib, 'The Technology and Economy of Mughal India', *IESHR*, January-March 1980, vol. XVII, no. 1, pp. 6-7, also in Devraj Chanana Lectures, Delhi, 1969.
157. See Mirza Muhammad Haidar Dughlat, *Tarikh-i-Rashidi*, pp. 47, 433. See also C.B. Hugel, *Travels in Punjab and Kashmir*, Jammu, 1972, pp. 116-19. There took place an immense construction activity chiefly in public works under Zain-ul-Abidin. N.K Zutshi, *Sultan Zain-ul-Abidin*, Lucknow, 1976, pp. 45-51. See also M.I. Khan, op. cit.
158. Zutshi, op. cit., pp. 115-51.
159. Sayyid Ali, 7-25.
160. Moharnmad Amin Kamil, *Noornama* (Kashmiri), Srinagar, 1965, pp. 29-34. S.K. Raina, *Kashmiri Bhasha aur Sahitya* (Hindi), Delhi, 1972, pp. 65-72.
161. B.N. Sopori. *Lall Vaakh*, Jammu, 1999, p. 145. See also Kotru, p. 19.
162. Raina, vol. 1, pp. 3-5. See also Krishna Raina, 1977, pp. 66-86, also Grierson 1920, pp. 1-2.
163. K. Santhanam, *An Anthology of Indian Literature*, Delhi, 1959, p. 341.
164. Keith Wilkes, op. cit., p. 79, discusses link between tools and social attitudes.
165. Jawaharlal Bhat, *Lalded Revisited*, Delhi, 2014. See Forward of the book.
166. Ibid., see also J,L. Kaul, *Lalded*, Delhi, 1973, p. 16; B.N. Sopori, *Voice of Experience, Lall Vakh: Lalleshwari of Kashmir (India)*, Jammu 1999 and N.J. Hangloo, 'Kashmiri Bhakti aur Sant Mirza Kak: Ek Samajik aur Sanskritik Adhyayan' (Hindi), unpublished Ph.D. thesis, Centre for Indian Languages, JNU, New Delhi, 1988.
167. For details see Baba Daud Mishkati, *Asrar-ul-Abrar* and *Rishi-*

nama (Persian Ms.), Research Department Library, Kashmir University, Srinagar. Also see Muhammad Amin Kamil, *Noornama* and Baba Nasib Kashmiri, *Rishi Nama* (Persian Ms.) Research Department Library, Kashmir University, Srinagar. Here it should be noted that while studying *Rishi-order* in Kashmir, the source material, available both at the Research Department Library, Srinagar and Iran, should be carefully examined. A careful study of the *Rishi* movement in Kashmir has been made by M.I. Khan under the title *Kashmir's Transition to Islam,* Delhi, 1994.

168. Muhammad Amin Kamil, 1965: 29-34; Raina, op. cit., pp. 65-72, 89-104.
169. Drabu, *Saivagma,* p. 47. For details see Jayratha's *Commentary on Tantraloka*, vol. I, pp. 46-52.
170. Mirza Haider Dughlat, *Tarikh-i-Rashidi,* p. 432, fn. 2.
171. Mohd. Noor Nabi, pp. 7-9. See also G.E. von Grunebaum, pp. 170-9.
172. Andre Wink, *Al-Hind,* vol. 1, 254; vol. 2, pp. 43-149.
173. Ibid.
174. Sayyid Ali, p. 34. The graves and *maqbaras* of these Sayyids are located in various parts of Kashmir and are in dilapidated condition.
175. Hangloo, *Situating Medieval Indian State,* pp. 5-25.
176. Sayyid Ali, op. cit., p. 29.
177. Ibid., pp. 2-7.
178. Ibid., pp. 3, 4, 6, 11.
179. Ibid., pp. 3-11.
180. This painting is available in India Office Library, London, but I have acquired it from Professor Harbans Mukhia formerly at Jawaharlal Nehru University, New Delhi.
181 Parmu, *A History of Muslim Rule in Kashmir,* pp. 11-113, note 87.
182. P. Masterson, *Atheism and Alienation,* London, 1964, p. 82.

3

The Sayyids, Sultans and the State: A Search for Legitimacy 1339-1470

In the first half of the fourteenth century, with the transfer of political power from the second Lohara dynasty to the Shahmir Sultans (AD 1101-1320), there seemed to be a general feeling among Kashmiris that the region of Kashmir would now register a comparatively peaceful era, while the establishment of a Sultanate would usher in an improvement in the conditions of people. However, after acquiring power, the Shahmir Sultans were more concerned about the legitimization of their rule. They preferred to promote Islam and felt that the patronization of the Sayyids was being more necessary towards perpetuation of their authority rather than any social transformation, thus affecting the socio-economic conditions of the people.[1] Behind the voluntary acceptance of Islam by the majority in Kashmir lay the expectation that the new rulers would overhaul the entire socio-economic and political system and respond to the immediate problems of the people. But while claiming the loyalty of their subjects the Shahmir Sultans were neither hostile to the old political structure for as long as it suited to them, nor to the growth of new institutions which helped them in the legitimization of their power. Therefore, the negligence of the Shahmir state in matters of social injustice and poverty at the lower end of society was not unjustified from their point of view. The ratification of their legitimacy was far more important and central to the Shahmir State, particularly when the administrative organization and control were insufficient to maintain social order or to undertake steps to improve the conditions of its subjects.

From the very beginning, the Sultans of the Shahmir dynasty (AD 1339-1470) felt that Islam was unquestionably a great issue in the establishment of the Shahmir Sultanate in medieval Kashmir. It becomes very clear from the fact that all Shahmir Sultans except perhaps Zain-ul-Abidin (AD 1420-70), thought that Islam was a secure political ideology for them and the law according to which they ruled.[2] In fact, all the Persian chroniclers on Kashmir are replete with evidences to this effect. In the past, the ideologies had been eliminated or set aside under the names of sects, heresies and religious errors. The hard and suggestive polemic between Sunnis and Shias is an excellent example of the ideological basis of the theological reason. Only modern critics of ideology can show that each orthodoxy is ultimately founded on an ideological postulate. The conversions from Brahminism to Islam were influencing the shift of the solidarity of various social groups from caste distinctions and other social disparities to a religious homogeneity. Sultan Shams-ud-din Shahmir (AD 1339-42) realized that the role of Islam was a political necessity, for once the majority of subjects had accepted Islam as a popular religion, the state needed to patronize it in order to complete itself as a State. Besides, the establishment of the Sultanate did not only involve the doings of those but also the response of those who were subjects. This necessitated the existence of the Sayyids creating and maintaining the hierarchies of dominance and deference.[3] True, that 'the democratic state, the real state, does not need religion for its political completion, on the contrary, it can disregard religion because the human basis of religion is realized in a secular manner'[4] But in some medieval societies with majority of subjects as Muslims (as in the case of Kashmir), the state recognized God as the Supreme Governor at least in theory.[5] In medieval Kashmir too, Islam was an integral part of the state system and the protest against the Sultan could be treated as protest against the Islamic tradition and punished by law to justify the role of the state and to enlarge it.[6] In this entire process, the Sayyids who worked as religious missionaries, reciters of the Koran and keepers of the traditions, the prayer leaders and Sufis in *khanqahs* played a very significant role. Gradually their preaching and teaching encompassed all aspects of life in medieval Kashmir. They took upon themselves the task of defining the nature of relations between the medieval state and society in Kashmir. The interference of the Sayyids in medieval Kashmir's polity is as old as Islam in Kashmir. Bul Bul Shah was the first person to have enjoyed royal patronage under King Rinchana (AD 1320-23) who accepted Islam. After him, the Sayyids of the Suharawardi order started dabbling in the politics of Kashmir more actively. Hence, from the very beginning. there was a relationship of mutual dependence. The Sayyids built a mass base and helped the state in the execution of its authority while the state maintained them with various grants. The Sultans solicited from the Sayyids, the formal legal acceptance of their politics in the form of the so-called *fatwas*. They included a wide range of areas in society, economy and polity.[7] They tended to emphasize that the newly-constructed Muslim community *Umma* was a divine trust and the political power of the Shahmir Sultans a divine gift. In strengthening such ideas for legitimization of the Shahmir Sultanate, the Sayyids were also the beneficiaries of the medieval stereotype, being regarded by the majority in Kashmir as spiritual, intelligent and learned. Consequently, they emerged as the most influential group not only in religious matters but also in the political affairs of the medieval state and in regulating the public order.[8] This dominance reflected Islamic orthodoxy as an official religion resulting from the collaboration of the large number of Sayyids as *ulama* with the state, in course of time.

To the Shahmir Sultans (AD 1339-1470), the Sayyids appeared to be self-motivated, as also largely the prime movers in maintaining the social order and the authority of state, becoming an integral part in the process. While justifying the primacy of his claim to governance, Sultan Shahmir (AD 1339-42) felt that the promotion and application of Islamic tenets in the affairs of the state was an ideal way of acquiring legitimacy for his rule. He tried to protect and promote the institution of the *Umma* by preaching the *Hanfia* doctrines, creating endowments for the upkeep of those who accomplished this task.[9] This popularization of the *Hanfia* doctrines at the hands of the Sayyids, provided him with an effective mechanism to acquire a cultural unity and defence, particularly at a time when the beliefs in innumerable gods, deities and rituals had been totally undermined. In the fourteenth century, the Kashmir Shahmir dynasty did not claim legitimacy by right of descent from the branch of Khalifas, therefore, the true basis of Shahmir rule was power, as illustrated by the Sayyids, who always stressed the authority of god as supreme and the *charisma* of the Sultan, the constitution of the community of solidarity which gave the Sultanate its cohesion.[10] To further drive home the fact that the Shahmir Sultanate was a necessary consequence of the spread of Islam in Kashmir, Sultan Shams-ud-din Shahmir struck coins and changed the *Laukika* calendar by applying *Yazdgird* to the offices of the medieval state.[11] He also ordered the *khutba* to be read in his name.[12] All these measures of the Sultan clearly reveal his desire to harness the functioning of the state to Islamic practices which were prevalent in other muslim sultanates. Dossuki rightly remarks:

> At the level of practice, Islam functions as an ideology. It is used in most cases consciously by a ruling class to legitimise its position, justify its policies, create consensus, generate mass support and

discredit opponents. In these endeavours the ruling class is highly supported to varying degrees by the official, *Ulama,* by the *Sheikhs* and by the *Imam.*[13]

This was the way Islam was used from above. From below Islam has been used mostly by militant groups as an instrument of opposition and change. They legitimized their opposition to the existing state of things with reference to Islam. This part of the Islamic revival can be interpreted as a response to the crisis of legitimacy of the ruling elite in many Muslim countries in the middle east and West Asia even today. In the present case of Kashmir, militancy can be defined as a reaction to the failure of the elite in substituting secular ideas of legitimization for traditional Islamic legitimacy. To this crisis of legitimacy was added immense social changes, unemployment and economic underdevelopment.

It is true that in the beginning, Sultan Shahmir tried to buttress the foundations of the Shahmir Sultanate by befriending important elements within the local nobility and sought their participation in the apparatus of the medieval state in Kashmir. He initiated this process by marrying his own son to the daughter of a local noble, Lakshimaka. The new calendar was known as *Kashmiri Sanah.*[14] Mohibbul Hassan says that the new calendar began with Rinchana's accession and conversion to Islam in AD 1324. According to him, it was used in all official correspondences. Later, however, it was abandoned by the Mughals.[15] He also chose Chaks and Magres to man the standing army.[16] His other measures included the abolition of all oppressive taxes and the reduction of land revenue to one-sixth of the total produce.[17] These measures should not be taken to imply a marked tendency towards secularizing of the nature of the state, because by then the state had not freed itself from the religious influence. Though these measures were tackled from a political standpoint, it does not mean that the state depended for its existence on the welfare of people. In other words, we can say that the state stood side by side with religion, again to justify its existence by developing a sense of responsibility, though this was abandoned after Sultan Shahmir.

But all these measures appear to have been essentially motivated by political ends. Because by the time he took over as Sultan of Kashmir, the Sayyids were not all that well-entrenched in Kashmiri society; therefore, the Sultan's dependence on such measures was merely to achieve initial political stability. Otherwise, his total silence over the existing tax structure, etc., would have resulted in unprecedented political opposition to his rule. However, if Sultan Shams-ud-din had been genuinely interested in improving the social conditions of people he would have initiated a fuller rationalization of the revenue system and also introduced various institutions (for public welfare) similar to those of Sultan Zain ul-Abidin (AD 1420-70), or of Emperor Akbar in the sixteenth century.[18] Until the Shahmirs ascendancy, the Turkish migrants had played practically no part in the political affairs of the valley. With the Shahmirs' ascendancy, that they continued to remain perfectly contented with the traditional trade and other tasks or showed interest in securing wealth and political careers, cannot be answered at the moment; however, that they would have been called upon to take charge of an area and aid the advancement of the Sultan's authority, also cannot be disputed. Similarly, the standing army was deployed to help the state to demonstrate its power and it also contained the growth of private power which would have otherwise been directed against the medieval state itself. In this regard one thing ought to be borne in mind: while considering Chaks and Magres (the most important families of the region's nobility) to raise his standing army, Sultan Shahmir took into account the dynamics of power relations of the twelfth and the thirteenth centuries, and therefore tried to exchange one controlling nobility for the other.[19] From the beginning of the Shahmir rule, these families of Chaks and Magres took upon themselves the fundamental role of structuring and restructuring power relations till ultimately the Chaks established their political dominance.[16]

During Sultan Shihab-ud-din's reign (AD 1355-73), a large number of Sayyids entered Kashmir as Sufis.[17] Most of these Sayyids had migrated to Kashmir from various parts of Persia and Central Asia not only because they were imbued with religious zeal, but to utilize the opportunities of power, wealth and prestige thrown up by the rule of the Shahmir Sultans in Kashmir. Besides, they were persecuted in various parts of Persia and Central Asia.[18] Sultan Shihab-ud-din made all arrangements for the rehabilitation of all those Sayyids who had migrated to Kashmir during his reign, thinking perhaps that they would give definite direction to the state in Kashmir in a very curious and an unexpected way. He granted large and fertile tracts of land for the maintenance of their establishments. Sayyid Hassan Simnani and Sayyid Haider were granted a number of villages in Kulgam pargana. The polity of pre-Sultanate Kashmir is replete with the role of the Dammaras, the Ekangas, Lavanyas and the Tantrins in the power relations of the state. It is most likely that Sultan Shahmir who served the pre-Sultanate State in Kashmir, though only for a short period in many, capacities, had fully understood the growing political aspirations of the Chaks and Magres and the ineffectiveness of others and therefore offered them important roles in building his standing army.

Nagam paragana was granted to Sayyid Taj-ud-din bin Sayyid Hassan.[20] He also opened a number of *madrasas* where Koran, *Hadith* and *Fiqh* were taught.[21] During Sultan Qutub-ud-din's reign (AD 1373-89), various families of Sayyids who entered Kashmir with their leader Sayyid Ali Hamadani in AD 1379 were also allotted lands.[22]Sayyid Jamul-ud-din Alai was given the Chitar area in pargana Khourpara. Generally our chroniclers have been more inclined to record the migration of the Sayyids, but how can one overlook the fact that the general discontent in Central Asia and Persia during this period could not have displaced the members of the official classes, the families of nobles, merchants, peasants, craftsmen and others who had fled to Kashmir with their retainers and other members of their establishments in search of sustenance. There are interesting anecdotes in our sources relating to the migration of the Sayyids to Kashmir. One author has attributed the migration of Sayyid Ali Harnadani to Kashmir to a dream in which Sayyid Ali was commanded to proceed to Kashmir to preach Islam.[23] Apart from the genuine problems existing in Central Asia, the Sayyids, as Muslim missionaries, seem to have been influenced by some other religion. Some points of contact did exist between Christianity and Islam. But one cannot go that far, because there is some uncertainty about influences and borrowings in early Sufism or mysticism. The example of Christian monks and monasteries in the western part of the Caliphate may well have impressed early Muslim Sufis, but this could hardly be true of areas like Iran or Central Asia, when we do not find any evidence of early Sufism in the West.[24] Perhaps what one needs to examine is the influence of Buddhism because the story of one of the early Sufis, Ibrahim-bin-Adham of Balakh (AD 777), is so much like that of Buddha that one wonders whether the biography of Ibrahim was fitted into the pattern of the Buddha. In fact, all that is indicated by Ibrahim and his disciple, Shaqiq AD 810 of Balakh, in the story of what Buddhists rather than Zoroastrianism preached and practised at that time. On the basis of this evidence, one can suggest that Sufism in Iran and Central Asia received its initial impulse from the Buddhist monks, perhaps the famous *Naubahar* Buddhist monastery or *vihara* in Balakh. Besides, Shihab-ud-din Suharawardi AD 1234, founder of a Sufi order, mentions a group of people in Khurasan called *Shaguffia*, who lived as ascetics in caves far from towns.[25] Sayyid Firuz was allotted Sempora and its surrounding villages in pargana Vihi.[26] Sayyid Kamal received the entire area of Naidkhai. Mir Sayyid Kazim was granted the area of Lethpora. Pargana Olar was endowed to Mir Sayyid Rukum-ud-din and Mir Sayyid Fakhr ud-din. Alarge Khankah was built at Shihab-ud-din pora in Srinagar and maintained by the revenues derived from other lands in Nagam pargana [27] Sayyid Jamal-ud-din who was well versed in Islamic theology, was made to stay in Srinagar to provide counsel to the Sultan and his subjects whenever necessary.[28] Mir Sayyid Mohammad Qurashi and Mir Sayyid Mohammad Abdullah were also granted land and other facilities in Bijbehara.[29]

All these endowments to the Sayyids and their *khanqahs* was also a way of providing for their families. The Sayyids were fortunate enough to have these fertile zones for farming, and to derive income from the voluntary labour of their disciples on these lands and also from the gifts of crafts produce and animals from the peasants and the artisans of their area.[30] Over a period of time, the Sayyids accumulated large fortunes built on the brutal system of unpaid labour of their disciples, while religious and secular grants and the subjection of peasants and craftsmen defined the social system within the valley. These grants later enabled the Sayyids to designate their heirs as administrators in perpetuity with a fixed income. The Sayyids gradually adopted the local tradition, conforming outwardly at least, to build the public character of their *khanqahs* and estates. Their endowments were free from the exactions of the Shahmir Sultans and their officials.[31] The Sayyids as missionaries in these various areas would not have confined their activity solely to the preaching of Islam. Under the cloak of Islam the *khanqah* popularized Persian writings, culture, traditions and other projects connected with social, economic and political organization of Kashmiri society. They found that religious fear was much more effective in a country where feudal or ancient traditions were dominant. Therefore the Islamic form of punishment appeared to them quite reasonable in controlling feudal tendencies and in defending the social order.

Although the relationship on these estates cannot be characterized as feudal in the strict western European sense of the term, there were many constraints on the utilization of the labour power of the peasants. The power of surplus extraction by the Sayyids was aided by the state, while the interests of people were subordinate to the state's interest. The medieval state in Kashmir was feudal in the sense that it did primarily serve the cause of surplus extraction by religious and secular elements while continuing to forge the process of sub-infeudation.[32] The generosity of the Shahmir Sultans in looking after the Sayyids won them their gratitude, and an influential place in the Muslim community of Kashmir who held the Sayyids in high esteem. However, this preferential treatment of the Sayyids by the Sultans cannot be attributed to their spiritual role, but was a direct consequence of the Sultan's desire to consolidate the medieval state in Kashmir, with the accompanying resources to maintain their monopoly of power.[33]

The evidence on the relationship of religion and state in medieval Kashmir is still incomplete, but there is much to indicate that the relationship was based on many reasons, probably the most predominant of them, in the practical sphere, was that Islam and the state must cooperate to protect and reinforce each other. In fact, those who would like to know how the two roles in polity (religious and political) in the world of medieval Islam were brought into play in the medieval processes of state formation, must start their investigation in earlier centuries. They must look back to understand the nature of the functioning of Islam in terms of institutions and ideas which developed with the death of the Prophet, the founder of Islam, and persisted down to modern times.[34]

Though the contribution of Islam in the medieval period was significant in the field of religion, law, philosophy, science, art and literature, it must be remembered at the same time that the tradition handed down was not necessarily the same for all parts of the Islamic world.[35] Popular practices and beliefs varied with different social situations. In the case of medieval Kashmir too, early Islam forced individual allegiance to depend upon the doctrinal legitimacy of the Sultan, not because the individual Sultan was possessed with any rights, but because it was the Koranic requirement. The efforts of the Sayyids indirectly demanded the absolute obedience of the people to the Shahmir Sultans as a religious obligation defined in terms of the Shariat and justified by the Koranic obligation: 'Obey God, obey Prophet and obey those with authority amongst you'.[36] And it was this obligation which the newly-established Sultanate in Kashmir came to acknowledge as an essential element for the maintenance of its authority. In course of time, the relations between the Shahmir Sultans and the Sayyids became close and complex, based on mutual need but with divergent interests. The Sultans needed legitimacy and the Sayyids, a privileged position. G.M.D. Sufi says that these Sayyids established hermitages all over Kashmir which served as centres for propagation of their religion, and through their influence definitely furthered the acceptance of Islam.[37] There developed many kinds of bonds between the Sayyids and the Sultans. Pledges of loyalty were expressed in oaths, and vows of gratitude were made for benefits received and in hope of future favours.

The Sayyids appear to have preferred largely to remain in the rural areas where they could root their establishments securely and also create the social basis of the power of the Sultanate. In urban areas too they developed into organizations and adapted to the conditions of urban life, deriving special advantages through their continuous links with the powerful rural-urban aristocracy.[38] Although the Sayyids differed radically in language, ethos and privilege from the largely Kashmiri-speaking people, yet they took much less time to grow into various dominant orders such as Suharwardiya, Qadri, Naqshbandi, etc., exercising a paramount influence on the social, economic, political and the cultural life of medieval Kashmiri society.[39] The importance of the role and functions of the Sayyids could scarcely be underestimated, since the entire Kashmiri society was intensely stratified on a social, economic and religious basis before accepting Islam.[40] In European feudalism also, the direct exploitation of monastic lands was consolidated in compact granges and practised by monks which conversely made their estates more productive. Savings derived from this rational organization or from their ascetic life could be used to extend and improve their patrimony. That is to say, these monks by putting into practice the letter and spirit of holy rule, unintentionally obtained a certain amount of surplus production. Trade developed as a necessary way of dealing with this surplus produce and this in turn provided further opportunity for territorial expansion. However, one consequence of this involuntary economic prosperity was a growing deviation from their original principles which led to transformation in the religious quality of their monastic life. Eventually they became landlords in receipt of rent like other seigneurial groups and at the same time caused the economy to decline.[41] The Sayyids certainly helped to rid medieval Kashmiri society of its divisive tendencies, and tried to build up a framework of a common social and normative order.

What one needs to emphasize here is that the emergence of the Sayyids as a ruling elite of Kashmir was not only visible in the multiplication of *khanqahs* but also in the above-mentioned orders and their participation in the functioning of the medieval state. The basis of these orders of the Sayyids were various social groups for whom the Sayyids acted as authoritative spokesmen in legal, social and religious matters. So diverse were the contacts of the Sayyids, that they played a crucial role in the integrating process through which social communication was carried on medieval Kashmiri society as a working whole.[42] All the Sultans were well aware of the importance of Islam in medieval Kashmiri society. Each of them diverted the influence of the religious establishments (*khanqahs*) towards their social and political goals and turned Islam into an instrument of state policy. The Sayyids provided in effect the Islamic legitimization for every act of the Sultan with whom they were pleased. Sultans like Shihab-ud-din (AD 1355-73), Qutub-ud-din (AD 1373-89), and Sikandar(*butshikan*) (AD 1389-1413), further sought to cultivate their personal images as devoted Muslims. It was under these Sultans that several of the migrant Sayyids, the so-called spokesmen of religion, found their way into the offices of the state which were otherwise the prerogatives of those who were part of the secular inheritance of state. In return, the Sultans received the general support from religious establishments; occasionally, when they intervened they found themselves in difficulties but such examples are rare. Hence Islam was closely connected with the Sayyids' compliance with the ruling elite in the Sultanate.[43] These Sayyids led the people in prayers in mosques and on religious occasions and came to form a distinct stratum in medieval Kashmiri society. As guardians of a shared system of beliefs, values and practices, they were spread out through the entire society, performing varied functions and attracting various degrees of public respect and allegiance.[44]

One of the prominent members of the Suharwardiya order Sayyid Ali Hamadani tried his best to set the pattern for his order, the members of which were allegedly prepared to die for their convictions, and thus marvellously initiated the application of Islamic tenets to the offices of the medieval state under the Shahmir Sultans.[45] He spared no trouble in asserting the position of the other members of his order and in justifying their necessity in all spheres of people's lives by seeking recourse to Islamic precedent and the Shariat.[46] Parmu observes,

> To Sayyid Ali Hamadani and his devoted band of Musalman disciples, the social and religious life of Kashmir was an anathema and an abomination, as it militated against Islam that was preached and practised in the name of the Prophet and pious *Khalifas*. They were too anxious to free Muslims of Kashmir from Hindu encrustrations. Therefore, Sayyid Ali took upon himself the task of transforming Kashmir. He first preached true Islam, preached and practised by the

Prophet to Sultan Qutub-ud-din, both by precept and example. He influenced him with his spiritual powers which he possessed in abundance. His sway over the mind of the Sultan was complete. At his instance his un-Islamic marriage was annulled. One of the two sisters was taken into wedlock after performance of *Nikah* (marriage) while the other was divorced for ever. He also induced the Sultan to adopt the Muslim style of dress and introduce it among Muslims subjects. Then he collected the important rules of *Shariat* for the guidance of the Sultan and his Muslim subjects and appointed his most truthful disciple as his religious mentor. Then he made a gift of his *Kulahi Mubarak* (cap or headgear) to the Sultan and blessed his progeny with long life.[47] To understand how the ruling class in a specific or particular region or a country rules, it becomes essential to discuss the nature of the political and ideological structures. According to Antonio-Gramsci, the dominance and hegemony of a social class does not and can not solely depend on physicial coercion.[48] However, class domination rests on an ideological consensus or general acceptance of primarily social conditions. Therefore, ideology has generally a very significant function in preserving dominance. In the case of medieval Kashmir, although the majority of the people had accepted Islam and there was hardly a problem of religious heterogeneity, yet in terms of economic and social levels, ideology had a significant role in integrating and converting divisive tendencies. Therefore, Islam acquired a significant role when it was used as a means of legitimizing existing social conditions. The Shahmir Sultans thought it fruitful to conceive of Islam as an ideology. It is interesting that Islam as a political ideology has at least two functions. On the one hand, it could function as a stabilizing force serving to maintain status quo and on the other, to serve as an agent of change and revolution.[49]

From the above account it is clear that the interference of the Sayyids in the affairs of the state under Sultan Qutub-ud-din had come more than halfway through. Now the issue was not only that of applying Islamic tenets to the affairs of the state, but also of the efforts of the Sayyids to control and direct the affairs of the state for their personal and political ends. They gradually began to embellish the Sultan's court and gave him a reputation for munificence and in return tried to obtain official positions in civil and judicial administration.[50] They existed above all to promote the interests of their own members through political competition, their first unifying political principle being the prospect of the material awards of land and offices of the medieval state for their various roles. They were strongly desirous of a mass following, although their reasons evolved over a period of time since the Sayyids who sought to win the peoples' support or could claim their allegiance in any particular area, were in a good position to claim a corresponding prominence at the Sultan's court.[51]

Under Sultan Qutub-ud-din (AD 1373-89), the medieval state made a solid advance towards the assimilation of the Sayyids as political ideologues which resulted in delimiting the access of a non-Sayyid nobility to the affairs of the medieval state in the long run.[52]

With Sultan Sikandar (AD 1389-1413), a period of permanent interaction commenced between Kashmiris and the people of Central Asia and Persia. Many more Sayyids entered the valley with their leader Mir Mohammad Hamadani; a dedicated preacher, Sayyid Mir Mohammad was accompanied by three hundred Sayyids when he arrived in Kashmir in AD 1393.[53] It was under the influence of the Sayyids that the Shahmir state subverted Hindu customs. Hindus were also denied official positions and music was banned totally in the kingdom. However, all these measures were for political reasons, not religious ones.[54] Like his predecessors Sultan Sikandar granted lands and made all the necessary arrangements to settle them in various parts of the valley. The *khanqah* of Mir Mohammad Hamadani in Alaud-din-pora in the heart of Srinagar was endowed various villages by Sultan Sikandar to provide subsistence to its inmates and for other expenses.[55] Sultan Sikandar's reign marked an era of very active participation of the Sayyids in the medieval state. Sultan Sikandar created the post of Sheikh-ul-Islam to head the department of ecclesiastical affairs, and the judiciary, and offered this to the Sayyids to enforce the Shariat on the Hindu converts in medieval

Kashmir.[56] Shariat, the divinely revealed law of God, had absolute authority. It preceded the state and was its law but there was no question of this law embodying the consent of those to whom it was applied.[57] For the establishment of the Shahmir Sultanate, Islam served as an ideology. The ideas of state, government laws regulating economic life, moral and ethical norms, jurisprudence, believers, behaviour and the entire mode of life of the Muslim community was based on Islam. However, this does not necessarily mean that the medieval state in Kashmir was an Islamic state. The specificity of the Islamic state is the existence of a special system of organs and institutions which fulfil the functions of the state, power and law and which consolidates a judicial system of norms, sanctioned by Islam and for the promotion of Islam purely for religious reasons. In the case of Kashmir, the promotion and patronization of Islam took place as it provided an effective political ideology, therefore, the promotion of Islam was not solely for religious purposes. The subjects of the Shahmir state had no right against the medieval state, only the expectation that the Sultan would at least act in conformity with the newly-established law in Kashmir. The combining of the post of Sheikh-ul-Islam with the judicial administration had very significant political overtones. The application of Muslim judicial law arrived at critical notions of legal equality in the eyes of Islamic law, and this would have helped to attract more and more people towards Islam and indeed towards the new political system. Therefore, the concentration of judicial powers in the hands of Sheikh-ul Islam was considered an important instrument in hegemonizing the population and in strengthening the centralizing spirit of the state's authority.

It seems that Sultan Sikandar was unfortunately under the impression that he was not a true Sultan by his own will, but by the grace of the Sayyids who could open up great public potential and consent to his rulership. He also believed that the execution of authority by the Sayyids would play a great role in future growth and perpetuation of his sovereignty. Because in the public eye, the extension of the authority of the Sayyids to the functions of the medieval state was seen as the fulfilment of divine precepts.[58] The Sayyids did not admit the existence of the medieval state under the Shahmir Sultans as an organization in its own right, but emphasized that the promotion and patronization of the process ofIslamization by whatever means, was a necessary component for the extension of the authority of Sultan in medieval Kashmiri society. They made him validate his claim to sovereignty by faithfully depending on their advice while dealing with affairs in the medieval state.[59] G.M.D. Sufi says that Sultan Qutub-ud-din had such a great regard for the cap given to him by Sayyid Ali Hamadani that he always wore it under his crown. The cap was passed on to succeeding Sultans and was finally buried with the dead body of Sultan Fath Shah in AD 1517. According to Sufi someone prophesied that the burial of the cap would be an indication of the end of the dynasty. It is a curious coincidence that the Shahmir dynasty came to an end at about this time. Such an approach has generated a wide range of questions central to the study of political history. In fact they centre around the functional relationship between power and mystical phenomena, which makes the notion of power essentially problematic, because sometimes the historian tends to treat the subject of ceremonial as fundamental while reconstructing history.[60]

Sultan Sikandar perhaps felt that Islam was the only basis of political unity and that it was the spread of Islam by the Sayyids which constituted the main claims to his legitimacy and the loyalty of his subjects. This underlines the fact that the stability of the medieval state in Kashmir was tied up with Islam as the right religion and its acceptance by the majority. In order to spread Islam, the Sayyid migrants kept on penetrating into wider areas of rural and urban society.[61] It was through this process that large sections of the rural poor owed allegiance to them for having controlled their social and economic life. Particularly when the Sayyids retained control of large proportions of cultivable waste in areas like Vihi, Nagam, Sempora, Tral, Nunwani, Chitar, Avanmpora, Naidkhai, Martand, Bijbehara, Khourpara, Lar, Pakh, Vachi, Soura, Kulgam, Biru and various other areas.[62] They include Mir Sayyid Haider, Sayyid Jamal-ud-din, Sayyid Kamal, Sayyid Kamal-Isfahani, Sayyid Jamal-ud-din Alai, Sayyid Feroz alias Sayyid Jalal, Mulla Ahmad Allami,Sayyid Ali Hamadani, Sayyid Azizulah, Mir Mohd. Hamadani, Sayyid Jalal-ud-din of Bokhara popularly known Makhdum Jehan, Sheikh Rukun-ud din Alam, Sayyid Tajud-din (a cousin of Mir Sayyid Ali Hamadani), Sayyid Masud, Sayyid Yousuf, Sayyid Hussain Simnani, Sayyid Ali, Sayyid Ahmed Isfahani, Sayyid Sayyid Mohammed Khawarzimi, Moulana Mohd. Sajad, Baba Haji Adham of Bokhara and Baba Hassan of Balakh.[63] The Sayyids gained unlimited and unrestricted access to power in the medieval state. They dominated all fields of human society and developed into a landed aristocracy within the medieval Kashmiri society. Reinforcing the close relationship between their order and various classes of society was a strong current of social mobility, and any entry into the body of Sayyids was influenced by the values implicit in Muslim notions of status, wealth and respect, almost universally available to them through the royal patronage of the Shahmir Sultans.[64] The extension of their influence into the secular areas of functioning also helped them to develop a fairly effective and coordinated system of action in their localities, and provided a basis for selective and orderly allocation of geographical spheres of political influence. They exercised a strong influence on administration. Any official, even if he desired to fulfil his administrative duties while standing aside from political intrigue, rapidly discovered that this was impossible; he had either to resign himself to official inactivity or to act according to the instructions of Sayyids to preserve his official position.

At the rural level too, they overshadowed the non-Sayyid nobles, although both derived their strength from the village extractions. The non-Sayyid nobles showed them respect, for the Sayyids had assumed extensive and arbitrary powers in the settling of disputes, divorces, punishments, and when they presided over various socio-religious occasions in their capacity of local Qazi, Mufti or Imams for they were well-versed in Muslim theology though at times unfamiliar with local traditions. Besides, the complete network of inter-family relations among the Sayyids also provided a ready-made machinery for arbitration of disputes which would have otherwise been referred to the court of the Shahmir Sultans.

Interestingly, whenever the Sayyids worked for the Sultans, they immediately exacted a price for their cooperation, and often used the occasion to increase their own power, wealth and prestige. Such assistance on all such occasions was solicited by the Sultan and not sought by the pre-emptive order.

Under Sultan Sikandar, the Sayyids sought a clear mandate from the Sultan to deal with all decisions. Their overriding influence led to civil strife which the Sultan was forced to put down with a strong hand.[65]

Therefore we are apt to think of Sultan Sikandar's reign as one of the interesting and critical periods in the history of the medieval state in Kashmir. For the Sultan struck upon all chords of duty incumbent upon him even though his contemporary chronicler Pandit Jonaraja does not dwell either objectively, or with critical appreciation, on his reign. The iconoclast fury of Sultan Sikandar seems to have shocked him more than anything else in the kingdom.[66] However, the chronicler has failed to notice the ideological significance of Sultan Sikandar's measures, which deserve some attention.

Sultan Sikandar's reign may appear despotic, but he was only vigorously trying to establish firm foundations for the Shahmiri State with the help of the Sayyids. The persecution of some of the Hindus and the destruction of some of their religious establishments under the instructions of

Sayyids, highlights the interdependence of religion, i.e. Islam and the state. The right religion (Islam) did help to generate political stability for the Shahmir Sultanate, but it also needed a coercive arm to enforce where persuasion did not work.[67]

However, it was during this process that the offices of the medieval state faced certain dangers incurred by the Sultan's submission·to the Sayyids. Zutshi aptly remarks,

> in the sweep of his religious enthusiasm enforced by exhortations of religious fanatics, Sikander was carried off his balance and committed excesses against non-Muslim subjects. The result was a wide-spread confusion in their ranks. The confusion became worse confounded under Ali Shah (AD 1413-1419), who while perpetuating the atrocities in a greater magnitude failed to stereotype the restructured government after the Islamic fashion, for he was a weak and an inefficient ruler.[68]

The Sayyids played their religious roles using political control and socio-economic monopolies. Though they saw themselves as proud and dignified, in actual practice they were impious and extortionist. By the end of Sultan Sikandar's reign, the Sayyids had become so powerful that they dominated both the secular and religious jurisdiction of medieval Kashmiri state and society so as to enjoy something of a politico-cultural hegemony. Their ambition soon found expression in political terms, primarily in competing alliances, each of which drew its recruits from several social levels of power, prestige and wealth to direcdy transfer political power into their own hands.[69] Sultan Sikandar's encouragement to Muslims and learned men, attracted to his court a large number of missionaries and scholars from Persia and Central Asian countries. They came in groups, the most important one was of 300 Sayyids and scholars led by Sayyid Mohammad Hamadani, the son of Sayyid Ali Hamadani. Soon they occupied the highest offices of the state. The Sultan came under the spell of Sayyid Mohammad and became his disciple in word and deed. The Sayyids resolved to dispel the darkness of infidelity in the kingdom and shaped the Sultan's attitude towards the non-Muslims.[70]

They found a suitable opportunity in the reign of Sultan Ali Shah (AD 1413-19). They joined hands with the Sultan's Prime Minister Saif-ud-din, a Hindu convert, in a scheme to extract taxes and to coerce the subjects of the Shahmir Sultans.[71] Sultan Ali Shah became totally ineffective when the Sayyids led by Mir Qaiser, directed the apparatus of the medieval state for their personal ends. Parmu observes, 'The Young Sultan's associates and advisers consisted mainly of Baihaqi Sayyids who had left their homeland in Subzwar led by Sayyid Mohd. Baihaqi, after being defeated by Timur.[72]

They threw Kashmir into a state of confusion by violating the wives of Kashmirees, subjecting them to all sorts of oppressions. Even the Sultans property was not spared.[73] Jonaraja says, 'Lofty houses, excellent horses, fine dresses, large gems and all that adorned the king (Ali Shah) were now wrested by the *Yavanas* (foreign Muslims) obviously they were accompanying Timur'.[74]

With this articulated emergence of the Sayyids as the ruling elite, the other non-Sayyid elements within the local nobility found their interests curtailed, their positions challenged and their power threatened. The rise and domination of the Sayyids was seen by them as political rivalry, while the dotting of multiple *khanqahs* on the surface of Kashmir appeared to be power centres manipulated in order to stage direct political ascendancy.[75] The non-Sayyid nobility was not easily satisfied with being relegated to important albeit prestigious political oblivion. Both the Sayyids and non-Sayyid nobility had definable political goals which set them at odds with the medieval Kashmiri state. With the increasing power of the Sayyids the state was proportionately weakened; therefore, not only did Sultan Ali Shah's ability to control the situation decline but so did his ability to rule. The conversion of the Chief Minister Suhabhata during Sultan Sikandar's reign is one of the interesting examples in this regard.[76] As a result the factional rivalry within the medieval Kashmiri nobility tended to increase, weakening the state further and rendering Sultan Ali Shah merely *primes interpares* among the institutions of medieval Kashmiri society. But the crisis at this stage was halted, though only for a while, by the succession of Shahi Khan, popularly known as Sultan Zain-ul Abidin (AD 1420-70).[77] The Qazi had a certain competence in penal matters and regarding certain acts which were specifically prohibited by the Koran and to which precise penalties were attached such as unlawful sexual intercourse and theft. He also had more general authority to punish acts which offended religion. In fact, most criminal justice, particularly in regard to matters which touched the welfare of the Sultanate were administered by the Sultan or his officials and not by the Qazi. The administration of justice was generally left to the Qazi, but the law was not so flexible as might appear from the law books. The Qazi mostly seems to have interpreted his role as a conciliator attempting to preserve social harmony by reaching on agreed solution to a dispute rather than applying the law strictly. However, the Sayyid as the Qazi was a central figure in the life of a city or pargana because he not only administered the law but was also responsible for division of property after a person's death in accordance with the medieval Kashmiri laws of inheritance and had the power of supervision given to him by the Sultan.[78] In his efforts to strengthen his claims to capture power, Zain-ul-Abidin depended on the non-Sayyid nobility. He entered into an alliance with the Thakurs and other local chiefs of southern Kashmir to wrest power from the rival claimant Yousuf Khan who was defeated and killed in AD 1418 at the Idgah in Srinagar. Mir Mohd. Hamadani was married to the daughter of Malik Saif-ud-din, a Hindu convert. Hassan Shah the son of Sultan Haidar Shah (AD 1470-2) was married to Sayyid Mirak Hassan Baihaqi's daughter.[79] Out of these chaotic conditions Sultan Zain-ul-Abidin tried to shape strong and coherent traditions to strengthen the foundations of the medieval state. Under him the state settled itself and found itself as it had never done before. Sultan Zain-ul-Abidin scrupulously prevented grabbing of the dictatorial powers by the Sayyids at his court.

He also did not hesitate to expel Sayyid Mak when the latter ignored the Sultan's abrogation of certain taxes, which some of the followers of the Sayyid Mak collected from the non-Muslim subjects for using the cremation ground.[80] He adopted a series of measures to create and promote a secular attitude in the state's dependent relationship with its subjects and this dependence was crystallized by promoting various institutions of public interest. Outwardly, he put on the semblance of a Muslim ruler by seeking the recognition of the Abbasiad Caliph of Egypt to provide a legal basis to his authority in the eyes of Islamic orthodoxy, even calling himself Amir-ul-Muminin.[81] He also recognized, though only in theory, the existence of *Zimmis* in his kingdom by realizing *jizya* according to the Islamic tradition. However, in actual practice he never collected even the one *masha* to which it was reduced from two *pals*.[82] As a ruler Sultan Sikandar was able and generous. He abolished many oppressive taxes like *baj* and *tamgah.* He is also said to have established schools and hospitals. He banned the use of wine and other intoxicants, prohibited gambling and also abolished *jizya.* This clearly indicates that he was interested in Kashmir's affairs.[83] Sultan Zain-ul-Abidin did establish the post of Sheikh-ul-Islam in his domain to enforce the Shariat but he never permitted his decisions regarding the state and societal matters to be influenced by the office of Sheikh-ul-Islam. Though Sayyid-ullah Shirazi was the Qazi (Chief Justice), it was Shirya Bhatta who headed the department. Ganapati Gaurak was appointed *Pradvivak* to further restrict Shirazi's influence.[84] Zutshi says, 'we are, however, placed in a comparatively much better position with regard to the organisation and working of the king's court. It was the highest court in the land, presided over by the Sultan trying civil and criminal cases. It was both the court of appeal and court of the first instance. As the highest court, its jurisdiction extended to the whole of Kashmir. It was composed of men belonging to different religions required to interpret the personal law of each individual accordingly.[85] It appears that Sultan Zain-ul-Abidin was politically a liberal who realized that the most obvious brakes on the affairs of state were the Sayyids. He thought that an elaborate administrative system and a strong standing army was essential to strengthen the basis of his power, and that this was impossible without the participation of the non-Sayyid nobility which was part of the secular inheritance. He felt more and more concerned about rebuilding their identity. To name a few, Tilka Acharya was one of the most important officials of the Sultan.[86] While Jaya Bhatta was the Sultan's treasurer, Shriya Bhatta and Ganapati Gaurak manned the judicial administration under the Sultan. Malik Autar Chand was the commander of the army. Kanch-Dammara was an important city prefect.[87] In fact Malik Saif-ud-din was an active supporter of the Sayyids who tried to assume more and more power when he found that Sultan Ali Shah was ineffective. It was at this time that the non Sayyid nobles like Ladi Magre found their power in the affairs of the state was restricted, and rebelled against the designs of Malik Saif-ud-din[88] The other important local nobles at his court were Nothsoma, Yodha Bhatta, Avtar Bhatta, Darya Khan, Sheik-noor-ud-din, Mulla Qazi Khan, Mulla Kabir Kashmiri, Sita Kantha, Siva Bhata, Mansur Bin Mohammad, Pandit Srivara, Mulla Ahmad Kashmiri, Mulla Nadri, Jonaraja, Karpura Bhatta, Rupya Bhatta, Sinha, Rajanak, Rig, Abhimanyu, Jamil Hafiz and others.[89]

In a very short time he rationalized and reformed the administrative system and put new vigour into the fiscal system. To ensure an adequate economic surplus for the maintenance of the state's expenditure, he took immense interest in agricultural production and the expansion of cultivable waste. Sirivara, the contemporary chronicler of Sultan quotes him: 'For the love that I have for my subjects I have augmented the production of my country threefold with the help of canals, extensive cultivation and by other means.[90] The promotion of crafts like metal work, wood work, wood carving, papier mache, carpet weaving, book binding, stone polishing, bottle making, gold beating, window cutting, and various other activities brought new foreign forms and revolutionalized the native taste.[91]

This gave an unusual turn to Kashmiri styles which owed much to Central Asian influence. In order to import new designs and skills, the Sultan invited artists from Sijistan, Iraq, Samarkand, Herat, Khurasan, Gilan, Balakh, Bokhara, Gujrat and various other parts of the world.[92] The caligraphists from Samarkand and Balakh were granted assignments of land in pargana Phag for their maintenance while they were in Kashmir, to develop new styles of calligraphy and painting. In painting, the new patterns developed under the Sultan were circular designs, plant forms, human forms, images of goddesses and various types of flowers and figures of birds and animals.[93] In fact, the non-Sayyid nobility does seem to have protested from the very beginning of the Sultanate when they found that the Sayyids were assuming more and more powers. For example, the rebellion of Lakshman Bhat during Sultan Jamshed's reign (AD 1342-3), and the revolt of the Lavanyas under Sultan Ala ud-din (AD 1343-54) should not be treated as isolated incidents.[94] Here it is necessary to mention that relations with these countries were limited not only to the exchange of periodic gifts but marked a widespread foreign influence in people's lives, and opened a new phase of development in technology and economy in Kashmir. His reign saw the emergence of the new towns which grew into the regional metropolis with its great concentration of officials, merchants, craftsmen and high level of commercial activity. In course of time there emerged a new economic elite who aspired political power.

With this attitude towards the neighbouring regions, Sultan Zain-ul-Abidin did not concentrate on any mighty military activities against them, for he felt that the political existence of small regions was necessary so long as they did not grow enough in wealth and power to challenge his legitimacy. He had no desire to merge them into his domain. His relations with Jasrat Khokhar and the other feudatories of Jammu, Naushera, Rajouri, Lohara, Ladakh, Kishtwar clearly indicate that this attitude of the Sultan towards them had an important ideological or legitimate justification for the existence of a political pluralism under one Sultan.[95] It was clearly as a result of discontent and factional fights among the local nobles that Ali Shah abdicated in favour of his son Shahi Khan who later adopted a soft attitude towards the non-Sayyid nobles. The Thakurs who supported his claims were the local nobility.[96]

Besides all these measures, what distinguished Sultan Zain ul-Abidin's ideology from that of the other Shahmir Sultans was the apparent fact that he concentrated on various aspects of education, culture and craft produce as a primary mechanism to maintain order in society: 'Zain-ul-Abidin was in theory the head of an absolute monarchy concentrating all executive, legislative and judicial powers in his hands. But in practice was a kind and a benevolent ruler and his rule was an enlightened autocracy.[97] Zutshi rightly says, 'His (Ali Shah's) decision to abdicate in favour of his son Shahi Khan was indeed the outcome of his utter indifference to the management of the state, the political affairs of which had gone against him to the extent that he preferred going on pilgrimage to being dethroned by Shahi Khan.[98]

Although the stability of the Shahmir State was achieved by Sultan Zain-ul-Abidin by balancing the power of the Sayyid and the non-Sayyid nobility, all this was only for a brief interval because after his death in AD 1470 the medieval state lost its hegemonic position because of the ceaseless efforts of the Sayyids and the rival factions of the local nobility, which with new cumulative strains, pushed the medieval state in Kashmir into a vortex of complete economic and social collapse, and from which it was ultimately rescued only by extension of Mughal rule.

Notes

1. *Rajatarangini,* vol. III, pp. 15, 26-7. Muhammad Qasim Firishta, *Tarikh-i-Firishta* (Persian), English translation by John Briggs under the title *History of the Rise of Muhammadan Power in India Till the Year 1612,* 4 vols., 1808, vol. IV, p. 389.
2. Sayyid Ali, *Tarikh-i-Kashmir,* pp. 1-9. Firishta, op. cit., p. 453; *Baharistan-i-Shahi* (anonymous), pp. 24-31.
3. Sayyid Ali, *Tarikh-i Kashmir,* pp. 1-20, 1984, pp. 43-4.
4. Karl Marx and F. Engels (on the Jewish question), *Selected Works,* vol. 3, Moscow, 1969, p. 157; see also by the same authors, *Islam in Critique,* Mosonnenve Larose, 1984. Even modern democracies both in India and America have not been spared by the ruling elements such as Narendra Modi and Donald Triumph respectively have also used religion for their legitimation like medieval polities.
5. H. Djait, 'Origins of Islamic State', in *Islam State and Society,* edited by K. Ferdinand and M. Mozaffari (Studies on Asian Topic), no. 12, London, 1988, pp. 74-82.
6. For details see Sayyid Ali, *Tarikh-i-Kashmir* and the description of *Baharistan-i-Shahi* (anonymous) of the Sultanate period.
7. Haidar Malik Chadurah, *Tarikh-i-Kashmir* (Persian manuscript), Research Department Library, Kashmir University, Srinagar (henceforth RDLKUS), pp. 98-100. For details see Hassan bin Ali, *Tarikh-i-Kashmir* (Persian), f. 101ab; and *Tazkirat-ul-Shura,* pp. 112-13.
8. Mohibbul Hassan, *Kashmir under the Sultans,* pp. 47-70. G.M.D. Sufi, *Islamic Culture in Kashmir,* Delhi, 1979, pp. 48-116.
9. Firishta, *Tarikh-i-Firishta,* p. 453.
10. Sayyid Ali, *Tarikh-i-Kashmir,* pp. 1-33.
11. Peer Hassan Shah, *Tarikh-i-Hassan* (Persian), 3 vols, 1885, RDLKUS. Urdu translation of vol. I by Moulvi Muhammad Ibrahim, Srinagar, 1957, vol. II, p. 151.
12. Firishta, *Tarikh-i-Firishta,* p. 453; Nizam-ud-din Ahmad Bakshi, *Tabqat-i-Akbari* (Persian), English translation by Barun Dey and B. Prashad, 3 vols., Calcutta, 1927, vol. III, p. 638. See also J. Rodgers, 'Coins of Sultans of Kashmir', *Journal of the Asiatic Society of Bengal,* vol. LIV, 1885, p. 26
13. A.E.H. Dossuki, 'The Islamic Resurgence, Sources, Dynamics and Implication', in A.E.H. Dossuki, ed., *Islamic Resurgence in the Arab World,* New York, 1982, pp. 17-18.

14. Jonaraja, *Rajatarangini,* vol. III, pp. 26-7; Firishta, *Tarikh-i Firishta,* p. 455; Nizam-ud-din Ahmad Bakshi, *Tabqat-i-Akbari,* vol. III, p. 638.
15. Mohibbul Hassan, *Kashmir under the Sultans,* p. 46
16. Firishta, op. cit., pp. 453-5.
17. Ibid.
18. N.K. Zutshi, *Sultan-Zain-ul-Abidin,* pp. 91-114.
19. Ibid.
20. Nizam-ud-din Ahmad Bakshi, *Tabqat-i-Akbari,* vol. II, p. 619. See also R.K. Parmu, *A History of Muslim Rule in Kashmir,* pp. 220-80
21. Jonaraja, *Rajatarangini,* vol. III, p. 26; Sayyid Ali, *Tarikh-i Kashmir,* p. 1, Sayyid Ali has based his information on *Tarikh-i Qazi Ibrahim,* but besides him no one has referred to this Persian chronicle in Kashmir's history
22. Mirza Muhammad Haidar Dughlat, *Tarikh-i-Rashidi,* p. 432
23. Zafar Badakshi, *Khulasat-ul-Manaqib* (unpublished Persian manuscript), RDLKUS, p. 573.
24. Richard N. Frey, *The Golden Age of Persia,* London, 1975, p. 158.
25. M.M. Sharif, *History of Muslim Philosophy,* Weisbaden, 1963, pp. 354-5.
26. Sayyid Ali, *Tarikh-i-Kashmir,* pp. 1-15.
27. Ibid.
28. Aba Rafi-ud-din Ahmad, *Nawadir-ul-Akbar* (Persian), RDLKUS, ff. 25-30.
29. Sayyid Ali, *Tarikh-i-Kashmir,* pp. 1-10.
30. Ibid.
31. Ibid.
32. Ibid.
33. Ibid.
34. Ibid
35. Ibid.
36. Ibid.
37 G.M.D. Sufi, *Islamic Culture in Kashmir,* pp. 37-8.
38. Ibid.
39. Muhi-ud-din Miskeen, *Tarikh-i-Kabir-i-Kashmir* (unpublished Persian Manuscript), RDLKUS, pp. 20-5.
40. Ibid. See also Sayyid Ali, *Tarikh-i-Kashmir,* pp. 1-15.
41. D. Knowles, *Monastic Order in England,* Cambridge, 1940, p. 349; see also L. Lekai, *The White Monks: A History of the Cistercian Order,* Kachee, 1963, pp. 209-10 and 230.

42. Sayyid Ali, op. cit., G.M.D. Sufi, *Islamic Culture in Kashmir,* pp. 32-69.
43. Ibid.
44. The death of Mohammad on 8 June AD 632, produced great consternation among the Muslims of Madina, but Abubaker his most senior friend and leader of the community, pacified them with these succinct words: 'if one worships who Muhammad died but if one worships God is living and does not die and then to *Umma* he added, stretch forth thy hand that I may swear allegiance to thee'. Richard J. Macarthy, *The Theology of Al Ashair,* Beyroth, 1953, pp. 115-16. Muhammad's mission as a messenger of Allah had ended but his political, economic, social and religious leadership of *Umma* needed a replacement. A Koranic verse had already divinely sanctioned such a procedure which stated 'oh *ye* who believe, obey Allah, obey the messenger and those of you who are in authority and if *ye* have a dispute concerning any matter refer it to Allah and the messenger, if you are (in truth believe in Allah and the last day that is better and more secure in the end'. Koran IV, 59. But soon Muslims were divided among themselves regarding the rules for the appointment of those in authority. However, the need for a successor to Muhammad was never questioned while Ali, Muhammad's cousin and son-in-law prepared for the burial of his body, the prophet's *suhabs* (companions) hurriedly convened a council in a roofed enclosure known as *Saqifa* of *Ban Saida.* A heated discussion ensued between the Muhajurun and the Ansar which led to the election of Abubakar as the successor. Abubakar thus became the Khalifa, the successor of the messenger of God and in this way the Caliphate was founded as an institution which had no equivalent and was destined never to have any outside the Muslim world. The Caliphate lasted for centuries and many things were subsequently changed, but the idea that the approval of the Caliph was a kind of contract imposing reciprocal obligation on the men elected and on his subjects, gained ground and became a fundamental concept once the Muslims had developed a juridical mentality. Laura Vecia Vaglieri, 'The Patriarchical and Ummayyads Caliphates', in the *Cambridge History of Islam,* ed. P.M. Holt, A.K.S. Lambton and B. Lewes, 2 vols., Cambridge, 1970, pp. 57-8. In fact, the Sayyids of the Shahmir Sultanate were not different from the *ulama* of the

Delhi Sultanate where the *ulama* as a distinctive religious group, were exerting enormous influence on statecraft because of the importance they attached to Koranic law in matters of statecraft. But it is interesting to note that this religious group was becoming too worldly in its *Weltanschaung* in spite of its excessive religious mindedness. The spirit of Koranic law which ought to guide them in their actual life as well as in matters of state was fast losing hold on them. The *Ulama* were identifying themselves with the crooked ways of kingship and were justifying their chicanery of politics which could not be sanctioned by Islam. Ishwar Topa, *Politics in Pre-Mughal Times,* Delhi, 1938, fn. 1, p. 94.

45. The Islamic conquerors brought monotheism with them. They possessed force and ideology. This inheritance presented problems when their rule over conquered lands in different regions had to be consolidated and regulated. The Ummayyads were able to rule for some time on the basis of traditional kinship cohesion, but such politics was far removed from original Islamic purposes. John A. Hall and C. John Ikenbery, *The State,* Open University Press, Milton Keynes, 1989, p. 31.
46. Koran, IV, p. 59
47. Parmu, *A History of Muslim Rule in Kashmir,* pp. 105-106. Dossuki, op. cit., pp. 111 and 271.
48. Ch. Monfee, 'Hegemony and Ideology in Gramsci', in Ch. Monfee, ed., *Gramsci and Marxist Theory,* London, 1980, pp. 47-8.
49. Dossuki, op. cit., pp. 111 and 271.
50. Sayyid Ali, *Tarikh-i-Kashmir,* pp. 9-23.
51. Only the Rishi order was indigenously founded by Sheikh Nur ud-Din Rishi. See Baba Daud Mishqati, *Asrar-ul-Abrar* (Persian) RDLKUS, f. 5la. See also for details Baba Nasib Kashmiri, *Rishi Nama,* RDLKUS. Sayyid Ali belonged to the Kubravi order. Qazi Noorullah Shustri, *Majalis-ul-Muminin* (Persian Ms.), RDLKUS, p. 286. Abdul Wahab Noori, *Fatuhat-i-Kubravia.* The Naqshabandi order was introduced in Kashmir during Sultan Sikandar's regin (AD 1389-1413) by Sayyid Hilal. Mohammad Azam Diddamari, *Tarikh-i-Azmi* (Persian), RDLKUS, p. 54. Sayed Niyamatullah Shah was the first to introduce the *Qadriya* order in Kashmir. See Mohammad Hussain Qadri, *Fatuahat-i Qadriya,* RDLKUS, f. 20a, also Mohi-ud-din Miskeen; *Tarikh-i-Kabir-i-Kashmir,* RDLKUS, p. 51.

52. Krishna Mohan, *Early Medieval History of Kashmir,* AD *1003-1171,* Delhi, 1981, pp. 211-26. V.N. Drabu, op. cit. By and large, the deference to social rank was still preserved in a degree unimaginable in Islam and the co-existence of affluence and extreme poverty was more sharply contrasted. The power of the medieval state was not made to aid only economic progress and surplus accumulation, but rather to serve the interest of enriching the politically powerful excessive consumption by the Sayyids and the spread of peasant wealth through political power.
53. Zutshi, op. cit., pp. 15-16.
54. *Baharistan-i-Shahi,* pp. 24, 31, Jonaraja, op. cit., pp. 59-74. Abdul Wahab, op. cit., f. 157b.
55. Mohi-ud-din Miskeen, *Tarikh-i-Kabir-i-Kashmir,* pp. 12-28.
56. G.M.D. Sufi, *Islamic Culture in Kashmir,* pp. 32-47.
57. Sayyid Ali, op. cit., pp. 3-10, Mirza Muhammad Haidar Dughlat, *Tarikh-i-Rashidi,* p. 432. Gusyam Mamed Ogly Kerimov, 'The Socio-Political Aspects of Modern Islamic Mission', K Ferdinand and Mehadi Mozaffari, eds., *Islam, State and Society,* pp. 44-5.
58. Sayyid Ali, *Tarikh-i-Kashmir,* pp. 1-16. Sayyid Ali Hamadani expected *Ammai-Khalaq* (majority classes) to strictly obey the laws prescribed by the *Asharite* system of Sunni theology, Sayyid Ali Hamadani, *Zakhirat·ul-mulk* (Persian), RDLKUS, pp. 6-7. The Shariat had grown up by a slow and complicated process of interaction between the norms contained in the Koran, Hadith, and the local customs and laws of communities brought under the rule of Islam. So there was a continuous process of mutual adjusnnent to the Shariat once it took its definite form and practice in Muslim society.
59. R.K. Parmu, *A History of Muslim Rule in Kashmir,* pp. 105-6. For details see Mohammad Azam Diddamari, *Tarikh-i-Azami,* p. 30.
60. G.M.D. Sufi, *Islamic Culture in Kashmir,* p. 38.
61. *Baharistan-i-Shahi,* pp. 29-30. There are plentiful references to show that the Sayyids acted in various capacities in secular jurisdiction of the Sultanate
62. Mohammed Khawarzimi, Moulana Mohd. Sajad, Baba Haji Adham of Bokhara, Baba Hassan of Balakh. Ibid., p. 34.
63. Ibid.
64. Ibid., p. 29. See also Sayyid Ali, op. cit., pp. 8-10.
65. Sayyid Ali, *Tarikh-i-Kashmir,* pp. 1-7, 25, 29. It seems the Sayyid

Ali Hamadani and his son Mir Mohammad Hamadani AD 1339 alone brought into Kashmir more than one thousand Sayyids to popularize Islam. Sufi, op. cit., p. 38

66. *Bharistan-i-Shahi,* pp. 29-31, Sayyid Ali, op. cit., pp. 10-12.
67. Ibid., p. 31.
68. The Shariat has grown a long way in maintaining the unity to *Umma* in its ethical and religious attitudes. It was therefore considered the principal duty of the Muslim government of the Sultans to enforce obedience to the Shariat. Also, the duties performed by Muslims in fulfilment of laws of Shariat were not invalidated. Ibn-ul-Bazaz, *Al-Kadariya,* Hyderabad, 1903, pp. 15-16
69. *Baharistan-i-Shahi,* pp. 23-4.
70. Abdul Wahab, op. cit., 156a, op. cit., p. 25, 29, 33.
71. Parmu, op. cit., p. 117. Haidar Malik Chadurah, *Tarikh-i Kashmir,* p. 29. See also Percy Sykes, *History of Persia,* 2 vols., London, 1992, vol. II, pp. 130-4.
72. Parmu, op. cit., p. 117
73. Sayyid Ali, *Tarikh-i-Kashmir,* pp. 1-20. Sufi, *Islamic Culture in Kashmir,* p. 37.
74. Sayyid Ali, op. cit., pp. 3-17.
75. Mohi-ud-din Miskeen, *Tarikh-i-Kabir-i-Kashmir,* pp. 21-5. All the Sultans extended their patronage to them during the Shahmir Sultanate
76. *Baharistan-i-Shahi,* p. 24. See also Malik Saif-ud-din. Suhabhata held a very important position at the court of Sultan Sikandar and Sultan Ali Shah (AD 1413-19), yet he only carried out what the Sayyids wanted. He had to strictly follow their instructions at every step. Jonaraja, op. cit., p. 60.
77. Zutshi, op. cit., pp. 36-7.
78. Ibid., p. 121.
79. Jonaraja, *Rajatarangini,* op. cit., vol. III, p. 60.

    Srivara, op. cit., pp. 184-5; see also Nizam-ud-din Ahmad Bakshi, *Tabqat-i-Akbari,* vol. III, p. 446. Also the exemption and enforcement of Islamic law would not have been possible without the appointment of the Sayyids as Qazis and Muftis. Sayyid Hassan Shirazi was the Qazi of Sultan Sikandar, Mir Mohd. Hamadani was the Sheikh-ul-Islam of Sultan Sikandar.
80. Jonaraja, *Rajatarangini,* op. cit., vol. III, pp. 59-74, Lieut. Col.

Newell, 'A Skerch of Muhammadan History of Kashmir', *JASB,* no. 5, 1854, p. 415.
81. Jonaraja, op. cit., p. 60.
82. *Tarikh-i-Kashmir, Munic Manuscript,* f. 70, Zutshi, op. cit., p. 71.
83. *Baharistan-i-Shahi* (anonymous), pp. 30-6.
84. Jonaraja, op. cit., stanzas 853-955.
85. Zutshi, op. cit., pp. 121-2.
86. Abdul Wahab, op. cit., f. 156a; *Baharistan-i-Shahi* (anonymous), pp. 29-30, Sayyid Ali, op. cit., pp. 9-15.
87. Nizam-ud-din Ahmad Bakshi, *Tabqat-i-Akbari,* vol. III, pp. 652-3. *Baharistan-i-Shahi* (anonymous), p. 54, Srivara, op. cit.
88. Jonaraja, op. cit., p. 61; Firishta, *Tarikh-i-Firishta,* pp. 467-8.
89. Zutshi, op. cit., p. 35.
90. Ibid., see also Jonaraja, op. cit., vol. III, p. 73.
91. Ibid.
92. Ibid., pp. 55-8.
93. Ibid., pp. 55-8. Nizam-ud-din, op. cit., pp. 653-9. Abul Fazl, *Ain-i-Akbari,* vol. II, p. 38. See also R.C. Kak, *Archaeological Survey Report (1906-7),* RDLKUS, pp. 163-4.
94. M. Hassan, op. cit., pp. 47-8. After the death of Hassan Shah (AD 1472-84), the Baihaqi Sayyids directly controlled the power of the state in AD 1519, Jonaraja, op. cit., pp. 65-70.
95. Haidar Malik, op. cit., p. 47; Firishta, op. cit., p. 468; *Baharistan-i-Shahi* (anonymous), pp. 29-64; Zutshi, op. cit., pp. 79-83.
96. M. Hassan, op. cit., pp. 67-70.
97. Zutshi, op. cit., p. 94.
98. Jonaraja, op. cit., 75-97. Firishta, op. cit., p. 468. Zutshi, op. cit., pp. 36-7.

4

The Incorporation of the Sultanate into the Mughal State

The incorporation of the Shahmir state into the Mughal Empire during the sixteenth century comes as no surprise to those who are aware of the ruinous conditions to which the medieval Kashmiri state and society were reduced under the Shahmir Sultans. After the death of Sultan Zain-ul-Abidin in AD 1470, the medieval state in Kashmir lost its hegemonic position and failed to register any steady progress despite the promising beginnings made by Sultan Zain-ul-Abidin.[1] The period from AD 1470 to 1586, was dominated by various factions of royalty and nobility. The claims of rival factions led by the Sayyids and the non-Sayyid nobility pushed the state into a civil war which lasted up to AD 1540.[2] In AD 1470 Haider Shah ascended the throne but the non-Sayyid nobles who did not like the idea, backed the claims of Adham Khan, the brother of Sultan Haider Shah (AD 1470-2), and tried to obtain control of the affairs of the Sultanate. However, Sultan Haidar Shah enlisted the support of the Sayyids to strengthen his position. He married his son to Sayyid Mirak Baihaqi's daughter and also assigned large jagirs to him in the parganas of Biru and Bangil) with absolute fiscal and administrative control. Sayyid Mirak Hassan Baihaqi was the most important leader among the Sayyids.[3] These measures of the Sultan not only aroused the further hostility of the non-Sayyid nobles (who hated the Sultan for lavishing money and affection on the Sayyids and his minions, but it also exhausted the financial foundations of the state.[4] During the brief period of his rule he acted only as a prodigal pleasure seeker and spent most of his time in his cups and in the society of women and musicians. As a result, he left the management of the state to corrupt worthless favourites who misguided the country.[5] He depleted the state's economic strength to the extent of leaving it utterly resourceless. Pandit Srivara, the director of the music department of the Sultan records 'owing to the exhausted state of treasury, the old copper *Panca-vimsatika* was somewhat reduced in weight'.[6] His lack of administrative skill allowed the chiefs of the outer hills to declare their independence and reduce the strength of the sovereignty of the Sultanate. Though Sultan Haider sent an army to subjugate the hill chiefs of Rajouri, Jammu and the Gakhar chieftains, it involved a lot of expense. The chief of Rajouri submitted without any resistance but the other two refused to recognize the suzerainty of the Sultan and therefore the Sultan did not gain anything except a few presents from the rulers of Rajouri, including his daughter, who was married to the Sultan.[7] When the country was financially so weak these futile attacks of the Sultan on the hill chiefs would have certainly worsened his declining economy.

The reign of Sultan Hassan Shah (AD 1472-84) saw an increase in the authority of the various factions of nobility at the expense of the state and society of medieval Kashmir. The Sultan gave various material awards to the non-Sayyid nobles to contain their ambition. Ahmed Yetu was given the title of Malik, with Nagam as his jagir.[8] His son Nauroz was appointed Amir-i-Dar (Lord Chamberlain) and given the title of Bahadur Malik. He was granted the jagir of Yech Pargana.[9] Jahangir Magre was given the command of the army and awarded the title of Shaukat Jung.[10] Khwaja Noor-ud-din was appointed Sheikh-ul-Islam and Khwaja. Muhammad got the post of Sadr.[11] Abhimanyu was allotted the entire pargana of Divasar as his jagir.[12] Divasar was the stronghold of Dammaras earlier. Thus the political ambition of the non-Sayyid nobility was manifested not solely through its links with the Sultan but also through the acquisition of lands and offices of the state. Not satisfied with this, the final goal of absolute power which presupposes a taste for dominion over men, revealed itself above all in the dynastic interests of most of these prominent families which had not initially enjoyed any real economic base. A well-recorded case of this kind is that of Malik Ahmad Yetu.[13] Abhimanyu and Malik Ahmad Yetu rose to high levels in the Sultans favour because they helped him in obtaining control of the Sultanate. But when Malik Ahmad became powerful and controlled all the offices at the court of the Sultan, his own associates felt jealous of him. He had them removed one by one from their positions on one pretext or the other. He got Abhimanyu blinded and thrown into prison at the orders of the Sultan. But ultimately when he exceeded the accepted norms, along with the members of family, he was imprisoned.[14] Initially he gave the impression of an enterprising noble who was always ready to range himself and his supporters alongside Sultan Hassan against the most dangerous men of the Sultanate. When Bahram the rival claimant to the throne returned to Kashmir, Malik Ahmad provided all assistance to Sultan Hassan Shah in his resistance against the enemy along with Tazi Bhat and other nobles.[15] But it was in this process that he also had all his rivals at the court of the Sultan eliminated. When the Sultan finally noticed the growing rebellious tendencies he was forced to revert to the help of the Sayyid nobility to crush Malik Ahmed Yetu.[16] Mohibbul Hassan says, 'Hassan Shah, who was watching those developments closely, did not approve of Ahmad's conduct and turned against him. Observing the change in the attitude of the Sultan, the minister's enemies felt encouraged and suggested that he should take away the guardianship of prince Yusuf from Ahmad. The Sultan acted on their advice but fearing rebellion, he won over the Sayyids and sought the support of Jahangir Magre to crush Ahmad,'[17] In fact, to play one group of nobles against the other, has been an all-time phenomenon in the ideological apparatus of the medieval state of Kashmir. Faced with such a tangle of private power groups, emerging from the individual local nobles, and the political aims of the Sayyids who were competing among themselves to create autonomous economic and military strongholds, the royal authority speedily declined, and failed to preserve its uneven supremacy in Kashmir. This further helped the rival camps of the nobles to set themselves up as the broad social basis of power in the state. This was possible not because the public owed allegiance to them for their actions but because they were economically not only capable of sharing in the maintenance of their establishments but also in the military protection of the state. The Shahmir Sultans from the very beginning of the Sultanate had entrusted all important positions and roles to the Sayyids, and allowed them to interfere in crucial matters of state's functioning.[18]

Sultan Haider Shah and Sultan Hassan Shah restored to the Sayyids the spheres of power within which the Sayyids sought to define their interests, with the moreorless obvious intention of strengthening their ties of kinship with the ruling aristocracy. For example, Sayyid Hassan Baihaqi was the father-in-law of Sultan Hassan Shah.[19]

After Sultan Hassan Shah's death, the Sayyids returned with renewed vigour to ravage the resources of the state and to directly control the power at the court of Sultan Hassan Shah's son, to whom they were related through his mother. They began progressively to transform themselves into a power with no other ambition other than that of generic hegemony over the whole of Kashmir.[20]This also resulted in co-operation among some of the factions of the non-Sayyid nobles who put up Fath Shah as their candidate to succeed Sultan Hassan Shah. But the Sayyids backed Sultan Hassan Shah's minor son Muhammad Shah and pushed the state into civil war.[21] In this civil war Muhammad Shah captured power five times: (i) AD 1484-6, (ii) AD 1493-1505, (iii) AD

1514-15, (iv) AD 1517-18 and (v) AD 1530-7; likewise Fath Shah also ruled three times (i) AD 1486-93, (ii) AD 1505-14, and (iii) AD 1515-17. The rival parties controlled the affairs of state in turns. There were successes and failures among both groups. The transfers of officials were quite common, the court became confused and the entire valley exemplified the general anarchy which finally dismantled the Shahmir state.[22]

According to Srivara, 'during the regime of Sayyids, accepting bribes was considered a virtue, oppressing the subjects was regarded as wisdom and addiction to women was regarded as happiness.[23]

The more the Sayyids claimed controlling functions in the Shahmir state, the easier was its destruction. The institutional framework set up by Sultan Zain-ul-Abidin was totally eroded. The long period of half a century reflects the heterogeneity of the means used, and of individuals and groups given privileges in order to guarantee the Sultans, one after the other (Muhammad Shah and Fath Shah), a network of ties meant to complement the unreliable collaboration of public officials. The social order was totally undermined and the subjects of the state at all levels were impoverished through exemptions, generous donations of land and its revenues, and also explicit concessions in perpetuity to these nobles. In AD 1534, the scarcity of food became so acute that a *kharwar* of *Shali* (paddy) could not be procured even for 10,000 *dinars.* In those times 1,000 *dinars* were equivalent to 10 *dams,* i.e. (8.25 of rupee). Even so, by all estimates, it was beyond the common man's capacity to accept this price hike.[24]

In fact, whatever role the state played in the medieval period, to improve the economic conditions of its people, it was influenced by the ideological tendencies dominant in the political economy of that period. On the one hand, the state's over-dependence on the various feudal families was likely to produce less than optimal results in the economic performance and growth, because of the very character of these families. The constant domination of these families in the society and polity of medieval Kashmir did not either deliberately deliver, or failed to deliver an adequate flow of benefits to the majority. On the other hand, the state itself frequently, articulated such feudalistic tendencies by assigning the land and its revenues with titles to a few families of both religious and secular natures, with which the political stability and effectiveness of a particular regime was linked. For these families the possession of land and its resources was not only the most important source of their wealth and power but also an index of their social status. The power of these families could not safeguard the territorial peace from external threats or guarantee internal security, but was only able to operate effectively in disrupting the growth of other centres of power within the sultanate. At individual points they did this everywhere, entering into rivalry or alliance with forces that denounced or recognized the supreme power of the state.

Although the state sought recognition from such feudal families, it also checked interference wherever its basis of power was threatened. The political economy of medieval Kashmir, which is the most significant aspect of the medieval state, concerns us here to the extent to which politics has influenced the economy in Kashmir and also the degrees to which the economic structure has become one of the main sources for sustenance of the medieval state. The sharp differences in the political stability between the state and the power management capabilities of the political elite were the important sources of variation in economic performance, irrespective of particular ideological impulses dominant there and the nature of political regime that organized state power. Among these families may be mentioned the Lavanyas now known as Loans, the Magres, the Chaks, the Dars, the Yetus, the Maliks, etc. But the pattern was complicated when some of the members of the nobility tried repeatedly to establish a dynasty or sought the help and cooperation of royal authority from outside the state.

During Sultan Fath Shah's third reign (AD 1515-17), Sultan Sikander Lodhi's (AD 1489-1517) help was sought by Muhammed Shah to obtain the throne for the fourth time. The very interesting case reflecting such tendencies on the part of the state is available to us in the expulsion of Sayyids and the confiscation of their assignments of the jagirs by Sultan Hassan Shah.[25]

From this time onwards, the Kashrniri nobles sought the help of external elements to settle their internal problems of power politics. This exposed the nature of affairs in the Sultanate and increased the subordination of the Shahmir state to the decisions made by the Sultans and emperors in Delhi. [26] For Kashmir polity, Delhi Durbar has operated from both ancient and medieval times.

In fact one can say that the metamorphosis of the medieval state in Kashmir after the death of Zain-ul-Abidin, until its incorporation into the Mughal Empire, began to increasingly reflect the discontinuous territorial hegemony. As if it was not enough to displace the Sultanate, the entire community of Kashmirees was further divided at the popular level by the introduction of the Shia creed.[27] The frequency of feuds among various factions of nobility, the Shia-Sunni conflicts with the occasional attacks on Hindus (though unmotivated by any theological reasons because from fourteenth century they were reduced to negligible minority), perhaps represents the most brutalizing, though certainly not a unique, impact on the overall societal format of Kashmir in the post-Zain-ul-Abidin's phase. Mir Shams-ud-din Iraqi entered Kashmir in AD 1484. He is considered the founder of the Noorbakshia order in Kashmir. During his lifetime in Kashmir, this order did not register much progress but Shams-ud-din Iraqi did succeed in converting a large section of population to the Shia creed. With this emerged the Shia-Sunni differences in Kashmir and the clashes became a constant phenomenon between the two sects. After the death of Shams-ud-din Iraqi in AD 1526, his two sons Mir Mukhtar and Mir Yehaya took keen interest in the Noorbakshia order. However, the Shia Sunni clashes assumed a more violent form and involved loss of men and material only after the arrival of Mirza Muhammad Haidar Doughlat, who ruled Kashmir for ten years (AD 1540-50).[28] It were probably these inner divisions which upset them (region's nobles) in any confrontation with the external forces. As a result, the Shahmir state was reduced to a non-state situation in the sense that all its institutions came close to extinction. Not surprisingly, therefore, the Kashmirees refused to recognize their future as something different and preferred the extension of the Mughal state to their own displaced regional sovereignty.

Our starting point now is Emperor Akbar (AD 1556-1605), the architect of the Mughal Empire. On 28 June 1586, Akbar sent Qasim Khan Mirbahar to Kashmir with instructions to 'practise enlightenment, justice and non-sufferance or wickedness and the accepting of apologies and the chastisement of evil'.[29] Despite the various interpretations that could have been and were made of this order, it is still difficult to believe that the incorporation of Kashmir into the Mughal state was carried out according to the strict instructions of Akbar and was therefore devoid of any military destruction and violence.[30] Careful scrutiny of sources reveals that some of the elements within the Kashmiri nobility were no less anxious than their Mughal counterparts, not to amaze the world with their might, but to capture court life which offered limitless access to power, wealth and moments of intoxicating splendour. Though they worked hard at this task, such an aura was never achieved and the total submission to the Mughal state was finally achieved in AD 1586. It was on16 October 1586, that Emperor Akbar was formally declared the sovereign of Kashmir.[31] Thus Kashmir became the *Subah* of the Mughal Empire.

However, by any historical standards no immediate amelioration of the sorry condition of the people could be expected at the hands of the Mughals; however, this extension of the Mughal rule did set in motion a series of measures in social, economic, political and cultural aspects of life in Kashmir, contributing significantly to the incorporation of this region into the Mughal Empire. The interest of the Mughals in Kashmir's polity had developed much before Emperor Akbar. During the civil wars, some of the Kashmiri nobles visited their neighbouring territories for help against their rivals in Kashmir. It was amidst these developments that Emperor Babur (AD 1526-30) started taking an interest in Kashmir's politics. During Kazi Chak's time, Babur sent his army to Kashmir but did not attain much success. Abul Magre, one of the local nobles, took shelter at the court of Babur and was later supported by Babur in his efforts to capture power in Kashmir. Babur sent Sheikh Ali Beg and Muhammad Khan to help him. When Abul Magre became the Chief Minister under Sultan Fath Shah, he rewarded the Mughal officials handsomely.[32] After Babur, with Humayun's consent, Kamran led an expedition into the valley in AD 1531. After Humayun's efforts Kashmir passed into the hands of Mirza Haidar Dughlat (AD 1540-50), a cousin of Babur. During the Chak domination also (AD 1550-86) Akbar's suzerainty was acknowledged. There are references to show that before the establishment of direct Mughal rule in Kashmir, Hussain Shah Chak sent some presents to the Mughal court and also gave his daughter in marriage to Prince Salim.[33] In AD 1573 Emperor Akbar sent his second mission to Kashmir. The members of this mission were Mulla Ashaqi and Qazi Sadr-ud-din of Kashmir. Sultan Ali Shah Chak (AD 1569-79) proclaimed Akbar as his sovereign and minted coins in his name. Nizam-ud-din Ahmad Bakshi says that all these missions succeeded without involving loss of men and materials.[34]

The process of incorporation rested on the ruthless efforts of the Mughal state which took the form of creating distinct staff, dependent on the Mughal imperial authority and loyal to it, as an effective instrument of policy pleading, cooperation, legitimization, and also of coercion as a means of acquiring the acquiescence of various sections of Kashmiri society.

Emperor Akbar formulated long-term goals which facilitated the social transformation in Kashmir. The most significant aspects of this process were:

(a) restructuring of the agrarian structure,
(b) expansion of handicraft production,
(c) administrative reorganization, and
(d) matrimonial relations.

The Mughal state in Kashmir tried to maintain economic and social stability as the basis of its political power. In AD 1589, Emperor Akbar sent a five-member team of Sheikh Faizi, Mir Sharif Ammuli, Khawaja Muhammad Hussain, Khawaja Shamsuddin Khafi and Kanwar Man Singh to Kashmir to formulate the pattern of land revenue assessment and to determine the nature and volume of collection.They scrutinized all revenue records of the entire Kashmir region.[35] There were some serious discrepancies in the earlier assessments worked under Yusuf Khan Rizivi, the first Mughal governor of Kashmir. The total revenue demand was fixed at half the produce and a reduction of two lakh *kharwars* was registered. The officials assisting Yusuf Khan Rizvi did not cooperate because it curtailed their chances of grabbing a large proportion of the peasants' produce to which they were used. but soon a local hindu Tota Ram, a Kashmiri *Peshkar* of Yusuf Khan Rizvi, complained about this to Akbar and the emperor sent Qazi Ali in AD 1591 to look into the problem. As a result, a new assessment was carried out and Akbar got Yusuf Khan Rizivi arrested during his visit to Lahore and Khawaja Shams uddin Khafi was made the new governor.The revenue administration Kashmir *Subah* was soon handed over to team which included Amad Beg, Muhamad Quli Beg, Hamza Beg, Hassan Ali and Muhammad Beg Aimaq of Badakshan.[36] This entire exercise was carried out under the supervision of Asif Khan. Asif Khan joined the court of Emperor Akbar in AD 1577. After some time when he was not given a *mansab* of high rank, he left Akbar and joined Muzaffar Khan of Bengal, but when Akbar offered him the *zat* rank of 2000 he rejoined Akbar's court. [37]He divided entire Kashmir into fourteen divisions and each division was kept under a *bitikchis*. This was all done to provide a great relief to the suffering peasantry that was severely exploited earlier.[38] The assessment of Asif Khan increased the new *jama* by 16392 *kharwars* and 5 *traks* but he provided a subsidy of 5 *dams* in each *kharwar*.So in actual practice there was no increase in *jama* but a reduction of 860034.5 *dams*. The *jama* was fixed at 3079443 *kharwarsout* of which 1011330.5 *kharwars* was to be paid in cash.[39] The Mughal state's capacity to incorporate the region of Kashmir into the Mughal Empire was also joined by the desires of those ambitious nobles of Kashmir who went to the Mughal court in the expectation of regaining their positions in Kashmir polity.[40] This included a large number of Kashmiri Pandits who were very well versed with Persian language and were preferred by the Mughal rulers. This feature of Kashmir polity continues even down to our own times and in the process makes the nature of centre-state relations more complex.

Although the local officials did not cooperate in the beginning, the team managed to prepare a very detailed report about the nature of land, its classification, production and appropriation, on the basis of the information available to them. The institution of revenue administration was thoroughly reorganized with the appointment of officials like Patwari, Tahsildar, Amil, Fotedar, Munsif, Qanungo, Chaudhri, Dewan, Mir Bakshi and others.[41] The new assessment of land and its revenues carried out by these officials, made it extremely difficult for some of the corrupt officials to continue their practice of depriving both the state and the peasants of their due shares.[42] There are some important aspects with which Akbar seems to have dealt intelligently. Although Akbar gave primary importance to some crucial issues like agrarian economy and trade, he always kept in mind that these were not the only issues which could help the Mughal state to elucidate or evaluate the State's claims to allegiance of its subjects. Perhaps he felt that the identification of social groups, the nature of their interests and the autonomy of the political groups did not adequately discriminate among different aspects of the superstructure. Because for him there were after all, equally pressing questions about the autonomy of the religion and its cultural aspects. Many of these institutions also claimed the allegiance of their members and attempted to sustain it through similar devices. He devoted his time to these areas also. Interestingly, it appears to be a typical case of political sociology, especially of a Marxist or a structuralist model, because it bears upon the relation between the state, action and social structure.[43]A Subahdar was appointed to protect and maintain the authority of the Mughal state in the entire region. For effective operation of administration, the Subah was made into Sarkars, Parganas, and Mahals.[44] When Nasq Gallabakshi was introduced as a system of assessment, the peasants and tenants benefited by this, being directly affected by the fluctuating nature of prices. Because under this system the losses arising out of the effects of drought, poor harvests, and other problems were borne by both the parties—the assignee and the peasants. The only bad feature of this method was that it involved a large number of officials in its working and the burden of maintaining such a large staff always fell on the peasant's shoulders.[45] Qazi Ali divided the Subah of Kashmir into 42 parganas. The various parganas were Srinagar, Islamabad, Ular, Ich, Advin, Inderkot, Bangil, Biru, Brang, Batu,·Phak, Trehgam, Devasar, Dachin, Sair-ul-Mawaiza, Sopor Soman, Shakroha, Showma, Shahabad, Kuthar, Khuihama, Khoi, Kamraz, Lar, Manchahama, Martand, Mohammudabad, Nagam, Wunts, Greater Tibet, Little Tibet, Gilgit, Barsal, Sarsal, Pakhli, Dardu, Doomyal, Damtur, Kashak, Kamlok, Kahel, Punch, Rajouri, Maruwardwan, Naushera and Banihal. The areas of Ladakh were included in the Mughal Empire by Jahangir.[46] The total demand was fixed at 30,63,052 lakh *kharwars* and

11 *traks* and out of this 9,01,663 *kharwars* and 8 *traks* were to be paid in cash at the commuted rate of 13-18/25 *dam* per *kharwar*. After AD 1594, a reassessment was carried out by Asif Khan at the instructions of Emperor Akbar.[47] The total revenue demand was fixed at half the produce and a reduction of two lakh *kharwars* was registered. The officials assisting Yusuf Khan Rizvi did not cooperate because it curtailed their chances of grabbing a large proportion of the peasants' produce to which they were used. Tota Ram, a Kashmiri *peshkar* of Yusuf Khan Rizvi, complained about this to Akbar and the emperor sent Qazi Ali in AD 1591 to look into the problem. As a result, a new assessment was carried out.[48]

When the emperor found that there was not much improvement in the condition of the peasants in the valley, he introduced some new reforms in AD 1597 to ascertain the nature and volume of the actual *jama*.[49] Careful consideration was given to the nature of land and the time span for which it remained under the plough. Perhaps Emperor Akbar had in view the serious ecological limitations which had always restricted the agrarian economy to a one crop pattern. After thorough investigation, the land revenue was fixed at one-third as the state's share.[50]

This was further subject to the changing nature of the harvest, a step very rarely conceded by the earlier Sultans. Apart from this, oppressive taxes like *sardarkhti, kahcharai, dastar-shumari, telicharagh, hasilihatar, chouthai, khadyar, baj* and *tamgah* were all abolished by Emperor Akbar.[51]

Abul Fazl remarks cash transactions not being the custom of the country, some part of *Sair Jihat* cesses, however, are taken in cash payments in kind and coins are estimated in *Kharwars* of *Shali* (rice) although 1/3 was the rate but in actual practice 2/3 are taken. *Baj* was a kind of toll tax and *tamgah* was demanded over and above the usual land revenue.[52] The cess of *Baj* and *Tamgah* were altogether remitted by his majesty which produced a reduction of 67,824.5 *kharwars* equivalent to 8,98,400 *dams*. For additional relief of husbandmen five *dams* as price of *kharwar* were thrown in under Emperor Jahangir (1605-1628). *Rasum-i-Faujdari* was also abolished.[53] The inscriptional evidence has been misinterpreted by R.K. Parmu in asserting the total abolition of forced labour in Kashmir, but the inscription on the main gate of Nagar Nagar Fort refers to the non-utilization of forced labour only for construction of this fort, but that does not necessarily establish the total abolition of forced labour or *begar* in other economic activities, as stated by Parmu.[54]

The original text of the inscription reads:

Binai Qjlai Nagar Nagar bud ba ahde padshahe dadgustar,
shahi Shahani A/am Shahi-Akbar Taalla Shana ha Allah Akbar. Shahanshahe Kidar a/am misalash Na bud ast-u-na khahad bud digar.
Karore-o-dah lakh az Makhaxan Firistad
Du sad ustadi Hindi Jumla Chakar. Na kardeh hech kas begar anjah Tamame Yaftand as makhzanash zar Chihil-o-chahar az juluse padshahi Hazar-o-shash ze tarikhe paigambar.

The foundation of fort town of Nagar Nagar was laid in the reign of just sovereign,
King of Kings, unique among past and present sovereigns of u'le world. One crore and
ten lakh were sent by him (Akbar)
from central exchequer with two hundred master builders and their servants.
No one was seized on *begar* (forced unpaid labour). All received their remuneration in the 44th year of his accession corresponding to 1006 of the Prophet, i.e. AH 1006.[55]

However, all the measures introduced by Akbar were meant to strengthen the basis of the Mughal state and its ability to rationalize the political, economic and administrative control in Kashmir region. Consequently, the Mughal state appeared to the public as more efficient than the Shahmir Sultans.[56]

From all these pieces of evidence it becomes amply clear that after Kashmir passed into the hands of the Mughals, the change in administration led to change in the land-based relations among various classes of Kashmiri society. The increase in the expansion of agrarian bureaucracy helped the Mughals to control the large proportion of surplus in the form of land revenue, and ensure the application of what Jadunath Sarkar calls the 'uniform administrative type throughout the length and breadth of Mughal empire'.[57]

This mechanism of setting up a common transferable machinery for all their dominions was both subtle and effective. Besides, the agrarian structure was a matter of comprehensive interest affecting all classes of Kashmiri society. It helped the Mughals to contain the conflicting interests of the region's nobility within the restructuring process of the agrarian system. The clear connection that I have stressed between the local political developments and the distribution of these opportunities should not, however, imply that one can mechanically deduce the distribution of power in the Mughal era from the differing economic strengths of the local landed aristocracy. Possession of land was certainly the instrument necessary for any local political power base, but this power base was not precisely commensurate with the extent of property. Therefore, the multiplication of the centres of power was influenced decisively by the individual tradition of authority conferred on these individuals and families by the Mughals to help the Mughal state in Kashmir.

For the locally dominant elements, the process of administrative reorganization threw up various positions of power prestige and wealth from Muqadams to Mansabdars.

Qazi Nurullah and Pandit Tota Ram were the Peshkars (deputies) of Mirzah Yousuf Khan (AD 1587-93).[58] Pandit Mahadav Koul was the Peshkar of Ali Mardan Khan, he was Governor of Kashmir for two terms (AD 1638-40 and AD 1650-7). He ruled for three months only.[59] Sudarshan Koul was the Peshkar of Inayatullah Khan (AD 1711-12). Fazal Khan (AD 1698-1707) is said to have recommended a large number of Kashmiris to the Mughal court for

Mansabs. Fazl Khan was the Mughal governor of Kashmir from AD 1698-1710. It is interesting to note here that it was during his rule that *Moi Mubarak* (sacred) Hair of the Prophet Muhammad was brought into Kashmir in AD 1699 by Khwaja Nooruddin Ishabari from Bijapur Deccan. Khwaja Nooruddin was a merchant, which clearly illustrates that the Kashmiri merchants visited various parts of south India as well.[60] Mir Ahmad Khan Hassan Beg, Muhammad Habib, and Muhammad Isaq Khan, were prominent among them. Muhammad Murad attained the position of Haft Hazari with Suwar rank of 10,000.[61] Abdul Fateh was appointed Dewan.[62] MullahAshrafheld the positions of Sadr and Dewan.[63] Mahesh Koul was appointed Chaudhry.[64]

Malik Ali, Malik Haidar were among the Jagirdars, Fateh Dar was a Muqadam.[65] Muqadam Fateh Dar is among those very few Kashmiri Muqadams who protested against the oppressive officials and brought their conduct to the notice of their superiors. Muhammad Yousuf Kawoosa was Sadar-i suba Kashmir.[66] Khwaja Hashim was Qanago-i-kul.[67] Qazi Saleem was appointed as Dewan. Mullah Habib, Mullah Haji Bandey and Abdul Karim were the Qazis. Qazi Khan held the post of Qazi-ul-Qazat during Aurangzeb's reign. Babrullah was the Thanedar, Muhammad Qasim and Muhammad Salim were the Bakshis.[68] Ali Akbar was Waqi Nawis.[69] Sayyid Maqsood was appointed to the post of Daroga.[70] Haji Muhammad Sayyid and Muhammad Rafi were among the Bayutatis.[71] Mullah Mazhari was appointed Mir Bahar.[72] These appointments were solely made by Mughal Subahdars of Kashmir but their choice of persons for such positions was qualified by the assessment of wealth and the position of the person concerned in a particular area. As a result, they mostly recruited from among the regional political elite on whom depended the governing apparatus of the Mughal state in Kashmir. The strife among these families would have otherwise assumed uncontrollable proportions and acted as an obstacle in the process of the growing incorporation of the region into the Mughal state. A more interesting, and sometimes highly informative, discussion on this aspect will follow from the analysis of expanded handicraft production and trade.

From the very beginning, the artisan production in Kashmir supplemented agriculture and thus formed a significant aspect of the region's economy. Agriculture was carried out only for four to five months a year, for the rest of the year the land remained under snow when no cultivation was possible. Under these circumstances craft production was the lone alternative, attracting the attention of people who had supplemented their income with agriculture from very early times. Abul Fazl mentions, 'There are artificers of various kinds, who might be deservedly employed in the greatest cities. The bazar system is little in use as brisk traffic is carried on its places of business.[73]

It was only with the extension of Mughal rule that trade and artisan production received encouragement and promotion. Emperor Akbar vigorously enforced internal freedom and external protection. Akbar took a keen interest in the shawl industry which was a source of sustenance to a large section of population in Kashmir. The shawl industry was one of the important sources of subsistence for both the rural and urban sections of Kashmir's population. With the Mughal occupation, the expansion of the market for shawls in various parts of India strengthened and further expanded the social division of labour involved therein. By the middle of the nineteenth century, when some of the European travellers and later some local historians unveiled the nature of labour involved in *shawl*-making, there were around seventeen persons whose labour was appropriated at various levels in producing a single *shawl* for the market.[74] He personally dictated the designs in the manufacturing process and even determined the colouring pattern. The interest of Emperor Akbar is recorded in *Ain-i Akbari:*

> His majesty improved this department in four ways. The improvement is first visible in the *tus shawls* which were made up of wool of an animal of that name . . . people generally wear it without altering

its natural colour. His majesty has had it dyed. Secondly in *Safid Alchas* also called *Tarahdars,* in their natural colours. The wool is either white or black. The stuffs may be had in three colours, white, black or mixed ... his majesty has given orders as Zardozi, Kalabtun, Kashida, Qalgha Bandhun chint, Alcha, Purzdar, to which his majesty pays much attention. Fourth, an improvement was made in the width of all stuffs his majesty had the pieces made large enough to yield the making of full dressess. His majesty encourages in every possible way, the manufacturers of shawls in Kashmir.[75]

These measures by Akbar promoted good trade between Kashmir and other parts of Mughal India. There is a large body of evidence to suggest that the merchants from Kashmir visited various parts of India frequently while merchants from other parts of India also set up business establishments in Kashmir. Mughal India received large supplies of Kashmiri products such as *zeera,* paper, shawls, papier mache articles, baskets, honey, forest products, saffron, rag-paper, furniture and woollen articles.[76] The principal commodity of export has been the Kashmiri shawl. The merchants from Mughal India completely monopolized the wool trade in Ladakh, Gilgit and central Tibet. They established links with direct producers by advancing loans. The warehouses were located in China, Turkistan, Lhasa and Tibet.[77] The Mughal nobility provided a good market for *pashmina* products. The imperial *farashkhana* always got large supplies of carpets, *dhuries* and various embroidered articles of silk and *pasham* wool.[78] Kashmir also exported large quantities of fruits to Lahore, Gujarat, Amritsar and Agra.[79] Amber beads were mainly sold to merchants from Surat and Ahmedabad. The royal kitchen regularly received supplies of Rajouri rice and fowls from Kashmir.[80] The other articles exported from Kashmir to other parts of India were feather, paper, colourful plumes, ink-stands, trays, walnut wood boxes, spoons, and silver horses (of both the local and imported variety).[81]

Kashmir exported saffron to China, Agra and also other parts of India, entering into competition at Patna with saffron brought from Nepal. In return it imported salt, paper, opium, cotton, yarn, silkworm eggs, turmeric, ginger, sugar, cloves, mace and doth.[82]

Under the Mughals Kashmir maintained good trade relations with Persia, Central Asia, Russia, Bhutan, Nepal, Bengal, Patna, Golconda and Bijapur. Internal trade also showed great progress which is reflected in the emergence of some of the new bazaars such as Saraffan Bazaar, Bangalia Bazaar, etc.[83] The aristocracy lived in urban areas which led to the expansion of towns. All these towns developed as secure shelters for various artisans. In the workshops of shawl merchants alone there were more than 2,400 looms to manufacture shawls. Similarly, the carpet industry also showed great progress and provided employment to a large number of people.[84] In fact, to ensure the security of increasing traffic between Kashmir and other parts of India, Emperor Jahangir had the main highway (Mughal Road) constructed. According to Abul Fazl, there were six routes which connected Kashmir with the rest of the world. The track route linking Central Asia to Mughal India passed through Kashmir. The Mughals maintained these various trade routes so well that even during winter months, merchants could travel through them. Besides this, Mughals also developed a large network of inns for merchants and travellers on the main highway.[85] During Jahangir's first visit to Kashmir in AD 1622, his camp followers and other members of his establishment did not require tents for their encampment. During the reigns of Shah Jahan (1628-58) and Aurangzeb (1658-1707) a chain of new inns were built and the old ones were repaired and kept under the control of the nobles.[86] These steps freed Kashmir from two serious limitations: (a) its seclusion from the wider world and (b) the scale of which men thought of distances. Markets in Mughal India beyond Kashmir became accessible, consequently what had seemed distant now seemed near. Kashmiri merchants travelled as far as Bengal to sell their ware and import salt. Henry Vansittart has made the careful observation that Kashmiri merchants in the Sundarbans in

Bengal advanced money and provided *malangies* to work on the salt pans. His estimate of duties on salt amounts to Rs. 30,000, and as he seems to have noticed, this process had been going on for years.[87] This evidence reinforces the impression that dealings such as advancing money must have involved wider and more enduring contractual procedures, which in course of time added a new element of strength and stability to an already existing process of reciprocity. These developments further removed the relative isolation of Kashmir, introducing a process of blending Kashmir's economic activity with a kind of generalized Indian economy. Since Kashmir economy was not predominantly given over to agriculture, as in other parts of India, expansion of the market provided a massive response to the growth of craft production. The expanding social differentiation created a mass of wage-receiving occupations. In course of time, these occupational groups recognized their social positions and served to enhance the legitimacy of the Mughal ruling class which promoted the kind of economy suitable to their needs. In addition, these groups, by the very nature of their relationship with the market economy, linked the interior of Kashmir with the rest of the country. These transactions between the Kashmiri and the non-Kashmiri elements were therefore interwoven with the formation of the nucleus of the Mughal State in Kashmir. The process of incorporation of the region of Kashmir into the Mughal empire and the political and administrative elaboration were linked together. These processes overlaid, alternated, and reinforced each other at every step and tended to form strong linkages between the Kashmir region and the Mughal state.

Such measures would not have been possible without bringing in the integrating processes of production, the emergence of a class of people highly dependent upon Indian goods and the predisposition to accept the new ideological influence, all contributing to the erosion of the concept of regional sovereignty.

The community of merchants within and beyond Kashmir had to cooperate with the Mughal ruling class to ensure the safety of their establishments and help the growth of the administrative system managing their lives. They also sought allies locally and in political institutions to achieve control over public opinion in order to direct the market economy from time to time. W.C. Smith remarks that the Mughal Empire was allied to middle class commerce as a secondary base of income, its primary base being land.[88] Thus the intrusion of the Indian merchants' goods broke the regional self-sufficiency of Kashmir and proved conducive to their economic dependence and psychological emancipation. In this case the political reordering of Kashmir around the growth of agriculture, trade and the reorganization of administrative network was slower and more precarious, but the local power was less capable of overcoming the deficiencies of public order in crisis and of resisting tendencies offered by the Mughal state towards its degeneration into the instruments of rural exploitation.

The encouragement of matrimonial relations between the Mughals and the Kashmiris was another aspect which helped the Mughal state to further test the loyalty of Kashmiri nobles to their new credo. Akbar married Shamas Chak's daughter during his first visit (AD 1589) to Kashmir.[89] The daughter of Mubarak Khan Chak was married to prince Salim.[90] During Shah Jahan's reign (AD 1628-58). Prince Murad married the daughter of the Malik of Shahabad. Prince Muhammad Sultan was married to the daughter of the Raja of Kishtwar. Prince Mohammad Azam took the daughter of Taju-ud-din of Rajouri in marriage while Raja Tamsen of Kishtwar gave his daughter to Shah Shuja.[91] Unfortunately our chronicles have recorded only a few cases which seemed to them more important from the point of view of their affiliation to the Mughal court.

But our oral tradition records that many more alliances were fostered between the Kashmiri merchant families and other social groups on the one hand and the Mughals on the other. 'The descendants of the Mughals may now be found among Mirzas, Begs, Mirs, Buch, etc.'[92] Since there was no feeling against inter-marriage this must have been an effective means to create an ever-widening social set-up. In these circumstances, the nobility, the merchants, and most of the urban groups whose sustenance was directly linked with the other parts of Mughal India and who exercised a paramount influence over the whole of Kashmiri society, created a climate to encourage this process. A more significant consequence was the natural inclination of all those involved in these commercial relationships on both sides, to absorb each other's cultural package for their personal advancement. Hence the economic forces were no longer alone in producing a lasting degree of ties with the Indian structure, since the incorporation of Kashmir into the Mughal state put various aspects of enterprise within the reach of Kashmiri society to its own advantage.

A close look at this situation reveals that these observations remain a little incomplete, because the cultural and religious aspects which were also involved in this long-drawn process of incorporation of Kashmir into the Mughal Empire have not been taken into account. In the course of the analysis, what is apparent is that from the time of the Mughal occupation, Kashmir became primarily dependent on the rest of India for her sustenance, despite the immensity of distances. The reorganization of administration, the new order of matrimonial relations, the increasing expansion of trade and craft-produce, and various other mutual pursuits nourished a new environment without in any way destroying Kashmir's basic identity.

Notes

1. K. Zutshi, *Sultan Zain-ul-Abidin*, Lucknow, 1976, pp. 11-51.
2. Pandit Srivara, *Jain Rajatarangini*, English translation by J.C Dutt, pp. 184-99. For details see Parmu, *A History of Muslim Rule in Kashmir*, pp. 175-206.
3. Firishta, *Tarikh-i-Firishta*, vol. IV, p. 475. Nizam-ud-din Ahmad, *Tabqat-i-Akbari*, vol. III, pp. 46-7.

4. Ibid.
5. Mohibbul Hassan, *Kashmir under the Sultans,* p. 99.
6. Srivara, op. cit., vol. III, p. 228. Apart from heading the music department of Sultan Haider Shah, Pandit Srivara left a detailed and interesting record of Kashmir's history from AD 1459 to 1486.
7. Ibid., pp. 198-200.
8. *Baharistan-i-Shahi* (anonymous), pp. 59-60. Firishta, op. cit., vol. II, p. 348. See also Sir Wolseley Haig, *Cambridge History of India,* vol. III, p. 285.
9. Srivara, op. cit., p. 206. The Yech pargana is mentioned in Sanskrit as *Ikshika.*
10. Ibid.
11. Mohibbul Hassan, op. cit., p. 99.
12. Ibid.
13 Srivara, op. cit., pp. 238-45.
14. Ibid.
15. Ibid., p. 211.
16. Ibid.,
17. Mohibbul Hassan, op. cit., p. 103.
18. Please see Chapter III for details.
19. Nizam-ud-din Ahmad, *Tabqat-i-Akbari,* vol. III, p. 446, ibid., p. 452
20. *Baharistan-i-Shahi,* pp. 59-61.
21. Parmu, op. cit., pp. 175-206.
22. Mohibbul Hassan, op. cit., pp. 106-24.
23. Srivara, op. cit., p. 250. Mohibbul Hassan, op. cit., pp. 106-24.
24. Suka Pandit and Prajayabhata, *Rajvalipatika* (Sanskrit), English translation by J.C. Dutt, *Kings of Kashmir,* vol. III, pp. 372-4.
25. Srivara, op. cit., p. 222, *Baharistan-i-Shahi,* pp. 60-1. The history of Kashmir during the medieval centuries is replete with such occurrences.
26. Suka, op. cit., p. 349. Firishta, op. cit., vol. IV, p. 351.
27. Abul Fazl, *Akbarnama,* vol. III, pp. 617-18.
28. Mirza Muhammad Haidar Dughlat, *Tarikh-i-Rashidi,* pp. 435-57.
29. Narayan Kaul Ajiz, *Mukhtsar Tawarikh-i-Kashmir* (Persian manuscript), RDLKUS ff. 58-9ab. See also Qazi Nurullah Shustri, *Majalis-ul-Muminin* (Persian manuscript), RDLKUS.
30. Abul Fazl, *Ain-i-Akbari,* vol. III, pp. 753, 770. It was on 16 October 1586, that Emperor Akbar was formally declared the sovereign of Kashrnir.

31. Ibid.
32 Firishta, op. cit., vol. IV, p. 491. Haidar Malik Chadurah, *Tarikh-i-Kashmir,* p. 175.
33. Abdul Qadir Badauni, *Muntakhab-ut-Tawarikh* (Persian), English translation by Lowe Ranking and Wolseley Haig, Calcutta, 1925, 3 vols., vol. II, p. 128.
34. *Tabqat-i-Akbari,* vol. II, p. 629. Mohammad Azam, *Tarikh-i-Azami,* RDLKUS, p. 82.
35. Haidar Malik Chadurah, op. cit., pp. 97-8. See also *Ain-i-Akbari* vol. I, pp. 105 and 502.
36. *Akbarnama,* vol. III, p. 1004.
37. Abul Fazl, *Ain-i-Akbari,* vol. II, pp. 570-1.
38. *Akbarnama,* vol. III, pp. 1085-6.
39. Abul Fazl, *Ain-i-Akbari,* vol. II, pp. 570-1.
40. Ibid.
41. Nath Pandit, op. cit., ff. 430-52, 532-4; Hussain Beg Khaki, *Tarikh-i-Kashmir* (Persian), f. 36a, RDLKUS. Jagat Rai Shujai, K. Saxena, *Khulasat-us-Siyag* (AD 1697-98), f. 18, Ms. 49, Subhanullah Collection, Maulana Azad Library, Aligarh. See also *Ain-i-Akbari,* vol. I, p. 209.
42. Abul Fazl, *Ain-a-Akbari,* vol. II, p. 570; *Akbarnama,* vol. III, p. 540. See also Pandit Birbal Kachru, *Mukhtasar Tarikh-i-Kashmir* (Persian manuscript), unpublished, RDLKUS, pp. 27-33.
43. On such aspects, a very interesting study has been carried out by N. Poulantzas, *Political Power and the Social Classes,* London, 1973.
44. Abul Fazl, *Akbarnama,* vol. III, pp. 830-2; see also *Ain-i-Akbari,* vol. II, pp. 366-7.
45. See Nath Pandit, *Gulshan-i-Dastur* (Persian manuscript) 2314, RDLKUS, f. 342a; Irfan Habib, *Agrarian System of Mughal India,* p. 239.
46. *Mukhtasar Tarikh-i-Kashmir* (Persian manuscript), unpublished, RDLKUS, pp. 27-33.
47. Abul Fazl, *Ain-a-Akbari,* vol. II, p. 570; *Akbarnama,* vol. III, p. 540.
48. Abul Fazl, *Ain-a-Akbari,* vol. II, p. 570; *Akbarnama,* vol. III, p. 540. See also Pandit Birbal Kachru.
49. Abul Fazl, *Ain-i-Akbari,* vol. II, p. 573. (AD 1605-27), Narayan Kaul Ajiz, *Mukhtsar Tawarikh-i-Kashmir;* Jahangir, *Tuzuk-i-Jahangiri;* English translation by A. Rogers and H. Beveridge (3rd edn.), 2 vols., Delhi, 1978, vol. II, pp. 137-56.
50. Abdul Majid Mattoo, *Kashmir Under Mughals,* Srinagar, 1988,

p. 155. *Kharwar* was a unit of measurement. Each *kharwar* was equal to 16 *traks* and each *trak* was equal to 5 *seers* and 83 *chattanks.*

51. Abul Fazl, *Ain-i-Akbari,* vol. II, p. 451. Jahangir also enhanced his rank to 5000 Zat. Jahangir, *Tuzuk-i-Jahangiri,* pp. 108-9.
52. *Ain-i-Akbari,* vol. II, p. 363.
53. Ibid., vol. II, pp. 726-7.
54. Parmu, op. cit. (AD 1597), p. 301.
55. Ibid.
56. Ibid., vol. II, pp. 366-7. Irfan Habib, *Agrarian System of Mughal India,* pp. 215-16.
57. For details see Jadunath Sarkar, *Conditions of Kashmiri People Under Muslim Rule,* Delhi, 1949 (monograph).
58. Sufi, op. cit., vol. I, p. 272. See also A.M. Mattoo, op. cit.
59. Mattoo, op. cit, pp. 99-107, ff. 73, 74.
60. Parmu, op. cit., p. 327. See also Mohammad Azam Diddamari, *Waqiat-i-Kashmir* (unpublished Persian manuscript), RDLKUS, pp. 155-6.
61. Mattoo, op. cit., pp. 129-30, fu. 20. William Irvine, *Later Mughals,* edited by J.N. Sarkar, 2 vols., Calcutta, 1922.
62. Ibid., p. 176.
63. Ibid., p. 193.
64. Kachru, op. cit., f. 417a.
65. Haidar Malik Chadurh, *Tarikh-i-Kashmir,* ff. 213-15.
66. Mulla Ahmad Bin-Abdus Sabur, *Khawariqus-Salikin* (Persian manuscript), AH 1109, RDLKUS, f. 119.
67. Mattoo, op. cit., p. 75.
68. Abdul Hamid Lahori, *Badshahnama,* edited by Moulvi Khair-ud-din and Abdul Rahim (Bib. Indica), 1860, 2 vols., vol. II, p. 362.
69. Mattoo, op. cit, pp. 73-6
70. Ibid., p. 129.
71. Ibid.
72. Badauni, *Muntakhab-ut-Tawarikh,* vol. III, pp. 344-5. See also Mohammad Azam, op. cit., p. 136.
73. Abul Fazl, *Ain-i-Akbari,* vol. II, p. 353.
74. G.T. Vigne, *Travels in Kashmir, Ladakh, Iskardu, Countries and the Mountain Courses of Indus and North of Punjab,* 2 vols., London, 1842, vol. I, pp. 127-30. William Moorcraft and W.G. Trebeck, *Travels in the Himalayan Provinces of Hindustan and Punjab, in Ladakh and Kashmir,* 2 vols., Delhi, 1971 (rpt.), vol. II, pp. 167-200. W. Moorcraft, *Tour Dairy,* Ms. EURD-265, India

Office Library, London, pp. 30-117. Among the local historians see, Mirza Saif-ud-din, *Akhbarat* (Persian manuscript), 13 vols. (1846-56), RDLKUS (unpublished). Also available with author in microfilm

75. Abul Fazl, *Ain-i-Akbari,* vol. II, pp. 97-8.
76. Habib, op. cit., p. 87.
77. A.H. Franke, *Antiquities of Indian Tibet,* 2 pts., Calcutta, 1927, pt. II, pp. 115-16. See also Ipolitio Desideri, *An Account of his Travels (1717-27 AD).* Filippo De Filippi, *The Travels of Ippolito Desideri of Pistoia, 1712-1727,* London, 1937, pp. 122, 123, 137, 292.
78. A.H. Lahori, *Badshahnama,* vol. II, p. 433.
79. Francisco Palsaert, *Ramoustrantie, Jahangir's India,* translated by W.H. Moreland and P. Geyl, Cambridge, 1925, p. 35.
80. Abul Fazl, *Ain-i-Akbari,* vol. I, pp. 34, 40, 44.
81. Badauni, op. cit., vol. III, p. 202. See also George Forester, *A Journey from Bengal to England, through the Northern Part of India,* Kashmir, 2 vols., London, 1826, vol. II, p. 22.
82. Palsaert, op. cit., pp. 35-6. See also Mufti Muhammad Murad Tang, *Tohfat-ul-Fuqara,* f. 43ab. Also Irfan Habib, op. cit., p. 87.
83. Azam, op. cit., p. 8.
84. Forester, op. cit., vol. II, p. 22.
85. Abul Fazl, *Akbarnama,* vol. III, pp. 538, 725. Abdul Hamid Lahori, *Badshahnama,* vol. II, pp. 212, n. 69. Fedrick Drew, *Jammu and Kashmir Territories,* London, 1895, rpt. Delhi, 1971, pp. 91, 94, 156..
86. Khafi Khan, *Muntakhab-ul-Lubab,* edited by Moulvi Kabir-ud-din Ahmad, Calcutta (Bib. Indica), 1860-4, vol. I, p. 301. Lahori, op. cit., vol. II, pp. 212, 469.
87. Henri Vansittart, *A Narrative of Transactions in Bengal (AD 1760-64),* 2 vols., London, 1930, vol. II, pp. 165-70.
88. Quoted from Sufi, op. cit., vol. I, p. 294.
89. Abul Fazl, *Akbarnama,* vol. III, p. 958.
90. Ibid., pp. 609,626. Prince Salim was also married to the daughters of lba Malik and Ali Rai, the Tibetan *zamindars.*
91. Mohammad Azam, *Waqiat-i-Kashmir,* p. 139. Lahori, *Badshahnama,* vol. II, pp. 434-5. J. Hutichson and Ph. Vogel, *History of Punjab Hill States,* 2 vols., Lahore, 1933, p. 686. Muhammad Saleh Kumbu, *Amal-i-Saleh,* 2 vols., Calcutta (Bib. Indica), 1932, p. 445.
92. M.I. Khan, *Perspectives on Kashmir, Historical Dimensions,* p. 129.

5

Conclusion

A review of the scope and general analysis of the processes involved in the growth of state formation and its functioning in medieval Kashmir, makes it amply dear that this region had become a rich productive area, perfectly capable of maintaining a viable independent regime much before the birth of the Christian era. Among other forces, the transition from tribal chieftaincy to the early formation of a state was speeded up by the Brahminical religion. It became a frame of reference within which a dominant group could foresee its political future. It established a process of absorption of varied tribal cults into an organized religio-cultural network and crystallized sufficiently to create a broader socio-political formation deriving legitimacy by patronizing the Brahmin and the Buddhist establishments. The Buddhists could not compete with the Brahminical elements in establishing their indispensability, nor could they maintain an earthly domination of the ruling class. Because Buddhism failed to produce a social infrastructure for the ruling elite, it did not fit into its schemes for perpetuating political power.

Although the Brahmins came to markedly occupy a significant position through their efforts in organizing social relationships, the nature of the state-society relations established by them was in the long run destructive to the region's economic development. The Brahmins associated with *agrahara*-based economy produced semi-servile dependencies at the popular leveL This helped them to develop as a part of the ruling aristocracy and to differentiate themselves from the common man not only by their wealth, culture and style of life, but also by legal and fiscal privileges and access to offices of state, possible only through the recommendations of royalty. Gradually, the state came to be dominated by influential families who monopolized public offices and concentrated power and wealth in their own hands.

But the imposing edifice of state came under severe strain from eighth century AD when the material base of the state was weakened. The state failed to gain regular taxes and even irregular tributes from various feudatories. The increasing transfer of tax-exempt land into the hands of the priestly (Brahmins) also threatened to outstrip the resources of state. With the rapid increase of expenditure, the entire tax system came under great pressure and various new levies were imposed. The religious establishments were brought under a tax network by the state, thus abandoning its role as promoter and protector of Brahminism, which it had used to derive legitimacy for its authority. However, despite it the state could not contain the dominance and challenges posed to its authority by the growth of private power of the Dammaras and other groups.

It was amidst this reversal of long-standing roles that Islam, the most potent force of all foreign influences, made its presence felt in Kashmir. The Islamic influence was by no means limited to the realm of ideology, for the Muslims had brought with them patronage of commerce and craft production, a minimum level of security, a new technology, and the institution of Sufism in which the individual could participate without withdrawing himself from the ties of family. The *khanqahs* with the donations of their supporters played an even more important role in turning away people from the Brahminical religion, which was highly ritual-dominated. This also marked the beginning of a great cosmopolitan period in Kashmir's history. There was widespread foreign influence. Regular communication was opened up with areas around Central Asia, Persia and Turkistan. These developments not only brought a new faith, i.e. Islam, but also a new level of sophistication in philosophical thought and theology. They also provided solution to some of the problems arising out of man's material needs. New arts, crafts and skills tended to link the people's lives with new economic activity. People withdrew their support from a political regime which was ridden with instability, court intrigues, frequent purges and the irrational and arbitrary violence of the ruling class. Eventually, all these changes brought to power the new Turkish Sultans who obtained a mass base when the majority accepted their faith in the entire region, in the expectation that the new regime would better their condition.

Unfortunately, the succession of the Sultanate did not mean any great change in the nature of the state's attitude towards its subjects. The Shahmir Sultans like their predecessors, derived legitimacy for their rule by making use of Islamic tenets among other things. The people owed allegiance to the Sultans not because they were co-religionists, but because the new religion of Islam had thrown up expectations, while covering a wide range of actual relationships. In this process the Muslim priestly class of the Sayyids emerged as the main body of intermediaries in regulating the State's attitude and the people's response. While carrying out this task, however, the Sayyids grew ambitious, and transferred the authority of the state into their own hands. The result was abroad-based disjunction which pushed the entire state and society into crisis from which it was ultimately retrieved by the extension of the Mughal rule to the entire region.

The Mughals discovered that depending on religion alone for legitimizing purposes, fostered a form of state-society relationship which did not help in any economic activity affecting the majority of the populace. The Mughals thus promoted craft production, commerce and agriculture by a variety of methods, thus abandoning religion as the only ideological method of perpetuating their power. They tried to restructure the institutional apparatus and encouraged market activity which made it easier for them to establish Kashmir's linkages with the rest oflndia. This too, was a secular ideological mechanism to ensure the total incorporation of the region into the Mughal state.

Bibliography

Persian Manuscripts and Translated Texts

Aba Rafi-ud-din Ahmad, *Nawadir-ul-Akhbar,* Research Department Library, Kashmir University, Srinagar (henceforth RDLKUS), AD 1723.

Abdul Wahab Noori, *Futuhat-i-Kubravia,* AH 118, Ms. no. 50, RDLKUS.

Abdus Sabur Mullah Ahmad Bin, *Khwariqus-Salikin,* AH 1109, Ms. Saburi, RDLKUS.

Abul Fazl, *Ain-i-Akbari,* Calcutta, 1872-3, English translation, vol. I by Blochmann, Calcutta, 1927, vols. II and III by Col. H.S. Jarrett, Calcutta, 1894, rpt., 1977.

______, *Akbarnama,* 3 vols., Calcutta, 1897-1913. English translation by H. Beveridge, Calcutta, 1897-1939.

Al-Biruni, *Kitab-ul-Hind,* English translation under the title *Al-Biruni's India* by E.C. Sachau, 2 vols., London, 1910, rpt., 1989.

Al Utbi, *Kitabul-Yamini* or, *Tarikh-i-Yamini,* Engligh translation by James Reynolds, London, 1869.

Ali, Hassan bin, *Tarikh-i-Kashmir,* RDLKUS, *Tazkirat-ul-Shura,* RDLKUS, AD 1600-1625.

Babur, Emperor, *Baburnama,* English translation by Henry Beveridge, Calcutta, 2 vols., 1904, 1907, 1911, rpt., 1979.

Badakshi, Zafar, *Khulasat-ul-Manaqib* (Persian), AD 1350, Urdu translation and edited by Sayyedh Ashraf Zaffar, Institute of Persian Studies, Islamabad, 1995.

Badakshani, Nur-ud-din, *Khulasat-ui-Muminin,* Teheran, AH 1299.

Badauni, Abdul Qadir, *Muntakhab-ut-Tawarikh,* Calcutta, 1865-9, English translation by Ranking, Lowe and Haig, Calcutta, 1925, 3 vols., rpt., Patna, 1973.

Baharistan-i-Shahi (anonymous), AD 1614, RDLKUS, Ms. 159.

Bakshi, Nizam-ud-din Ahmad, *Tabqat-i-Akbari,* 3 vols., Calcutta, 1927, Lucknow edn., 1920.

Bhandari, Sujan Rai, *Khulasat-ui-Tawarikh,* Delhi, 1918.

Chadurah, Haidar Malik, *Tarikh-i-Kashmir,* AD 1622, RDLKUS.

Diddamari, Mohammad Azam, *Waqiat-i-Kashmir,* also known as *Tarikh-i-Azmi,* RDLKUS, AH 1303. Urdu translation under *Tarikh-i-Kashmir Azmi,* by Munshi Ashraf Ali, Delhi, 1846.

Dughlat, Mirza Muhammad Haidar, *Tarikh-i-Rashidi,* RDLKUS, English translation by Sir E. Denison Ross with Introduction by N. Elias, London, 1895.

Firishta, Muhammad Qasim, *Tarikh-i-Firishta* (Gulshan-i-Ibrahimi) Lucknow, AH 1321, English translation by John Briggs under the title *History of the Rise of Muhammadan Power in India Till the Year 1612,* 4 vols., Calcutta, 1808, rpt., 1966.

Gulbadan Begum, *Humayunnama,* English translation with text by A.S. Beveridge, London, 1902, rpt. in India by Idarah-i Adabiyat-i Delhi, 1972.

Hamadani, Sayyid Ali, *Gayat-ui-Makan,* (AD 1314-1384) RDLKUS, also available at the Raza Library, Rampur.

———, *Zakhirat-ui-Mulk* (mid 14th century), RDLKUS.

Hassan, Shah Peer, *Tarikh-i-Hassan,* 3 vols., 1885, RDLKUS. Urdu translation of vol. I by Moulvi Muhammad Ibrahim, Srinagar, 1957.

Hussain Beg Khaki, *Tarikh-i-Kashmir* (n.d.), RDLKUS.

Ibn-ul-Bazaz, *AI-Kadariya,* Hyderabad, 1903.

Jagat Rai Shujai, Kayath Saxena, *Khula, satus siyaq,* AD 1697-8, Ms. 49, Subhanullah Collection, Maulana Azad Library, Aligarh Muslim University.

Jahangir, Emperor, *Tuzuk-i-Jahangiri* (Persian), AD 1609, English translation by A. Rogers and H. Beveridge, 3rd edn., 2 vols., Delhi, 1975.

Kashmiri, Baba Nasib, *Rishi Nama,* (AD 1631-32), RDLKUS.

———, *Tazkira-i-Mashaikh-i-Kashmir* (19th century), RDLKUS, 1640.

Kaul, Narayan Ajiz, *Mukhtsar Tawarikh-i-Kashmir,* (AD 1710-15), RDLKUS.

Khafi Khan, Muhammad Hashim, *Muntakhab-ul-Lubab,* edited by Moulvi Kabir-ud-din Ahmad, Calcutta, 1860-4, rpt.

Khan, Muhammad, *Iqbalnama-i-Jahangiri,* Calcutta, 1915.

Kumbu, Muhammad Saleh, *Amal-i-Saleh,* 2 vols., Calcutta, 1932.

Lahori, Abdul Hamid, *Badshahnama,* edited by Moulvi Khair-ud-din and Abdul Rahim, 2 vols., Calcutta, 1860.

Matin, Muhammad Ali Khan, *Tazkirat-ul-ulma* (n.d.), RDLKUS.

Mishkati, Baba Daud, *Asrar-ul-Abrar,* AD 1653-4, RDLKUS, no. 40/ 1177.

Miskeen, Muhi-ud-din, *Tarikh-i-Kabir-i-Kashmir,* AD 1892, RDLKUS.

Miskeen, Saif-ud-din, *Tarikh-i-jadwali,* early 20th century, RDLKUS.

Mohd. Sayuddin Kashmiri, *Tarikh-i-Jadwali,* AH 1322, RDLKUS.

Munshi Muhammad Kazim, *Alamgir Nama,* Calcutta, 1865-7.

Naqshbandi, Kh. Muin-ud-din, *Maqamat-i-Mahamadiya,* AD 1457, RDLKUS.

Nurullah Shustri, Qazi, *Majalis-ul-Muminin,* AD 1610, RDLKUS.

Pandit Birbal Kachru, *Mukhtasar Tarikh-i-Kashmir,* 1949 (unpublished), RDLKUS.

Pandit, Nath, *Gulshan-i-Dastur,* Persian Ms. 2314, AD 1754-55, RDLKUS.

Qadri, Mohammad Hussain, *Fatuhat-i-Qadriya,* 1882 (unpublished), RDLKUS.

Qazvini, *Badshah Nama,* 1636, Asafiya Library, Hyderabad.

Sahabadi, Mulla Shah Muhammad, *Tarikh-i-Kashmir,* AD 1590, Indian Office Library, London.

Saif-ud-din, Mirza, *Akhbarat, 1846-1856, Akhbarat wa Murasala Jat Siyasi wa Mulkidar Ahdi Maharaja Gulab Singh,* Persian Ms., unpublished, 13 vols., RDLKUS. Also available with author in microfilm.

Sayyid Ali, *Tarikh-i-Kashmir,* AD 1579, RDLKUS. Urdu translation is available with author in manuscript.

Shams Shah Nawaz Khan, *Massir-ul-Umara,* 3 vols., Calcutta, English translation by H. Beveridge, revised and completed edition by Dr. Beni Prasad, Calcutta, 1911-41.

Tang, Mufti Muhammad Murad, *Tohfat-ul-Fuqara,* Ms. RDLKUS, rpt., Delhi, 1973.

Tazkirat-ul-Shura, *Baksh-e-Awwal,* Sayyid Hasamuddin rashidi (1st published by Iqbal Academy, Lahore, 1967).

Sanskrit Manuscripts and Printed Texts with Translations

Abhinava Gupta, *Tantra Sara* (Sanskrit), edited by Pandit Mukundram Shastri, Bombay, 1918.

———, *Tantra Loka* (Sanskrit), KSTS, Bombay, 1925.

Jonaraja, Pandit, *Rajatarangini* (Sanskrit), English translation by J.C. Dutt, under the title *Kings of Kashmir,* Calcutta, 1879-98, rpt., 1990. Its Hindi translation which has been done by Raghunath Singh, Varanasi, 1972 has also been used in this book.

Kak, R.C. (ed.), *Gandharva Tantra,* Kashmir Series of Texts and Studies (henceforth KSTS), Srinagar, 1934.

Kalhana Pandit, *Rajatarangini* (Sanskrit), English translation with notes by M.A. Stein, 2 vols., Westminster, 1900, rpt., 1961 and 1979.

Kaul, Pandit Madhusudan Sastri (ed.), *Malinivijayottara Tantra,* KSTS XXXVII, Bombay, 1922.

Khemendra, Pandit, *Desopadesa,* edited by Pandit Madhusudan Kaul Sastri, KSTS, Poona, 1923.

———, *Lokprakasha,*RDLKUS, Kashmir. German translation of some extracts by A. Weber, Indische Studies XVIII, 1989. Also edited by Pandit Jagadhar Zadoo Sastri, KSTS, 75, Srinagar, 1947, French translation by J. Bloch (*Le lokaprakaca*), Paris, 1914.

———, *Samayamatrika,* edited by Pandit Durga Prasad and K.P. Parab, Kashmir manuscripts 10 (2nd edn.), Bombay, 1925, translation, Johann Jacob Meyer and Das Zanberbuch der Hetaren, Chicago, 1903.

Manka, *Srikanthacarita* (with commentary by Jonaraja), edited by Pandit Durga Prasad and K.P. Parab, KM. 3, Bombay, 1900.

Mrgendratantra, KSTS, no. I, Bombay, 1930.

Netra Tantra, KSTS, nos. XLVI, LXI, Bombay, 1926.

Nilmata Purana, English translation by Ved Kumari Gai, Srinagar, 1973, edited by K. De Vreese, Leiden, 1936, and R.L. Kanjilal and Pandit Jagadhar Zadoo, Srinagar, 1928.

Somadeva, *Kathasaritsagara,* English translation: *Ocean of Stream of Stories* (ed.) with notes by N.M. Penzer and E.H. Tawney, 10 vols., London, 1924; Indian edn. by Durga Prasad and K.P. Parab, Bombay, 1930.

Somananda, *Paratrimshika* (with commentary by Abhinava Gupta), edited by Pandit Mukundram Sastri, KSTS, no. 18, Bombay, 1918.

———, *Sivadrsti,* Kashmir Sanskrit-Granthavali (with the Vrtti by Utapaladeva), edited by Madhusudan Kaul Sastri, KSTS, val. 54, 1934.

Srivara, Pandit, *Jain Rajatarangini,* English translation by J.C. Dutt under title *Kings of Kashmir,* vol. III, Calcutta, 1935, rpt., 1990.

Suka Pandit and Prajayabhata, *Rajvalipatika* (Sanskrit), English translation by J.C. Dutt, *Kings of Kashmir,* vol. III, Calcutta, 1935, rpt., 1990.

Svacchanda Tantra, KSTS, nos. XXXI, XXXVIII, XLIV, XLVIII, LI, LIII, LVI, Bombay, 1921, 1923, 1926, 1927, 1930, 1933, 1935 respectively.

Published Works in English and Other Indian Languages

Anderson, P., *Lineages of Absolutist State,* London, 1974.

_____, *Passages from Antiquity to Feudalism,* London, 1974.

Arnold, T.W., *Preaching of !slam,* London, 1912.

Aron, R., *The Imperial Republic,* London, 1974.

Badie Bed, P. Birnbawn, *The Sociology of State,* Chicago, 1983.

Bagchi, P.C., *India and China,* Calcutta, 1944.

Bamzai, P.N.K., *A History of Kashmir,* Delhi, 1962.

Banerjee, J.N., *Development of Hindu Iconography,* Calcutta, 1956.

Banerjee, S.C., *Cultural Heritage of Kashmir,* Calcutta, 1965.

Bapat, P.V., *Twenty-five Hundred Years of Buddhism,* Government of India Publication, Delhi, 1956.

Bazaz, Ibn-al, *AI Qadriya* (Urdu), Hyderabad, 1903.

Bendix, R. (ed.), *State and Society,* California, 1973.

Bhandarkar, R.G., *Vaishnavism, Shaivism and other Minor Religious Systems,* Strassburg, 1913.

Brown, Percy, *Indian Architecture,* Calcutta, 1942.

Bus-Stone, *History of Buddhism,* translation from Tibetan into English by E. Obermiller, Heidelberg, 2 vols., 1932.

Bull, H., *The Anarchical Society,* New York, 1977.

Buller, G., *Detailed Report of Town in Search of Cultural Heritage and Sanskrit Manuscript of Kashmir,* Bombay, 1877.

Calleo, D., *Beyond Hegemony,* New York, 1987.

Cannadine, David and S. Price, *Rituals of Royalty,*Cambridge, 1987.

Carniero, R.L., 'A Theory of Origin of State', *Science,* vol. 169, 1970.

Classen, H.J.M. and P. Skalnik, *The Early State, Models and Reality,* The Hague, 1978.

Crone, P. and M. Cooked, *Islamic Haggarism,* London, 1977.

Crone, P., *Pre-Industrial Societies,* Basil Blackwell, 1989.

Cunningham, Alexander, *Archaeological Survey Report,* vol. II, London, 1863-4.

_____, *The Ancient Geography of India,* London, 1871.

Dass, S.K, *Shakti or Divine Power,* Calcutta, 1934.

David, J.B. and T.N. Clark, *Culture and its Creators,* London, 1977.

Demerath, N.J. and Philip H. Hemmod, *Religion in Social Context,* New York, 1969.

Desideri, Ipolitio, *An Account of his Travels (1717-27 AD),* London, 1937.

Dossuki, A.E.H., *Islamic Resurgence in the Arab World,* New York, 1982.

Doyle, M., *Empires,* New York, 1986.

Drabu, V.N., *Kashmir Polity,* Delhi, 1986.

———, *Saivagamas: A Study of Socio-Economic Ideas and Institutions,* Delhi, 1990.

Drew, Fedrick, *Jammu and Kashmir Territories,* London, 1895, rpt. Delhi, 1971.

Farquhar, J.N., *An Outline of Hindu Religious Literature,* London, 1919.

Fergusson, J., *Tree and Serpent Worship,* London, 1873.

Filispo De Filipi, *Travels,* London, 1937.

Forester, G., *A Journey from Bengal to England, through the Northern Part of India,* Kashmir, 2 vols., London, 1826.

Francisco, Palsaert, *Remoustranite: Jahangirs India,* translated by W.H. Moreland and P. Geyl, Cambridge, 1925.

Franke, A.H., *Antiquities of Indian Tibet,* 2 pts., Calcutta, 1927.

Frey, R.N., *The Goldm Age of Persia,* London, 1975.

Frey, H., *Religion and Revolt,* Manchester, 1984.

Gaily, Jean-Claude (ed.), *Kingship and the Kings,* London, 1989.

Gellener, E., *Plough, Sword and Book,* London, 1988.

Gellner, David N., *Monk, Householder and Tantric Priest,* Cambridge, 1992, 1st Indian edn. 1993.

Gibbs, M., *Feudalism,* London, 1949.

Gladwin, F., *The History of Jahangir,* Madras, 1930.

Grierson, G., *Lalavakini,* London, 1920.

Grunebaum, G.E., *Classical Islam (600-1258),* London, 1970.

Habib, Irfan, *Agrarian System of Mughal India,* Bombay, 1967.

Habib, Mohammad, *Sultan Mahmud of Ghaznin,* Aligarh, 1927.

Hall, J.A. and C.J. Ikenbery, *The State,* Canada, 1989.

Hangloo, R.L., *Agrarian System of Kashmir,* Delhi, 1995.

Hangloo, R.L. (ed.), *Situating Medieval Indian State,* Delhi, 1995.

Haig, Sir Wolseley, *Cambridge History of India,* vol. III, London, 1928, p. 285.

Hassan, Ahmad, *The Doctrine of ijmah in Islam,* Lahore, 1976.

Hassan, Mohibbul, *Kashmir under the Sultans,* Srinagar, 1967, 2nd edn. 1974.

Hiuen-Tsang, *Si-yu-ki*, English translation by S. Beal, *Buddhist Records of the Western World*, 2 vols., London, 1884.

Hugel, C.B., *Travels in Punjab and Kashmir*, Jammu, 1972.

Irvine, William, *The Army of the Indian Mughals*, Delhi, 1962.

_____, *Later Mughals*, 2 vols., edited by J.N. Sarkar, Calcutta, 1922.

Kak, R.C., *Archaeological Survey Report (1906-7)*, RDLKUS.

Kamil, M.A., *Noornama* (Kashmiri), Srinagar, 1965.

Kamudi, *Kashmir, Its Cultural Heritage*, Bombay, 1952.

Kane, P.V., *History of Dharmasastra*, 4 vols., Pune, 1960.

Kaul, A., *The Kashmiri Pandit*, Calcutta, 1924.

Kaul, J.L., *Lalded*, Delhi, 1973.

Keithwilkes, *Religion and Technology*, Oxford, 1972.

Khan, M.I., *History of Srinagar*, Srinagar, 1978.

_____, *Perspectives on Kashmir, Historical Dimensions*, Srinagar, 1983.

_____, *Kashmir's Transition to Islam*, Delhi, 1994.

Khosla, S., *History of Buddhism in Kashmir*, Delhi, 1974.

Knowles, D., *Monastic Order in England*, Cambridge, 1940.

Kosambi, D.D., *Introduction to the Study of Indian History*, Bombay, 1956.

Lawrence, W.R., *The Valley of Kashmir*, London, 1895.

Lekai, L., *The White Monks, A History of Cistercian Order*, Kachee, 1963.

Levin, G.M., Bongard, *Mauryan India*, Delhi, 1985.

Lewes, B., P.M. Holt and A.K.S. Lambton, *Cambridge History of Islam*, Cambridge, 1970.

Lovejoy, P.E., *The Ideology of Slavery in Africa*, London, 1981.

Mabbett, Ian, *Pattern of Kingship and Authority in Traditional Asia*, Australia, 1985.

Macarthy, R.J., *The Theology of Al Ashair*, Beyroth, 1953.

Mann, M., *Sources of Social Power: A History of Power from the Beginning to AD 1760*, 2 vols., Cambridge, 1986.

Marcell, M., *The Gift*, London, 1954.

Marco Polo, *The Book of Sir Marcopolo*, edited· and translated by M. Yule, 2 vols., London, 1903.

Marshall, Sir John, *Mohanjodaro and the Indus Civilisation*, 3 vols., London, 1931.

Marx, Karl and E Engels, *Islam in Critique*, Mosonnenve Larose, 1984.

_____, *Selected Works*, 3 vols., Moscow, 1969.

Masterson, P., *Atheism and Alienation*, London, 1964.

Mattoo, A.M., *Kashmir Under Mughals*, Srinagar, 1988.

Mohan, Krishna, *Early Medieval History of Kashmir, AD 1003-1171*, Delhi, 1981.

Monfee, Ch. (ed.), *Gramsci and Marxist Theory*, London, 1980.

Moorcraft, W. and W.G. Trebeck, *Travels in the Himalayan Provinces of Hindustan and Punjab, in Ladakh and Kashmir*, 2 vols., rpt., Delhi, 1971.

Moorcraft, W., *Tour Diary*, Ms. EURD, India Office Library, London.

Narayan, Brij, *Social Lift of North India*, Delhi, 1966.

Nazim, M., *Sultan Mahmmud of Gazna*, Delhi, 1971.

Naudou, J., *Buddhists of Kashmir*, Delhi, 1980.

Oberoi, J.P.S., *Politics of Kaula Kings*, Manchester, 1962.

Oddie, G.A., *Religion in South Asia*, Delhi, 1977.

Panday, K.C., *Abhinavgupta, Historical and Philosophical Study*, Banaras, 1951.

Parmu, R.K., *A History of Muslim Rule in Kashmir (1320-1819)*, Delhi, 1969.

Petrshevski, I.P., *Islam* v *Irane*, vols. VII-XV, Venkaleh, Leningrad, 1966.

Poulantzas, N., *Political Power and the Social Classes*, London, 1973.

Price, J.R.F., *Rituals and Power, the Roman Imperial Cult in Asia Minor*, Cambridge, 1984.

Raina, G., *Lala Pakini* (Urdu), 2 vols., Srinagar, 1959.

Raina, K., *Hindi aur Kashmiri Nirgun Sant Kavya ka Tulnatmak Adhyayan* (Hindi), Delhi, 1977.

Raina, S.K., *Kashmiri Bhasha aur Sahitya* (Hindi), Delhi, 1972.

Rao, T.A.G., *Elements of Hindu Iconography*, 2 vols., Madras, 1914.

Ray, S.C., *Early History and Culture of Kashmir*, Calcutta, 1957.

Reinard, *Memoirs Surl' Inde* (French), Paris, 1849.

Rizvi, S.A.A., *A History of Sufism in India*, 2 vols., Delhi, 1978.

Rodgers, C.J., *The Copper Coins of the Sultans of Kashmir*, JASB, XLVIII, 1879.

Russel, J.W., *Modes of Production in World History*, London, 1988.

Santhanam, K., *An Anthology of Indian Literature*, Delhi, 1959.

Sarkar, J.N., *Conditions of Kashmiri People Under Muslim Rule*, Delhi, 1949 (monograph).

Saxena, K.S., *Political History of Kashmir*, Lucknow, 1974.

Sender, H., *The Kashmiri Pandits*, Oxford and Delhi, 1988.

Service, E.R., *The Origins of State and Civilization*, New York, 1975.

Sharif, M.M., *History of Muslim Philosophy*, Weisbaden, 1963.

Stein, M.A., *Ancient Geography of Kashmir*, Calcutta, 1899.

Stepan, A., *State and Society,* Princeton University Press, 1978.
Sufi, G.M.D., *Islamic Culture in Kashmir,* Delhi, 1979.
———, *Kashir,* 2 vols., Lahore, 1949.
Sykes, P., *History of Persia,* London, 1922.
Tejomayananda, *Introduction to Kashmir Shaivism,* Delhi, 1974.
Temple, R.C., *The Word of Lalla, The Prophetess,* Cambridge, 1924.
Terborn, G. *What Does The Ruling Class Do When It Rules?* London, 1978.
Todd, J., *Annals and Antiquities of Rajasthan,* London, 1914.
Topa, I., *Politics in Pre-Mughal Times,* Delhi, 1938.
Vansittart, H., *A Narrative of Transactions in Bengal* (*AD 1760-64*), 2 vols., London, 1930.
Vigne, G.T., *Travels in Kashmir, Ladakh, Iskardu, Countries and the Mountain Courses of Indus and North of Punjab,* 2 vols., London, 1842.
Vogel, Ph. and J. Hutichson, *History of Punjab Hill States,* Lahore, 1933.
Wallerstein, I., *The Politics of the World Economy, the State, the Movements and the Civilization,* Cambridge, 1984.
Watters, Thomas, *On Yuan Chwang's Travels in India,* 2 vols., edited by T.W. Rhy Davids, London, 1904.
Wilson, H.H., *Hindu History of Kashmir,* Calcutta, 1960.
Yule, M., *The Book of Sir Morcopolo,* 2 vols., London, 1903.
Zutshi, N.K., *Sultan Zain-ul-Abidin,* Lucknow, 1976.

Published Papers

Ashrafyan, K.Z., 'Historical Significance of Turkish Conquest', in *Kunwar Mohammed Ashraf: An Indian Scholar and Revolutionary,* edited by H. Kruger, Delhi, 1969, pp. 56-77.
Classen, H.J.M., 'The Internal Dynamics of Early State', *Current Anthropology,* vol. XXV, no. 4, August-October 1984, pp. 365-79.
Djait, H., 'Origins ofIslamic State', in *Islam State and Society,* edited by K. Ferdinand and M. Mozaffari, London, 1988, pp. 74-82.
Dossuki, A.E.H., 'The Islamic Resurgence, Sources, Dynamics and Implication', in A.E.H. Dossuki, ed., *Islamic Resurgence in the Arab World,* New York, 1982, pp. 17-25.
Frey, H., 'Religion as an Ideology of Domination', in *Religion and Revolt,* Manchester, 1984, pp. 15-30.
Geertz, C., 'Centres, Kings and Charisma, Reflections on the Symbolics

of Power', in *Culture and its Creators,* edited by J. Ben David and T.N. Clark, Chicago and London, 1977, pp. 34-72.

Habib, Irfan, 'The Technology and Economy of Mughal India', *IESHR,* vol. XVII, no. 1, January-March 1980, pp. 1-34.

Kerimov, G.M.O., 'The Socio-Political Aspects of Modern Islamic Mission', in K. Ferdinand and M. Mozaffari, eds., *Islam, State and Society,* London, 1988, pp. 39-52.

Khan, M.I., 'Impact ofislam on Kashmir in Sultanate Period, 1320-1586', *Indian Economic and Social History Review,* vol. 2, no. 23, 1986, pp. 87-206.

Kosambi, D.D., 'Origins of Feudalism in Kashmir', in *Journal of Bombay Branch of Asiatic Society (Fifteenth Anniversary Volume),* Bombay, 1957, pp. 108-20.

Laibman, David, 'Modes of Production and Theories of Transition', in *Science and Society,* vol. XLVIII, no. 3, Fall 1984, pp. 257-94.

Monfee, Ch., 'Hegemony and Ideology in Gramsci', in Ch. Monfee, ed., *Gramsci and Marxist Theory,* London, 1979, pp. 255-88.

Mukhia, Harbans, 'Communalism: A Study in its Socio-Historical Perspective', *Social Scientist,* no. 1, August 1972.

Newell, Lieut, Col., 'A Sketch of Muhammadan History of Kashmir', *Journal of the Asiatic Society of Bengal,* no. 5, 1854, pp. 70-5.

Price, S.R.F., 'Rituals and Power', The Roman Imperial Cult in Asia Minor, Cambridge, 1984, pp. 70-5.

Rizvi, S.A.A., 'Islamic Proselytization from Seventh to Sixteenth Centuries', in G.A. Oddie, ed., *Religion in South Asia,* Delhi, 1977, rpt. 1992.

Rodgers; J., 'The Square Silver Coins of Sultans of Kashmir', *Journal of Asiatic Society of Bengal,* vol. LIV, 1885, pp. 92-139.

Singh, S.D., 'The Early Development of Kingship in Pre-Muslim India', in Ian Mabbett, ed., *Pattern of Kingship and Authority in Traditional Asia,* Croom Helm, London and Monash University Press, Melbourne, 1985, pp. 85-107.

Unpublished Thesis

Hangloo, N.J., 'Kashmiri Bhakti aur Sant Mirza Kak: Ek Samajik aur Sanskritic Adhyayan' (Hindi), Ph.D. thesis, Centre for Indian Languages, JNU, New Delhi, 1988.

Index

Abbasiad Caliph 143
Abdullah, Mir Sayyid Mohammad 129
Abdullah, Sayyid 140
Acharya, Tilka 144
Agamas (Shaivite Tantricism) 19, 21, 25, 27, 34, 36, 37, 38, 97, 98, 106
agrahara of Bedra 40; of Jalura 39; of Sanara 39; of Katimusa 40
agrahara, confiscation of 73
agrahara-based economy 43, 79, 180-1
Ahmed Yetu 155
Ain-i-Akbari 170-1
Ajaka 43
Akasa 39
Akbar 161-4, 166, 167, 170-1, 174
Akbar, Ali 169
Aksavala 39-40
Alai, Sayyid Jamul-ud-din 127
Ali, Malik 169
Ali, Qazi 163, 165, 166
Amir-i-Dar (Lord Chamberlain) 155
Amir-ul-Muminin 143
Ammuli, Mir Sharif 163
Amrit Prabha 40
Ananta 44, 51, 81, 86
Ashoka 23, 25, 26, 39, 95, 96
Ashraf, Mullah 169
Ashrafyan, K.Z. 77
Atrani, Sayyid Jamal-ud-Din 108
Aurangzeb 169, 172
Avantivarman 40, 49, 50, 85, 87, 96

Baihaqi, Sayyid Mirak 154
Baihaqi, Sayyid Mohd 141
Baj tax 143, 166
Baladitya 40
Bandey, Mullah Haji 169
Beg, Mir Ahmad Khan Hassan 169
Bhata, Siva 144
Bhatphalguna 43-4
Bhatt, Kumarila 96
Bhatta, Avtar 144
Bhatta, Jaya 144
Bhatta, Karpura 144
Bhatta, Rupya 144

Bhatta, Shriya 144
Bhatta, Yodha 144
Bindusara 20
Bodhisattva Nagarjuna 26
Bodhisattva, Dhyani 96
Brahmanism 13, 14, 16; patronization of 13, 23, 96, 180
Brahmin Bhatphalguna 43-4
Brahmin Mitrasaraman 43
Brahmin Raka 44
Brahminical religion 180
Brahminism 66, 68, 76, 93, 95, 99, 104, 108, 122, 181
Brahmins: cultivation of the holdings 44-5
Buddhism 21, 23-5, 27, 33, 64, 67, 68, 74-7, 93-6, 98, 106, 112, 128, 180
butshikan (idol breaker) 73

Cakravarman 50, 81
Canpaka 43
Central Asian culture 92
Chak, Mubarak Khan 174
Chouthai tax 166
Conversion 65
cultural exchange 93

Damarapatis 49
Damaras: rebellions of 85
Dammara 47-9
Dammara Dhanva 49
Dammaras, dominance in Kashmir polity 47-53, 83, 85, 110, 127, 156, 181
Dammaravisayas 49
Dar, Fateh 169
Dastar-shumari tax 166
deshadhyakshas (heads of areas) 82
deshadhyakshas 41-2
Devasarman 43
Dhanna the Jat 64
Dhanva, Dammara 49
Dossuki, A.E.H. 124

Ekangas 52, 67, 77, 83, 85, 89, 96, 110, 127

Fakr-ud-din, Mir Sayyid 129
Fateh, Abdul 169
fatwas 123
Fazal Khan 168-169
Fazl, Abul 166, 170, 172
feudal families 159
Fika-i-Ahvat 110
Firuz, Sayyid 128
free communal kitchen (*langar khanah*) 93

gashqa 70
Gaurak, Ganpati 143, 144
Gayat-ul-Makan 110
Gonda dynasty 39
Gopaditya 40
gramadhyakshas (heads of villages) 82
Gunavarman 24, 67
Gupta, Abhinava 96

Habib, Muhammad 169
Habib, Mullah 169
Hafiz, Jamil 144
Haft Hazari 169
Haidar, Mailk 169
Haldra 41
Hamadani, Sayyid Ali 70, 102, 107, 127, 137, 138

Hanfia doctrines 124
Harsha 39, 43, 46, 51-2, 74, 81, 86, 91, 95, 102
Hashim, Khwaja 169
hasilihatar tax 166
Hassan, Sayyid Taj-ud-din bin Sayyid 127
Hazrat Baba Zain ud-Din 108
Hindu or Muslim fundamentalists 65
Hussain, Khawaja Muhammad 163

Ibrahim-bin-Adham of Balakh 128
Iranian Sufis 71
Islam in rural Kashmir 68
Islam, conversion to 63-112: Batmaloo Saheb 68; conversions from Brahminism 66; Kashmiri Hindus 65; *rishis*, tradition of 68; state formation in 67
Islamic orthodoxy 123-4
Islamic tenets 134-5

Jahangir 165, 167, 172
Jamal-ud-din, Sayyid 129
Janaka 39
Janakaraja, Dammara 86
Jayaka Dammara 47
Jayapida 43, 49, 80
Jizya 70, 71, 101, 143
Jonaraja 71-4, 81, 86, 101, 141, 144
Jushka 23

Kahcharai tax 166
Kalasa 51, 81, 86
Kalhana 26, 35, 36, 40, 44-52, 72, 75, 76, 79-81, 85, 87-92
Kalhana's *Rajatarangini* 76
Kalima 103
Kamal, Sayyid 108, 128, 138
Kanch, Dammara 144
Kanishka 23
Kantha, Sita 144
Kanyakubja 52, 89
Karim, Abdul 169
Kashmir: *agrahara*-based economy 180-1; Brahmin, patronization of 13; Brahminism 66, 68, 76, 93, 95, 99, 104, 108, 122, 181; Buddhism, spread of 21; Dammmaras, dominance of 47, 51-53; economy 173; endowments to Sayyids 129; impact of Islam 14; Islam, conversion to 63-5, 69; legitimacy, search of 122, 124-5, 137; Mughal state 16-17, 161-2, 164, 167-9, 173-5; Mughals, social transformation by 163; Muslim migrants 14, 93; Nagas, tribal foundation 18; non-Naga tribes, intrusion of 20; political economy of 158-9; pre-Sultanate period 18-54; religious life 24, 33, 38, 74, 94, 133; Sayyids, intereference in State affairs 123, 134; Sayyids, patronization of 121; Shah-mir dynasty 124; Shahmir Sultanate 122-5, 136; social base of power 63-112; state

and society 123, 140, 154, 155; state formation 18, 25; Zain-ul-abidin reign 103-4, 142-6; under Mughals 172
Kashmir: Bikshus 25; Brahmin 39, 98; Buddhism 95-6; Hindu migrants 65; merchant families 174-5; Muslims 111; Pandits 27, 32, 35, 66, 99, 164; polity 160; Shaivism 27, 30; society 175; valley, territorial limits of 20-1
Kashmiri Sanah 125
Kashmiri, Mulla Ahmad 144
Kashmiri, Mulla Kabir 144
Kashmiris: 14, 27, 29, 67, 90, 92, 93, 99, 107, 121, 135, 168; Buddhism, acceptance and contribution 24; and Mughals, matrimonial relations between 174; nobles 160; tribal social formation 31
Kawoosa, Muhammad Yousuf 169
Kayasthas, malpractices by 81
Kazim, Mir Sayyid 128
Keshva 44
Khadyar tax 166; Khafi, Khawaja Shamsuddin 163
Khalifas 124
Khan, Adham 154
Khan, Ali Mardan 168
Khan, Asif 163, 164, 166
Khan, Darya 144
Khan, Fazal 168
Khan, Inayatullah 168
Khan, Mirzah Yousuf 168
Khan, Muhammad Isaq 68, 169
Khan, Mulla Qazi 144
Khan, Shahi 142, 146
khangahs 101
khanqah 71, 103, 107-9, 123, 129, 132, 135, 141, 181
kharwar of *Shali* (paddy) 158
Khokhar, Jasrat 146
King Godhara, 39
King Samkaravarman 80-1
Koranic obligation 131
Kosambi, D.D. 25, 51
Kottarajas 49, 100-1
Koul, Mahesh 169
Koul, Sudarshan 168
Kriya Pradhan 106
Ksemgupta 86
Kushana kings 23

Lakshimaka 125
Laleshwari 72
Lalitaditya 40, 43, 48, 90
Lalleshwari 104-6
langar-khanah 101
Lavanyas 15, 52, 67, 69, 77, 83, 84, 85, 89, 91, 96, 101, 110-11, 127, 145, 159
lingam in a *yoni yantram* 28-9
Lodhi, Sultan Sikander 160
Lohara dynasty 38, 50, 52, 87, 121

madrasas 101
Magre, Jahangir 155, 156
mahatmyas 94-5
Mak, Sayyid 143
Malik Ahmad Yetu 156
Malik-Saif-ud-din 101
malini 106
Malinivijayuttara Tantra 37
Manka 43
Maqsood, Sayyid 169

Masterson, P. 111
Mazhari, Mullah 169
medieval Kashmir: Islam, contribution of 130-1; religion and state 130
Megvahana 40
Mihirakula 39
Mihirakula 39, 75, 77, 95
Mir Mohammad 71
Mir Sayyid Kazim 128-9
Mir Shams-ud-din Iraqi 160
Mirbahar, Qasim Khan 161
Mitrasaraman 43
Mlecchas 68, 74, 91
Mohammad, Mansur Bin 144
Mohammad, Sayyid Mir 135, 142, 154
Mohibbul Hassan 156
monotheistic religion 99-100
Muffakhari Iran 93
Mughal India 171
Mughal Subahdars of Kashmir 169
Mughals and the Kashmiris, matrimonial relations between 174
Murad, Muhammad 169
Muslim judicial law 136
Muslim settlements 93

Nadri, Mulla 144
Naga kingdom 20
Nagam paragana 127
Nara 86, 95
Narendratiya 40
Nasq Gallabakshi 164
Nature (*Prakriti)* 29
Naubahar Buddhist monastery or *vihara* in Balakh 128
Nauroz 155
Neolithic culture 29
Netra Tantra 45
Nila Naga 19-20
Nilmata Purana 19-20, 26, 30, 35, 80
Nizam-ud-din Ahmad Bakshi 162
non-*agrahara* holdings 79
non-Sayyid nobles 138-9
Noor-ud-din, Khwaja 155
Nothsoma 144
Nurullah, Qazi 168

Panca-vimsatika 155
Pandit Mahadav Koul 168
pari passu 54
Parmu, R.K. 69, 133, 141, 167
Partha 81
phallic emblems 28
Phallic worship 28
political instability 14
politico-economic anarchy 95
post-Karkota period, political history of 83
Prakasha ideology 37
prayopavesa (hunger strikes) of the Brahmins 85
pre-Mauryan period 21
Pre-Sultanate Kashmir 18-54: *agraharas* 39; animals, domestication of 29; Brahmin *parsada* (corporation) 36; Buddhist Tantric rituals 33; class division 23; complex state formation 18; *Great Exegesis* (*Mahavibasha*) 24; Kashmiri religious elite 24; *Malinivijayuttara Tantra* 37; matriarchical society 29-30; Nagas, tribal foundations of

18-19; non-Naga tribes, intrusion of 22; one-crop economy 35; polyandry 30; *Prakasha* 37; religiosity 33; *Saivagamas* 35, 106; Samkarvarman's time 46-7; Shiva-Shakti cult 33; South East Asia, Indianized communities of 25; tribal level state formation 21; two-tier social format 21; *Vimarsha* 37
primitive Kashmiris 27, 67
purohitas 98-9

Qaiser, Mir 141
Qasim Khan Mirbahar 161
Qasim, Muhammad 169
Qureshi, Sayyid Mohammad 108
Qutub-ud-din 127, 133-4, 135, 137

Rafi, Muhammad 169
Rajanak 144
Rajatarangini 47, 51, 53, 72, 76, 85, 87-9
Raka 44
Rasum-i-Faujdari 167
regional sovereignty 161, 173
Rig Veda 28, 33
Rinchana 93-4
Rizivi, Yusuf Khan 163, 166
rudabarudi (forced labour) 46
Rukum-ud-din, Mir Sayyid 128-9
rural-urban aristocracy 131

Sacinara 39-40
sadhakas (disciples) 83
Sadhangula 20
Sadhangula 20
Saif-ud-din, Malik 70, 101, 141, 142, 144
Sair Jihat cesses 166
Saleem, Qazi 169
Salhana 43, 51
Salim, Muhammad 169
Samanta 44
Samgram Dammara 50, 86
Samgram Raja 46, 81
Samkarvarman 40, 45-6, 49, 86, 107
Sangramraja 44
Sardarkhti tax 166
Sarkar, Jadunath 168
Sarvastivada School of Buddhism 95
Sayyid Hassan Simnani 127
Sayyid Mak 143
Sayyid migrants 137
Sayyids 70, 73, 78, 94, 96, 101-3, 107-12, 121-46, 154-8, 160, 182
Sayyid-ullah Shirazi 143
secular *agraharas* 78-9
Semgupta 43
Shaguffia 128
Shah Jahan 172, 174
Shah, Bul Bul 100, 123
Shah, Fath 157, 158, 160, 162
Shah, Haider 154, 155, 157
Shah, Muhammad 157-8
Shah, Sultan Ali 141-2, 144, 162
Shah, Sultan Hassan 155-7, 160
Shahmir dynasty 73, 86, 101, 122, 124, 137
Shahmir state 63
Shahmir Sultanate 14, 84, 103, 122, 123, 124, 125, 136, 140, 149

Shahmir Sultans 15, 101, 121-4, 127, 129-31, 133-4, 137-9, 141, 146, 154, 157, 167, 182
Shahmir, Sultan Shams-ud-din 122, 124, 126
Shaiva Acharyas 97
Shaivism 29-30, 33, 54, 69, 74-6, 95, 97, 98, 106-7, 112
Shaivite Acharayas 33
Shaivite *mathas* 84
Shaktaism 68, 76, 95
Shankaracharya 96
Shariat 69, 131, 133, 136, 143
Shavite *acharyas* 95
Sheikh Nuruddin 106
Sheikh, Faizi 163
Sheikh-ul-Islam 136
Sheik-noor-ud-din 144
Shias 122
Shia-Sunni conflicts 160
Shihab-ud-din Suharawardi 128
Siddhatantra 106
Silk Route 103-4
Simnani, Sayyid Hussain 127, 138
Singh, Kanwar Man 163
Sinha 144
Skandkas, role in the revenue administration 46
Smith, W.C. 174
social differentiation 173
Srikantha Charita 43
Srimadhaka 20
Srinagar 40, 68, 75, 88, 93, 101, 103, 104, 108, 129, 135, 142
Srinagara town, foundation of 23
Srivara, Pandit 72, 144, 155, 158
Sufi saints in East Bengal 63-4
Suhabhata 73-4, 86, 101, 141
Suhadeva 81, 92
Sultan Ali Shah Chak 162
Sultan Qutb-ud-din 108
Sultan Shams-ud-din Shahmir 122, 124-6
Sultan Shihab-ud-din 73, 101, 127, 128, 129, 133
Sultan Sikandar 70-4, 101-4, 135-7, 139-41, 143
Sultan Zain-ul-Abidin 72-3, 103, 126, 158, 160
Sultans of the Shahmir dynasty 122
Sunnis 122
Sura 49, 87
Suraymati, Queen 41
Sussala 44, 46, 52, 81, 85, 91-92, 95
Suvarna 39
Svacchanda Tantra 41
Swami Tejomayananda 97

Tamgah tax 143, 166
Tantra sect 98, 106, 112
tantric gurus 97
Tantric literature 21-2
Tantrins 15, 47, 50, 52-3, 67, 77, 80, 83, 84-5, 89, 96, 110-11, 127
Tarikh-i-Kashmir 73, 102
Tejomayananda 97
Telicharagh tax 166
Tota Ram, Pandit 163, 166, 168
Trika Shaivism 27
Tunjana 40
turushka 74, 91
Turushkas 90-1, 95

ulama 15, 124, 125

Umma 123-4
Unmattavant 81
Urwat-al-Waga 101
Utkarsha 81

Vaishnavism 76, 95, 97
Vakpushtha 40
Vansittart, Henry 172
Vedic Aryans, mythic-religious concepts of 74
vihāras 95
Vikramaditya 40, 90-1
Vimarsha 37

Yasaskara 41, 44
Yavanas (foreign Muslims) 141
Yetu, Ahmed 155, 156, 159
Yusuf Khan Rizivi 163, 166

Zain Rajatarangini/Jain Rajatarangini 71-2
Zain-ud-din, Hazrat Baba 108
Zain-ul-Abidin, Sultan 69, 72, 103-4, 122, 142-3, 144-6, 154, 158, 160
Zakhirat-ul-Mulk 110
Zimmis 143
Zulachu/Zulqadr Khana 92
Zutshi, N.K. 70, 140, 143, 146